Being and Not Being

Being and Not Being

End Times of Posthumanism and the Future Undoing of Philosophy

Richard Iveson

ROWMAN & LITTLEFIELD
Lanham • Boulder • New York • London

Published by Rowman & Littlefield
An imprint of The Rowman & Littlefield Publishing Group, Inc.
4501 Forbes Boulevard, Suite 200, Lanham, Maryland 20706
www.rowman.com

86-90 Paul Street, London EC2A 4NE, United Kingdom

British Library Cataloguing in Publication Information Available

Library of Congress Cataloging-in-Publication Data Available

ISBN 978-1-5381-8822-4 (cloth)
ISBN 978-1-5381-8824-8 (ebook)

For Maoki, the best of us

Contents

Acknowledgements

I am very grateful to all those who have helped with the writing and publishing of this book, particularly given the extreme patience such support ultimately involved. I began this project while a postdoctoral research fellow at the University of Queensland in 2014, initially in the Centre for Critical and Cultural Studies and later as part of the Institute for Advanced Studies in the Humanities. I would also like to thank Lynn Turner and Stefan Herbrechter for their ongoing support of my work, as well as Sarah Campbell, Natalie Mandziuk, Yu Ozaki, and Lynn Zelem at Rowman & Littlefield.

I want to thank too my brother Greg Hainge for his friendship, unwavering support and constant belief throughout the nine years of writing, without whom this book would never have been written. I remember (of course) your comment all those years ago about the rarity of genuine minds, and at last I have the chance to thank you properly.

Finally, my thanks go to my family. In particular, my sincere thanks and gratitude go to Jo for her help and support that went well beyond all reasonable limits, and to Makiko and Maoki for everything they do and everything they are.

Parts of this book originally appeared in the following publications, which have graciously allowed them to be reprinted here:

A slightly shorter version of the reading of Leibniz's principle of reason in the introduction can be found in my chapter 'Posthumanism and the Ends of Technology,' in *Palgrave Handbook of Critical Posthumanism*, ed. S. Herbrechter, I. Callus, M. Rossini, M. Grech, M. de Bruin-Molé, and C. John Müller (New York: Palgrave Macmillan, 2022), 1021–1043.

An earlier version of chapter 3 was originally published as 'Of Times before Tomorrow: Contingency and the Life of Machines,' *Culture, Theory and Critique* 61, no. 1 (2020): 37–63.

Part of the conclusion originally appeared in the chapter entitled 'Technology,' in *Edinburgh Companion to Animal Studies*, ed. Ron Broglio, Lynn Turner, and Undine Sellbach (Edinburgh: Edinburgh University Press, 2018), 504–517.

Introduction

Relative Reason

> Modern technology pushes toward the greatest possible perfection. Perfection is based on the thoroughgoing calculability of objects. The calculability of objects presupposes the unqualified validity of the *principium rationis*. It is in this way that the authority characteristic of the principle of reason determines the essence of the modern, technological age.
>
> —Martin Heidegger, *The Principle of Reason*

Speaking in 1956, philosopher Martin Heidegger poses what he calls the *world-question of thinking*, the answer to which will ultimately decide 'what will become of the earth and of human existence on this earth' (*The Principle of Reason*, 129). Are we, he asks, to remain in thrall to the mindless enchantment of calculative thinking, or are we instead 'obliged to find paths upon which thinking is capable of responding to what is worthy of thought' (129)? We thus find ourselves situated at a fundamental crossroads with regards to the future, tasked with the enacting of a decision unlike anything that has gone before. Long before the concept of the Anthropocene became common academic currency, Heidegger here correlates the instantiation of this world-question of thinking with the advent of a new historical epoch founded for the first time upon the rapacious procurement of any and all potential resources. Given the recklessness of calculative thinking that is the driving force behind the globalizing project of postindustrial capitalism, it should come as no surprise that the urgency of this call to cognitive arms has only increased over the course of the intervening decades. In parallel with this increase in urgency, however, developments in digital technologies have further transformed globalizing processes of consolidation out of all recognition and thus, if we are to hope to respond to Heidegger's world-question today, it is necessary also to move beyond Heidegger's existential analytic with its basis in the privileged form of the uniquely human Dasein.

The history of reason in the West tells the story of the quest for a perfect accounting of the world around us, one that, once properly codified, will disclose a perfectly ordered and orderly future, at which point this future becomes available to human knowledge and thus subject in its entirety to human control. From Plato to Descartes and from Leibniz to Einstein, to truly accede to the universe of reason is to erase all possibility of chance, to resolve fundamental uncertainty and to restrict the role of indeterminacy to that of a simple heuristic impulse signaling only that the grand narrative of reason is not quite yet complete. This is the normative ideology of causal determinism in a nutshell, and I would like to think that this is a vision of the world and of the future that very few of us would wish to inhabit. Despite this, however, and despite Heidegger's warning shot all those years ago, we remain to this day in thrall to the very same ideology of the future, bewitched by the promise of control over the calculable.

To break free of the spell of reason is no simple task, however, and this brings us to a second major challenge facing us today. In what is perhaps something of a kneejerk reaction to the underlying problem identified by Heidegger's world-question of thinking, it has become a commonplace of contemporary posthumanist and new materialist discourse to decry the simplistic human–animal binary, while at the same time maintaining an absolute and constitutive disjunct between living beings and nonliving things.[1] Indeed, the reductive reasoning of this latter pairing is not infrequently celebrated as proof of the overcoming of liberal humanism and anthropocentrism both, thus playing its own part in what today is a largely triumphal discourse built around the defining role of *autopoiesis*—a role predicated upon the reduction of infinite ways and forms of being to that of a single 'life.' While the importance of the ongoing deconstruction of the human–animal dichotomy is undeniable, when considered in isolation or when taken as an end in itself it is nonetheless rendered toothless for the most part. The reason for this is simple insofar as, just as deconstruction discloses the illegitimacy of the traditional human–animal antonym, so too it necessarily discloses the illegitimacy of the normative structuring of simple ontological dualism in *all* of its myriad forms of exclusion. Hence, it is important to stress from the start the incommensurability of what follows with the vitalisms and animisms that carry aloft recent theories of vibrant matter and affective embodiment. The deconstruction of the traditional human–animal binary is, in other words, but a first step and wholly insufficient on its own.

As we shall see, moving beyond the reductive metaphysical blueprint that decrees as both absolute and undeniable the division between embodied lifeforce and its absence brings along with it a profound shift in the ways we engage critically and ethically both with the world around us and with the future. No longer distracted by the chimera of the *élan vitale*, we inevitably find ourselves occupying a very different terrain and a very different landscape, one in which *all* physical processes retain the chance of giving rise to novel emergence, and which in so doing disclose an inhuman and mutilating formal power at work at the very heart of being.

RISKING IT ALL

The future, Heidegger tells us, is in the balance. More specifically, the balance of futures rests with the question of *risk* as productive of exclusion. The promise that is the chance of a future, in other words, requires us to collectively refute such manifold delusions of safety constructed upon an entirely baseless ideology and policed by a politics of exclusion. As with the contemporary resurgence of vitalisms, to fail to address the posthumanist 'world-question' of thinking in this manner risks failing to address the corresponding reduction of the practically infinite array, disarray and diversity of inclinations to that of a single inclination as definitive of the peerless triumph of global capitalism today and tomorrow. This is the risk that we know by the name of the Anthropocene: a vision of the world ordered up and down and front to back by calculative thinking in the guise of a promise to safeguard the present from the vagaries of the future by way of predictions based upon naïve causal calculus. Ultimately, however, such promises to keep our present safe from future risk are simple ideological fictions, sleight of hand productions of a fabricated need that, in the end, puts everything at risk.

Contrary to all such appearances, contingency is definitive of the structure of being itself, from which it follows that any predictions about the future founded upon present or habitual states of being are *necessarily* subject to possible error. As we shall see, to *be* is to be fundamentally *un*safe; subject to a profound structural unpredictability from which nothing is ever safe and which inscribes a prior ethical demand common to biological and technological systems alike. As a result, the 'rules' of critical and ethical engagement are transformed insofar as we can no longer lay claim to the legitimacy and the usefulness of decisions made today and tomorrow on the back of predicted futures that erroneously presume the absolute determinability of all beings unilaterally deemed to lack the alchemical privilege definitive of life.

If we are to escape from this normative logic of life, one of the first hurdles to be overcome concerns our general anxiety about the speed and complexity of technological innovation. In this regard, the perceived potential of biotechnologies makes very clear exactly what, if anything, remains of ethical choice today insofar as it explodes the myth of linear causality considered as fully determining in the case of any entity we care to classify as lacking the ephemera of a lifeforce. Instead, contemporary notions of living technologies and technological lifeforms mean that we are now obligated—philosophically, ethically and politically—to recognize that the future effects of animate and inanimate causes alike can by definition never be predicted with absolute surety.

THE LONG SLEEP OF REASON

In *Before Tomorrow: Epigenesis and Rationality* (2014), philosopher Catherine Malabou seeks to address three urgent questions that reveal within contemporary Continental philosophy the outlines of three areas of 'incomprehensible silence' (1). Notably, the first of these questions concerns time: 'Why has the question of time lost its status as the leading question of philosophy?' (1).[2] In the wake of Martin Heidegger's late decree in *On Time and Being* that time ultimately 'vanishes' as a question, writes Malabou, 'no one asks this question anymore, no one has taken up the problem by developing afresh a decisive concept of temporality, be it with or against Heidegger' (1). While strictly speaking Malabou's claim is of course hyperbole, she is nonetheless correct in bringing to light the recent disappearance of time as the fundamental question of philosophy. Whether this silence can be described as incomprehensible, however, remains to be seen.

If we are to respond to Malabou's challenge and engage anew with the question of time today, we must first of all ask after the status of the principle of reason. Fittingly perhaps, Heidegger delivered a lecture course and summary standalone address on precisely this question in 1955–56. Entitled *Der Satz vom Grund* or *The Principle of Reason* (1991), the address begins in a somewhat belligerent mood:

> The principle of reason reads: *nihil est sine ratione*. One translates this with: *nothing* is *without* reason. What the principle states can be paraphrased as follows: everything has a reason, which means each and every thing that is in any manner. *Omnes ens habet rationem*. Whatever happens to be actual has a reason for its actuality. Whatever happens to be possible has a reason for its possibility. Whatever happens to be necessary has a reason for its necessity. *Nothing* is *without* reason (117).

In fact, continues Heidegger, 'what the principle of reason states is commonplace, and because it is commonplace, it is immediately illuminating' (117).[3] What the principle of reason states, in other words, is so obvious as to be perceived immediately and with utmost clarity by everyone. So much so, however, that just what, exactly, the principle states is not expressly posited as a principle or law until the seventeenth century, when Gottfried Wilhelm Leibniz "recognized the long-since commonplace idea 'nothing is without reason' was a normative principle and described it as the principle of reason" (118). So, asks Heidegger, what of the two thousand three hundred years of philosophical endeavor in the West that preceded Leibniz's eventual validation of the principle of reason? What is it about 'this little principle [that it] needed such an extraordinarily long incubation period' and, more to the point, why have we 'scarcely thought at all about this curious fact' (118)? Perhaps, suggests Heidegger with heavy irony, this unusually long incubation period is preparation for an equally unusual awakening, 'a quickening to a wakefulness that no longer admits of sleep, least of all, an incubation' (118). Mirroring Malabou's question of time, Heidegger's question addressed to the long sleep of reason here similarly resounds as a negative or paradoxical echo that reveals the outlines of a further area of incomprehensible silence within contemporary Continental philosophy in response to both the possibility and the plausibility of the principle of reason *as* a reasoned and reasonable principle. Moreover, as we shall see when addressing the death of Socrates in the first chapter, with this analogous pairing of reason with wakefulness and unreason with sleep, Heidegger in fact calls time on the entire metaphysical tradition in the West.

With this in mind, we can now elucidate a brief overview of the project embarked upon here. In subjecting itself to profound critique through its absence of rational foundation, it will be argued, reason must then decree that the existence of an immutable law, concept or cause is necessarily impossible. Based initially upon these two interlinked proclamations—that reason subjects itself to profound transformation and that no law, concept or cause is absolute and therefore invariable—it then becomes possible to address anew the conditions of unprecedented emergence into being and which, in turn, pose significant challenges to normative ethical practice as traditionally conceived in the West. Notably in this regard, the operative categories of 'living' and 'natural' remain with us only under extreme duress, yet the exclusive taxonomies to which these outmoded categories give rise continue to blindly justify the uses to which 'things' are being put with little or no ethical consideration. In order to remedy this ethical blinding that both enables and inheres within the categories and taxonomies of life and nature, a philosophical analysis of the machinery and machinations of novel emergence is indeed overdue. Furthermore, it will be argued that there exists a preliminary constitutive relation between the ethical and technological domains insofar as the process of emergence into being also orders an ethics of technological innovation.

THE RENDERING OF REASON

Staying for the moment with the belatedly staged principle of reason, Heidegger notes that for Leibniz this new principle is not simply one among many, but is rather 'one of the supreme fundamental principles, if not the most supreme one' (118). As to why this is so, continues Heidegger, we must look to the complete formulation of Leibniz's supreme new principle, that of the *principium reddendae rationis sufficientis*, which Leibniz glosses as 'nothing exists for which the sufficient reason for its existence cannot be rendered' (cit. 120). Clearly there is a lot more going on here than an as yet unexpressed but nonetheless immediately self-evident claim that 'everything has a reason.' Ironically, a significant part of this 'lots more' concerns the possibility or otherwise of immediacy itself. For Leibniz, truth describes the correctness of judgement, and it is reason alone that renders an account [*reddendae rationis*] of the truth of judgement. By its rendering of accounts, in other words, reason justifies the correctness of this or that judgement and, as such, declares this or that judgement to be true and, inversely, that any and all judgements are therefore untrue until such time as they are accounted for by reason. However, the need to justify judgement by the rendering of accounts raises a further question: To whom or what must these accounts be rendered? Heidegger's elegant answer is simple but nonetheless crucial: reasons are rendered 'to humans who determine objects as objects by way of a representation that judges' (119). From this point onward, writes Heidegger, all of 'modern thinking' experiences the human 'as an I that relates to the world such that it renders this world to itself in the form of connections correctly established between its representations—that means judgements—and thus sets itself over against this world as to an object' (119). As the newly appointed custodian of reason and arbiter of what does and does not count, the human thereafter establishes itself amid and against a world of objects that is now *literally of no account* but which exists solely for a representing subject.

This brings us to the fourth term in Leibniz's complete principle of reason, the *sufficientis*. Here, the question of sufficiency serves as a final check and balance imposed by reason upon otherwise all too human accounts of judgement. It rules, in short, as to the legitimacy or otherwise of accounts that lay claim to truth status. As such, it is better understood as a test of *adequation* insofar as it determines whether this or that account can be considered as *adequate* for the secure establishing of objects. From this moment forth, it is not only truth but also *existence itself* that now entirely depends upon human cognition. Only the completeness of the account, writes Heidegger, 'hereafter vouches for the fact that every cognition everywhere and at all times can include and count on the object and reckon with it. . . . The principle now says that every thing counts as existing when and only when it has been securely established as a calculable object for cognition' (120). We can therefore paraphrase Leibniz's grand principle as follows: *Every thing in the world exists only insofar as we (humans) have reasoned it so*. The principle of reason thus betrays the profound idealism of its founding, while the supposedly objective 'test' of sufficiency is shown to be nothing other than a blunt yet supremely effective ideological tool.

Leibniz's principle of reason thus serves to establish the 'objectness' or 'thingness' of everything else that exists as constitutively excluded *from* 'the human' and therefore wholly calculable *by* 'the human.' At the same time that the world of objects is pressed into being, in other words, every object in that world is declared fully comprehensible and thus entirely predictable. As the condition of their existence, reason now thoroughly determines the inhuman realms of matter, nature and artifice—and all this despite the fact that the principle of reason is not in the strict sense a causal principle. Less obvious, however, is that the determinist constraints introduced and maintained by the principle of reason are inevitably put to work on *both* sides of the human–nonhuman divide. As Heidegger writes:

> When Leibniz first expressly and completely formulated the principle of reason as such a Principle, what he thereby articulated is the fact that human cognition, in a decisive and unavoidable manner, had come to be taken up into the claim of the *principium rationis* and held in the sway of its power. The *principium rationis*, the principle of reason, becomes the fundamental principle of all cognition. This means: dominated by the *principium rationis* (120).

Put simply, in expressly formulating the principle of reason as a rigid and universal Principle, Leibniz inevitably constrains cognition itself to the dictates of its own fundamental principle. Hence, in the very process of constituting human cognition as ontologically distinct from the fully comprehensible and calculable objects that populate the natural, material and artificial realms, Leibniz in the same moment subjects human cognition to the demands of reason. Both despite and because of its exalted ontological difference, cognition must thereafter render reasons sufficiently adequate to justify its *own* existence. Human cognition, in other words, must now securely establish itself as a calculable object in order to account for its existence as singularly incalculable. The paradoxical circularity quickly becomes dizzying.

Nevertheless, since its formulation Leibniz's supreme principle has proven incomparably powerful. 'In the history of humanity,' writes Heidegger, 'the authority of the powerful fundamental principle becomes more powerful the more pervasively, the more obviously, and accordingly the more inconspicuously the principle of reason determines all cognition and behavior' (121).

This, he continues, "brings to fruition nothing less than the innermost, and at the same time most concealed, molding of the age of Western history we call 'modernity'" (121). Moreover, it does so through the machines, myths and contrivances of what we know today as modern technology. This is because the perfection to which technology tends above all consists 'in the complete-ness of the calculably secure establishing of objects, in the completeness of reckoning with them and with the securing of the calculability of possibilities for reckoning' (121). In its triumph of unqualified validity, the *principium rationis* thus determines the essence of our modern technological age.

In one respect, as Heidegger notes, Leibniz's translation of a 'barely thought' notion into an all-conquering fundamental principle marks the end of a curiously extended period of incubation. In another, however, this marks but one more somnambulist stage in the continuing incubation of reason in the West. Rather than a decisive step—be it causal, dialectical or teleological—along the way to a perfect accounting of the world and thus of its perfectly predictable future, this continuing incubation of reason serves only itself inasmuch as it serves ultimately to demonstrate its own absent foundation. In other words, and as I will endeavor to show over the course of this book, *reason subjects itself* to a profound and profoundly uncertain transformation. Just as reason at the close of the nineteenth century ultimately decrees the death of the God it was initially constructed to slavishly serve, so too reason ultimately decrees the death of *life* as a distinct—and distinctly privileged—ontological category today.

EINSTEIN'S INSANITY: THE RECIPROCITY OF THE RATIONAL, THE INSTRUMENTAL AND THE PREDICTABLE

Recalling Malabou's provocative allegation about the contemporary loss of primacy accorded to the concept of time, we follow in detail here Heidegger's challenge to the normative adequation of reason when he asks whether we should 'give up what is worthy of thought in favor of the recklessness of exclusively calculative thinking and its immense achievements' (*The Principle of Reason*, 129). For Heidegger, as for us, the stakes clearly could not be any higher insofar as it is the future itself that is at stake. In order to 'enter on a path of reflection,' writes Heidegger, we must first try to reflect on the principle of reason in such a way as to 'come to terms with the distinction that holds before our eyes the difference between mere calculative thinking and reflective thinking' (122). Moreover, he continues, such reflection begins by attending to that which, as the herald of the Anthropocene, conceals itself in the naming of the 'atomic age': namely that, for the first time in its history, 'humanity interprets an epoch of its historical existence on the basis of the rapacity for, and the procuring of, a natural energy' (122).

Thinking as calculation and the rapacity for procuring natural energy are for Heidegger the indissociable markers of modernity, and the tyrannical governance of the calculable is nowhere more in evidence than in the commonplace definition of insanity—famously if erroneously attributed to Albert Einstein—as 'doing the same thing over and over again and expecting a different result.' Of course, the authority accruing to the name Einstein in the modern era is unparalleled, making it *somewhat* ironic therefore that this authority should be usurped here in defence of pre-modern—i.e., *Newtonian*—physics insofar as the corollary definition of the rational entailed by this claim consists therefore in knowing the effect of every cause in advance.[4] The rationale of calculation, in short, demands an entirely deterministic and thus wholly predictable universe in order to function. In this way, perfection becomes synonymous with the absolute calculability of objects and, insofar as modern technology is perceived as coming closest to this engineered perfection, 'the authority characteristic of the principle of reason' thereafter comes to 'determine the essence of the modern, technological age' (121).

At base, Leibniz's principle of reason thus serves to *instrumentalize* the entire universe insofar as it is deemed as existing outside of human reasoning and as such is subject to the singularly unambiguous dictates of causal determinism. Moreover, as a corollary of this fundamental determinism by calculable relations of cause and effect, time and temporal affects abruptly vanish from our mechanist universe, which runs just as well backward as it does forward. The consequences of the symmetrical conception of existence are far from innocuous. Not least, if we *also* keep with tradition in supposing that we can never approach being except through time, then essential timelessness inevitably renders being itself as essentially timeless, that is, as fully determined stasis. In short, the stalled reciprocity of the rational, the instrumental and the wholly predictable condemns the universe to a moribund state of profound immobility.

Enchanted by the abstraction of calculative *ratio*, we forget to ask what for Heidegger is the 'world-question' of thinking and instead remake the earth in our image: as a material repository, a world of nature configured as mere 'stock' in solitary service to our rapacity for the material, and then we forget that too. While we will address the various roles—moral and political as well as metaphysical—attributed to the concept of nature along with the insidiousness of its violence in detail in the second chapter, it is sufficient at this early stage to simply gain a sense of 'the force of the demand that threatens to overpower us through the principle of rendering sufficient reasons' (123). Such is the dominance of Leibniz's commonplace little principle, that is, of modernity itself.

And what, we must ask, of the future? Can we really afford to forget that also? Here, we stay with Heidegger insofar as we too must ask: What is the instrumental itself? 'Wherever ends are pursued and means are employed,' writes Heidegger in *The Question Concerning Technology* (1954), 'wherever instrumentality reigns, there reigns causality' (6). At this point, Heidegger addresses a crucial coda to the principle of reason: 'But suppose that causality, for its part, is veiled in darkness with respect to what it is?' (6). Returning to the logic of insanity mistakenly attributed to Einstein, it is not by chance that this logic specifically defers to the (already insane) expectation or anticipation of a breakdown of determined causal relationships. However, what concerns us here—and what still today remains largely veiled in darkness—is that of a causality *more* insane than insane, insofar as the effective event is precisely that which cannot be expected or anticipated—an unpredictable break *with* determinist causality that is not however the breakdown *of* causal relations. While this will be addressed in detail over the course of this book, we already have a sense of how the potential inscription of irreversible and unpredictable formal events at the structural level of being inevitably requires philosophy to once again turn its attention to the question of time. Moreover, as both existential possibility and prior condition, time in this way ceases to be in slavish service to superlative human folly, no longer available for expropriation as a uniquely human property (whether real or irreal) and no longer a simple accident of existence (human or otherwise).

EXISTENCE WITHOUT PRECEDENCE: QUESTIONS OF TIME AND TECHNOLOGY

Time, it will be argued, is real and inclusive, meaning that nothing, including all physical and natural laws, stands outside of time. The question of time is thus a question of relation, key to which are the concepts of immediacy and mediation. Tightly bound up with the concept of timeless being, immediacy was long deemed the exclusive property of Nature understood as the set of all living entities other than the human, with the loss of immediacy being considered the (bargain) price paid by humankind upon its constitutive Epimethean secession into the sociotechnological realm of Culture. Today, however, this concept of immediacy is in the process of being radically reworked.

One key aspect of this reworking of immediacy concerns the prior conditions of novel emergence. Put another way, what things have to happen and what conditions must be met in order for some radically 'new' being to emerge into existence? Whatever its form may become in time, for an innovation to be truly innovative the very possibility of its existence must, everywhere prior to its material emergence, be literally unthinkable. It must, in other words, be in being without precedent. But *does* it necessarily follow that 'being without precedent' is the same as 'being without condition'? We have to be careful on this point. Prior to its timely emergence, such a being is by definition impossible and inconceivable (the latter terms being in a strict sense synonymous in this instance). Furthermore, the sense of this previous impossibility and inconceivability only comes into being alongside the (impossible and inconceivable) emergence of novel being—and this, it should be noted, holds regardless of whether we are talking about cultural objects, natural things or lively technologies and everything in between.

To exist without precedent. Can we really conclude from this that only true novelty, alone among beings, exists without condition? And if so, are we also to conclude from this definitive lack of determining historicity that the process of its emergence into being is therefore uniquely and paradoxically *im*mediate? Clearly, such a claim is counterintuitive in the extreme, not least because the very concept of 'process' is defined in the first instance by a 'taking up' of time. That said, however, the concept of process already presumes a particular conception of causality that either gives rise to temporal succession or, at the very least, functions in tandem. Hence, if causality indeed remains veiled in darkness with respect to what it is, then so too must the process of 'process' be veiled in darkness with respect to what *it* is also.

So where does this leave us today? As will be argued at length in the first chapter, in order to even begin to respond to such questions, it is necessary first of all for us to move beyond the normative metaphysical sophistry that opposes biological life to inanimate matter. This is not intended as a particularly provocative statement, although some readers will likely deem it to be so based on what they perceive as the inherent danger of any theory founded upon an ontological 'flattening' that seeks to erase the absolute distinction that constitutes life via the exclusion and negation of matter. Such uneasiness is not surprising in the least insofar as the presumed existence of a secure distinction dividing life from nonlife—together with its correlates subject from object and being from thing—is not only a staple throughout Western philosophy, but also serves as the ground upon which the entire edifice of liberal morality, ancient and modern, is constructed. While counterintuitive perhaps, it will be argued here that the production and reproduction of this simple distinction in fact serves to *necessarily exclude the possibility of ethics*. Ethical possibility, in short, *can begin only following* the collapse of the living-nonliving binary, just as ethical accountability therefore begins only on the condition that we are done with life entirely.

As a preliminary theoretical and ethical step, the extension of formal processes of individuation as constitutive of *all* forms of being—irrespective of whether such forms are labeled living, dead or nonliving—can be seen to accord very closely with contemporary research being proposed from within the physical sciences. Of these, most important are the realist arguments for pilot wave theory and spontaneous wave function collapse in quantum theory along with—and often overlapping—theories posed by proponents of far-from-equilibrium thermodynamics, all of which refute the timelessness of classical physics in favor of contingency and irreversibility on both microscopic and macroscopic levels of being. However, while the strange temporalities described by dissipative structures serve as privileged examples in what follows, they must nonetheless await the final chapter before being addressed directly and in detail. That said, Dorian Sagan and Eric Schneider's definition of metastable flow systems provides us with a very useful introduction. Metastable processes, they argue, 'underlie the things we mistake for things. Selves are not closed or isolated but arise as metastable open systems in a sea of energy and flows. . . . [W]e too are metastable flow systems with billions of years of history as dissipative structures' (*Into the Cool*, 112). Neither simple being nor simple thing, every given *form of being* instead describes an open energy-driven processual structure, at once product and producer of material cycles and self-reinforcing networks. Only on this basis, it will be argued, does it become presently possible to address the concept of immediacy as it pertains to the emergence of entirely novel forms of being.

Before we move on, however, there is a critical coda to this claim that should be recalled throughout. Whereas metastable systems are constitutively open, this does *not* mean they are open to an infinite polymorphism. Rather, the emergence of novel forms or patterns must nonetheless remain always dependent upon prior historical states. Formal plasticity, in other words, inscribes the potential for unpredictable transformation as a constitutive condition of metastable systems but, insofar as this potential is a consequence of the material cycles that structure forms of being through iterative feedback loops, this transformation—while discontinuous and nonlinear—is nonetheless constrained by historicity, that is, by the *memory* of prior states of being. While this will be further clarified over the course of the chapters to follow, for the moment it suffices for us to note both that the *a priori* potential for any metastable system to become wholly other to itself is a defining property of being, and that this potential is dependent upon prior forms of being. As Sagan and Schneider write, 'the emergence of whirling energy-dependent systems, their path-dependent growth and history, and even a sort of reproduction to make use of increased energy flux, are not just properties of life' (130).

SIMULTANEITY IS INDISTINGUISHABLE
FROM MAGIC

Returning to the role of immediacy as it relates to the emergence of novel forms of being, by turning to the physical sciences we discover that the functioning of both spatial and temporal simultaneity is in fact indistinguishable from magic. While I will introduce several such examples of problematic immediacy in what follows, for now it is helpful to pay particular attention to Sagan and Schneider's discussion of the fluid systems of Taylor vortices, the process and significance of which will be explored at length in later chapters. Put simply, Taylor vortex flow refers to the regular yet unpredictable patterns that emerge when a thin layer of fluid is trapped between two rotating cylinders. Most interesting here are the terms by which Sagan and Schneider describe the emergence of these new states (patterns) of being.

In a section entitled 'Evolution and Memory,' they note how the 'rotated fluid progresses through a series of near-instantaneous jumps, from one pair of flow patterns to the next. . . . As the rotation rates increase or decrease, different numbers of vortex pairs and/or number of waves appear. Near-magical jumps from state to state are observed' (*Into the Cool*, 129). While we can likely assume that the notion of 'progress' as it is used here refers only to a chronology of observed events and not to a willed or externally determined teleology, the question of proximity nonetheless gives rise to a number of significant concerns. On two occasions within a single paragraph Sagan and Schneider employ the same hyphenated prefix in describing the transformation from one state to another, first as 'near-instantaneous' and then again as 'near-magical.' Just what is meant by this somewhat clunky prefix inevitably remains obscure: How close must one thing or one state of being have to be to another, exactly, in order for them be considered 'near'? By simply changing the scale of reference, this problematic becomes even clearer when we ask just how near is near in the nanoscopic realm of subatomic quanta.

In describing an abrupt replacement of one metastable state or form of being with another in the same *physical* location, Sagan and Schneider are clearly referring to proximity in *time* rather than proximity in space. At the same time, their idiosyncratic use of the hyphen in this case is telling. Serving to bind the two terms closer than close in a defiance of formal convention, the hyphen visually and grammatically reenacts the very sense it is meant to convey, that of a closeness in time that goes so far beyond mere proximity as to border on the magical. More precisely, it is the apparent simultaneity of the supplemental form of being with that which it supplements that bestows upon these transitions and transformations their apparent magic. Instantaneity, in other words, is synonymous with magic insofar as it describes a formal dislocation in space *but not in time*, and as such breaks with all traditionally accepted rules of causality. The magic of the instantaneous and the simultaneous—that is to say, of the immediate—thus inheres not in the speed or the timeliness of its coming, nor in the brevity of its appearing, but is rather to be found in its paradoxical time*less*ness. Magic, in other words, describes the impossibility of atemporal emergence. We can now better understand the role played by the qualifying prefix 'near-' in Sagan and Schneider's account of fluid dynamics. Something akin to an involuntary stutter, it serves to paper over what would otherwise be a far more serious breach of formal convention—that of classical causality—with the hyphen serving to further guard against its decoupling at some time down the line.

Change takes time: as a principle, this seems at least as immediately obvious as 'nothing is without reason.' Ironically then, it is the apparent immediacy of the statement that again marks out its normative function as an unqualified success. Regardless of how quickly or how slowly a transformation is effected, the transformation of one form into another must necessarily occur both in time and over time—this all seems eminently reasonable, an incontrovertible fact and as such unworthy of mention. On this, Sagan and Schneider would clearly agree, and yet equally clearly, they nonetheless *do* feel it to be worthy of mention. In this instance, however, 'near-' does not in fact signify a determined relation of forms, but instead attests only to an unquestioned *faith* in the sufficient adequation of the governing laws of classical physics with the actual functioning of external reality. Stated simply, the normative principle of reason decrees that whatever *appears* contrary to scientific law cannot therefore *be* that which it nonetheless appears to be.

That said, however, the temporal simultaneity of forms of being cannot be so easily dismissed as a mere illusion awaiting its time of sufficient adequation or as a consequence of constraints inherent in the current state of technological progress. What, in other words, if the simultaneity of forms is neither an error of perception nor an error of measurement, the resolution of which in the future requires only time in the present? Even without the obvious irony of any claim to have sidestepped the question of simultaneity by deferring it to the future, the problematic of temporal simultaneity has long occupied, and continues to occupy, a fundamental place in quantum theory since its inception at the start of the twentieth century. Most notably, temporal simultaneity is at the core of two of its strangest and most contested concepts: superposition and entanglement. The former refers to the simultaneous 'stacking'— i.e., superpositioning—of two or more differently configured states of being, while the latter refers to entangled states of being that instantaneously affect each other despite any amount of physical distance between them. This 'spooky action at a distance' of entangled states thus demonstrably refutes the causal principle of contiguity, which claims that states of being can only be directly influenced by other states of being that are nearby in both space and time. Ignoring for the moment the severe conflict with special relativity that results, we can nonetheless summarize this very simply: *simultaneity is nonlocal both in time (superposition) and in space (entanglement)*.

Theoretical physicist Lee Smolin offers a more nuanced account of entanglement, describing it as a 'property of a quantum state of two or more systems, where the state indicates a property shared by those systems that is not just the sum of properties held by the individual particles' (*Einstein's Unfinished Revolution*, 299). In addition to the problem of faster than light interactions presupposed by nonlocal entanglement, Smolin here highlights the further crucial point that, insofar as they are entangled, the sum of such states is always greater than that of its parts. Entanglement, in other words, describes a relational property and state that always exceeds the determinable properties and states of an individual system, which, insofar as it is without relation, thus remains constrained by the principle of locality. Hence, to be entangled is to be indeterminate.

Recalling the 'near-magical' phase states occupied by Taylor vortex patterns in fluid mechanics, it will be argued in what follows that such patterns may in fact serve, if not as an indubitable example of macroscopic superposition per se, then at least as a macroscopic *model* of superposition insofar as the micro- and macroscopic distinction necessarily breaks down as we attempt to close in on a simple line of demarcation, only to disclose instead a continuum of metastable systems and configuration spaces or, in the language of thermodynamics, energetic forms of negentropic decoherence.

In order to better understand this, Smolin's account of the restricted principle of precedence provides a particularly useful setting from which to begin our analysis of novel emergence. According to classical mechanics, the laws of physics are entirely deterministic and as such preclude any possibility of genuine novelty emerging anywhere in the Newtonian universe. As Smolin writes, all that ever happens is 'rearrangements of elementary particles with unchanging properties by unchanging laws' (Unger and Smolin, *The Singular Universe*, 466). However, continues Smolin, determinism is in fact only necessary in a very limited set of circumstances wherein multiple iterations of the same in the past make it possible for us to reliably predict the outcome of multiple iterations of the same in the future. This predictive reliability is thereafter taken as proof of the existence of universal timeless laws of nature that ultimately order all change. But this, writes Smolin, is 'an over-interpretation of the evidence' (466). Reliability, in other words, is not the same as certainty. Rather than providing empirical proof of the existence of underlying and unchanging physical laws, the reliability of prediction requires only that there be a principle that measurements which repeat processes which have taken place many times in the past yield the same outcomes as were seen in the past. Such a *principle of precedence* would explain all the instances where determinism by laws works without restricting novel processes to yield predictable outcomes (466).

Put more simply, the principle of precedence states only that the *probability* of correctly predicting the future outcome of a given process increases significantly following many successful iterations of a particular process all yielding the same outcome. While this probability may indeed *approach* 100 per cent, it cannot, however, ever *be* 100 per cent insofar as no state or process of being can ever exist in sovereign fashion outside of its relations with other states and processes of being. Echoing the challenges posed to classical causality by Humean empiricism in the eighteenth century, Smolin here argues that quantum mechanics demands a different way of thinking about causality, one that compels us to let go of illusory certainties. This difference takes two forms. First, prior iterations of a state or system can no longer be assumed to offer 'unique predictions for how the future will resemble the past' but rather 'only a statistical distribution of possible outcomes in the future' (466). Second, insofar as entanglement 'involves novel properties shared between subsystems which are not just properties of the individual subsystems,' the future forms of entangled individuals cannot therefore be predicted by any knowledge of the past (467).

So, what does this all mean from the perspective of novel emergence? In contrast to the absolute preclusion of novelty described by Newtonian mechanics, the probabilistic distributions and entangled states of quantum theory describe instead a universe that can never be wholly constrained by its prior states of being. Rather, as Smolin writes, quantum mechanics discloses at the atomic level 'the possibility that novel states can behave unpredictably because they are without precedent' (467). The restricted principle of precedence, in other words, ultimately makes space for the possibility of novel emergence. Hence, writes Smolin,

> we can have a conception of a law which is sufficient to account for the repeatability of experiments without restricting novel states from being free from constraints from deterministic laws. *In essence the laws evolve with the states.* . . . Only after sufficient precedent has been established does a law take hold, and only for statistical predictions. Individual outcomes can be largely unconstrained (467, italics added).

Clearly, the potential for emergence without precedent in Smolin's account cannot be reserved as the defining property of biological or organic forms of *life*. Rather, as an indeterminate property arising from relational entanglement, the potential for unprecedented emergence becomes instead the property of all forms of existence. While the material functioning of this formal power as yet remains obscure, we nonetheless begin to gain a sense of how ethics may indeed have a fundamental role to play with respect to the emergence of genuine technological innovation.

In beginning to make connections between emergence without precedent, the historicity of technicity and the creative evolution of forms of being, we are better able to understand how it is that reason must subject itself to profound transformation and, in the process, return the concepts of time and causality to the forefront of contemporary philosophical concerns by ensuring that the operative categories of life and nature cease to serve as blinds behind which exploitation is left to run rampant in the absence of all ethical regulation.

Chapter 1

Ends of Life

Death of Socrates

Today's deconstructive orthodoxy, as is well known, discloses as unfounded and therefore illegitimate the exclusivity constitutive of encapsulated metaphysical binaries. In practice, however, what too often gets overlooked is the necessary corollary of this disclosure: that deconstruction discloses as fundamentally unsound the *structuring* of simple ontological dualism itself. While perhaps appearing negligible at first, it is in fact this distinction between two closely drawn disclosures that proscribes the folly of an unwitting repetition and replacement of metaphysics in the guise of an ever more profound or ever more essential antithesis. Stated as simply as possible, the deconstruction of a given ontological dualism must also entail the deconstruction of ontological dualism as a legitimate ordering structure.

In order to interrupt in this way the ideological exclusivity that is the operative function of encapsulated relation, which is to say of simple difference, we will thus turn our attention first to the ends of life, before then moving on to the ends of nature in the next chapter. As already noted in the introduction, the ontological 'flattening' that follows the deconstruction of an absolute distinction dividing biological life from inanimate matter is perceived by many as inherently dangerous and, indeed, it is not at all difficult for us to understand just why this is so. Since the dawning of philosophy in the West, as we shall see in this chapter, the constitution of life upon the exclusion and negation of nonlife has been considered integral to the safeguarding of truth and value as well as the foundation of anthropocentric privilege. As such, the deconstruction of the life–matter binary is seen as throwing open the doors of reason to the limitless specters of cynicism, sophistry and immorality. By contrast, however, it is rather the production and reproduction of the simple life–matter binary that stymies the transformation of reason by itself. The possibility of ethics, it bears repeating, *follows* the disarticulation of the living–nonliving binary.

Before returning again to the fatal crucible of the ancient Greek *agora*, there are a couple of provisos to bear in mind. First and most important, the deconstruction of the simple living–nonliving binary does *not* in any way involve the 'promotion' of inanimate objects to the status of living beings (animism) or the 'demotion' of living beings to the status of 'mere' things (mechanism). Such thinking only makes sense within the confines of a pre-established ontological dualism. This is not what is at stake here. With admirable clarity, philosopher Claire Colebrook demonstrates the incommensurability of all such approaches. In its triumphant championing of a return to life, affect or 'the lived,' she writes, contemporary posthumanisms have unwittingly brought back 'one grand whole' of interconnected systems of observation, in which

> '[m]an' is effected as that animal who would be especially poised to read the logic of life, and this because of his capacities for speech and sociality; it is the creation of man that enables a certain concept of life. When man is destroyed to yield a posthuman world it is the same world *minus humans,* a world of meaning, sociality and readability yet without any sense of the disjunction, gap or limits of the human. Like nihilism, the logic is metaleptic: the figure of man is originally posited in order to yield a sense or meaning of life, and yet when man is done away with as an external power what is left is an anthropomorphic life of meaning and readability (*Death of the Posthuman*, 164).

If we are ever to break free of our enchantment to this reactive and metaleptic logic of life, argues Colebrook, it is important to understand that, while it may only be known or given from within life, the *sense* of an ethical imperative is nonetheless 'irreducible to life' ('Fragility,' 257). There is, she continues, 'something like a formal power that dislocates humanity from itself, that opens humans to an infinite or non-living future' (257). We first encountered this 'something like' a formal power in the introduction, where it is initially described as an as yet obscure material function that inscribes the potential for unprecedented emergence as a property common to all forms of entangled existence. It is the same malevolent and inhuman formal power that for Colebrook opens thought to a future in which 'it is no longer enslaved and enclosed in Cartesian self-presence of the dead system of a solely human language' (257). More recently, Colebrook further clarifies this obscure formal power as 'another counter-logic of artifice that is not quite counter to life, but that is perhaps best thought of as a destructive and inhuman force within figurations of artifice' ('All Life Is Artificial Life,' 1).

While it will be argued at length that processes giving rise to novel emergence indeed disclose an inhuman and mutilating formal power as their condition, it is important at this early stage to stress the incommensurability of such an argument with the vitalisms and animisms that carry aloft recent theories of vibrant matter and affective embodiment. Just as there is no *life* in general, as Colebrook affirms, then so too there is no *matter* in general. Whereas the fetishized boundaries and borderlines of ontological dualism necessarily presuppose that a prior ethical differentiation has already taken place, ways of being are instead composed of radically differing configurations, intensities and multiplicities 'in which different speeds and economies open different and incompossible systems' (*Death of the Posthuman*, 166). Put simply, and despite the extraordinary longevity that reaches its pinnacle with Leibniz in the eighteenth century, the constitutive binaries definitive of metaphysics inevitably doom it to failure before it can even begin.

BEGINNING, AGAIN

It is precisely because of this extraordinary longevity, however, that we are compelled to return to the site of this originary failure. How did this even happen? How is it, in other words, that the inevitable failure of metaphysics in fact *preceded* metaphysics itself? What strange causality is at work here? What begins as a simple, albeit somewhat ignominious desire to circumvent circular reasoning will, as we shall see, propel Western philosophy along a long—and ultimately futile—search for adequate knowledge and a sufficiency of proof.

We can trace the inauguration of Western philosophy to a very precise moment in the collected dialogues of Plato. Unsurprisingly, it concerns the safeguarding of philosophy as a unique site of truth uncontaminated by cynicism and sophistry. Philosophical truth, in other words, begets itself in and as an attempt to safeguard itself from unwanted incursion. What certainly is surprising, however, is that this safeguarding of truth in fact depends upon an eminently unreasonable act of *faith*, with its border security built upon the exclusion of nonbelievers and with sophistry, dog-philosophy and cynical self-interest newly castigated as the blinds of incorrigible infidels. As we shall see here, metaphysical reason opens already under the cosh of death and dissolution, to which Socrates, in a dance of death all his own, responds by first excluding *equality* from the empirical world of equal things before then extrapolating this process in order to posit *property* as a pure ontological concept constituted through the exclusion of ontical properties insofar as the latter are all necessarily impure. And with this simple Socratic two-step, the production of a restricted system of ownership outside of societal control thereafter becomes possible.

The argument from exclusion is initially staged in response to a variant of the sophistic 'trick' argument posed to Socrates in *Meno* (80d–81e), and then reiterated in greater depth in *Phaedo*, wherein it is further posed as a corollary of the argument from opposites (70d–81a).

THE TRUTH OF VIRTUE

In the midst of a discussion concerning the proper sense of virtue, Socrates gently chides his interlocutor Meno for bringing up what he calls 'a debater's argument' (80e). Socrates first summarizes Meno's argument as stating 'that a man cannot search either for what he knows or for what he does not know. He cannot search for what he knows—since he knows it, there is no need to search—nor for what he does not know, for he does not know what to look for' (80e–81a). While Socrates flatly dismisses the argument as unsound, the stakes of the challenge posed to truth and knowledge here vastly exceed the dialogue's primary concern with the concept of virtue. In fact, Meno is here abruptly calling on Socrates to prove the possibility of adequate knowledge. Socrates, in other words, is being called on to do nothing less than to safeguard philosophy—as the proper realm of truth and knowledge—from the rhetoric and technical trickery wielded from a position of cynical self-interest. Hence, with the rebuttal of Meno's sophistic relativism, philosophy is here being called upon to save it*self*.

So, just how is it that Socrates becomes both the inaugurator *and* the savior of Western philosophy in one and the same moment? To better understand this, it will be necessary to restage the argument as it is more broadly posed in the *Phaedo*. Hardly fortuitous, this argument quickly turns to an examination of the relation between life and nonlife, and between the living and the dead. Similarly nonfortuitous, the dialogue in question between Socrates and his interlocutory tag-team of Cebes and Simmias in *Phaedo* follows exactly the same two-step pattern found in *Meno*.

Beginning in both cases from the concept of 'true virtue,' Socrates first invokes 'the mysteries' in support of his position—the Eleusinian mysteries in *Meno* and the Dionysian mysteries in *Phaedo*—and then moves on to consider the existence of the soul before concluding with the claim that true knowledge can never be *dis*covered but only ever *re*covered. That said, however, there is one obvious difference between the two accounts: there is no practical demonstration of knowledge as recollection in *Phaedo* but rather only a recollection of its previous demonstration in the *Meno*, and in this case it is recalled not by Socrates but by Cebes. Ironically, in this case recollection without reiteration of prior proof leads us not toward true knowledge, but serves instead to mutely gloss over a fundamental problem left unresolved in the earlier dialogue with Meno. In other words, the profound hesitation between knowledge as empirically learned and knowledge as recollection of atemporal truths that undermines Socrates's argument in *Meno* is nowhere to be found in the *Phaedo*, obscured from view by way of a timely failure of recollection. In place of hesitation, there is now only the proper domain of philosophy, disposed already in the first instance to the essential and immaterial realm of Ideas.

While ostensibly dealing with the possibility or otherwise of attaining true virtue amid such everyday material distractions as pleasures, pains and fears, Socrates in fact begins his account in the *Phaedo* by subtly but nonetheless dramatically shifting what is to be meant by the concept of virtue itself. Virtue, he says, first and foremost must be excluded from all *material* or *bodily* economies of exchange. This is the first move in the metaphysical two-step, a general mechanic that thereafter avails itself without limit. Across its every reiteration, one operative ideology reigns supreme: the constitutive exclusion as inherently inferior of material and bodily economies of exchange. We can now better understand why Socrates first sets out his stall with the concept of true virtue in both *Meno* and *Phaedo*. The single 'valid currency' for which all worldly distractions should be exchanged, he argues, is quite simply wisdom. We only have 'real courage and moderation and justice and, in a word, true virtue, with wisdom, whether pleasures and fears and all such things be present or absent' (*Phaedo*, 69b). While this is somewhat unclear given that Socrates states first that distractions of the body can be validly exchanged *for* wisdom only to claim immediately afterwards that the attainment of wisdom in fact renders all corporeal affects and passions irrelevant, from the larger context we can understand Socrates as saying that the acquiring of true wisdom or true knowledge ultimately nullifies any and all such worldly exchange. Such material and bodily economies of exchange, says Socrates, only ever produce 'an illusory appearance of virtue; is in fact fit for slaves, without soundness or truth' (69b).[1]

What is interesting about Socrates's delineation of true virtue in particular is the apparent exchangeability of wisdom itself, which is here deemed synonymous with a whole raft of diverse concepts including courage, moderation, justice and virtue. Virtue, it would now seem, is in fact an exchangeable property after all. This muddies the water considerably, and hence it is ironic indeed that this admixture of terms serves the precise function of introducing the concept of *purity* into the dialogue: '[I]n truth,' Socrates says, 'moderation and courage and justice are a purging away of all such things, and wisdom itself is a kind of cleansing or purification' (69b–c). Based upon nothing more than this alleged identity or association with a series of otherwise unrelated concepts, wisdom is thus likened to a pure state of being with the processual recollection of knowledge becoming akin to that of a cleansing purge. As such, the way is now open for Socrates to define the realm of philosophy

as one of purity and true faith. There are, he says, and 'as those concerned
with the mysteries say, many who carry the thyrsus but the Bacchants are
few. These latter are, in my opinion, no other than those who have practiced
philosophy in the right way' (69c–d). Here, Socrates credits the Dionysian
Bacchants with the correct practice of philosophy solely on the basis of the
apparent depth of their faith in contrast to those who merely cultivate the
appearance of faith, thus defining the practice of philosophy—that is, the
correct processual recollection of knowledge—as a ritual purging that, on the
condition that it is accompanied by absolute faith, serves to cleanse the soul
of all physiological distraction.[2]

Equally important, Socrates's rallying of the Bacchants as fellow travel-
lers in the search for truth and thus wisdom serves to introduce and at once
legitimize the theological concept of the immortal human soul. Whereas in
Meno Socrates invokes two theological sources in support of his thesis—cel-
ebrants of the Eleusinian Mysteries in the first instance and then 'priests and
priestesses' more generally (81b–c)—in *Phaedo* the Bacchants end up doing
double duty as practitioners of ritual purification and true believers in the
immortality of the human soul. With this, the dialogue on virtue quickly turns
to an examination of life and death.

THE TRUTH OF IMMORTALITY

While seemingly innocuous, the introduction of the state of the soul into
the discussion at this point is of fundamental importance to what is to follow. Referring once again to 'those who established the mystic rites for us,'
Socrates comes to their defence, stating they 'were not inferior persons but
were speaking in riddles long ago when they said that whoever arrives in the
underworld uninitiated and unsanctified will wallow in the mire, whereas he
who arrives there purified and initiated will dwell with the gods' (*Phaedo*
69c). Having been only recently sentenced to die by an Athenian court,
Socrates might well be forgiven at this point for waxing somewhat lyri-
cal as regards his imminent 'arrival yonder,' but Cebes fortunately steps in
before too long. Socrates, he says, everything else you said is excellent, but
it remains very hard 'to believe that the soul still exists after a man has died
and that it still possesses some capability and intelligence' (70b). While such
a belief would doubtless offer 'much good hope' (and presumably most of all
to those who, like Socrates, find themselves abruptly confronting their own
imminent extinction), as far as the rest of us are concerned it still 'requires
a good deal of faith and persuasive argument' (70b). So, how does Socrates
respond to having the process of wisdom exchange described by Cebes as a

mishmash of consolation, strong faith and persuasive argument? 'What you say is true, Cebes, but what shall we do?' (70b).

Indeed, what shall we do? Socrates's answer is the argument from opposites, which in turn provides the prior condition for the argument from exclusion and therefore the basis upon which Western philosophy will construct itself. In the hope of correcting Cebes's persistent scepticism regarding the indestructibility of the human soul, Socrates recalls 'an ancient theory that souls arriving there [the underworld] come from here, and then again that they arrive here and are born here from the dead' (70c). In turning now to the two parts and pair of corollary proofs that make up the argument from opposites initiated with this mythic recollection, our task will be to see if it is indeed based upon sound logical principles, or whether it rests in truth upon nothing more than a combination of hope, faith and persuasive rhetorical techniques.

Here, then, is the argument for the immortality of the human soul posed by Socrates:

> If that is true, that the living come back from the dead, then surely our souls must exist there, for they could not come back if they did not exist, and this is a sufficient proof that these things are so if it truly appears that the living never come from any other source than from the dead (*Phaedo* 70c–d).

Socrates opens here by saying that living beings must emerge from dead beings—that life, in other words, must have death as its necessary condition—since its demonstration serves as sufficient proof of the indestructibility of the human soul. While this claim already breaches the limits of every attempted anthropocentric or vitalist closure, as we shall see, for the moment let us stay with the argument put forward by Socrates. Here, he exhorts Cebes to not simply confine himself to humanity, but to 'take all animals and all plants into account' and, indeed, 'all things which come to be' so as to 'examine whether those that have an opposite must necessarily come to be from their opposite and from nowhere else' (70d–e). Socrates then proceeds to offer several examples in support of his claim: that which becomes larger must first have been smaller; that which becomes weaker must first have been stronger; that which becomes swifter must first have been slower; that which gets worse must first have been better; and that which becomes more just must first have been more unjust. Adding nothing further than this list of seemingly self-evident examples, Socrates then quickly and prematurely claims to have 'sufficiently established that all things come to be in this way, opposites from opposites' (71a).

With this initial point supposedly made, Socrates thereafter draws Cebes's attention to 'a further point' that needs to be considered, which is that 'between each of those pairs of opposites there are two processes: from the one to the other and then again from the other to the first' (71b). Opposites, in other words, come to be each from the other. Hence, for each oppositional pairing there must be two *reciprocal processes* of generation, corresponding to the back and forth exchanges between the two. Once again, Socrates follows up this second claim with a bombardment of rapid-fire examples. Between the larger and the smaller, he says, are processes of increase and decrease, and 'so too there is separation and combination, cooling and heating, and all such things' (71b). Here, however, we find a clear privilege being afforded to one pair of opposed terms and processes in particular, that of being asleep and being awake—an opposition that ultimately delivers to Socrates' argument all of its forward motion. To be awake, he says, 'comes from sleeping, and to sleep comes from being awake. Of the two processes one is going to sleep, the other is waking up' (71d). Moreover, insists Socrates, it is '*in the same way* about life and death' (71d, italics added). In the case of the latter, he continues, 'one of the two processes of becoming is clear, for dying is clear enough, is it not? . . . What shall we do then? Shall we not supply the opposite process of becoming? Is nature to be lame in this case?' (71e). On this point, Cebes is of course quick to agree that, yes, dying is 'certainly' clear enough and that nature will 'most surely' not prove to be lame but instead provide a necessary process of becoming that is opposite to that of dying. This process, Socrates then clarifies, can only be that of 'coming to life again' and, as such, it therefore follows that this must be 'a process of coming from the dead to the living' (72a).

At this point, Socrates pauses to sum up his argument so far: if we accept, as we must, that the process of dying exists, then we must also accept that the process of 'coming to life again' also exists, meaning it is agreed 'that the living come from the dead in this way no less than the dead from the living, and, if that is so, it seems to be a sufficient proof that the souls of the dead must be somewhere whence they can come back again' (72a). On this basis, Socrates then offers a second proof in support of his thesis. If dying and coming to life again are *not* in fact reciprocal processes engaging in perpetual back and forth exchange, then 'all things would ultimately be in the same state, be affected in the same way, and cease to become' (72b). If not for the mirrored processes of dying and 'alive-ing,' in other words, the universe and all things within it must sooner or later succumb to a state of moribund stasis wherein the possibility of change no longer exists. To understand this, however, we must first examine more closely Socrates's privileged example of reciprocal processes, falling asleep and waking up. If the process of falling asleep exists but the process of waking up does not, argues Socrates, it is readily apparent that there must inevitably come a time wherein every waking thing is asleep and will remain so for eternity. 'In the same way,' he continues, 'if everything that partakes of life were to die and remain in that state and not come to life again, would not everything ultimately have to be dead and nothing alive?' (72c–d). Hence, and in conjunction with the obviousness of mortality, it is the very existence of living beings in the world *today* that, according to Socrates, sufficiently proves his claim that 'coming to life again in truth exists, the living come to be from the dead, and the souls of the dead exist' (72d–e).

THE SLEEP OF THE DEAD

But does it really? Has Socrates actually provided sufficient proof in this case? As we know, Socrates first claims to have sufficiently proven the argument from opposites, according to which everything comes into being from its opposite and from nowhere else. Our question here is deceptively simple: *Is* this an argument from opposites? Ironically, the answer to this question will ultimately depend on how we understand the lexical term 'opposition.' It is, in other words, a question of *rhetoric*—the very subject traditionally dismissed by philosophy as the shelter of cynicism and sophistry.

In rhetorical discourse it is necessary to distinguish between several types or modes of opposition, with the most germane in this case being *binary* antonyms, *graded* antonyms and *relational* antonyms. Whenever the notion of opposites is raised, it will most likely be in reference to the concept of binary antonyms, also known as complementary antonyms. A binary antonym names a mutually exclusive or 'encapsulated' lexical pairing in which each term is the antithesis of the other and whose complementary meanings do not lie on a continuous spectrum. Common examples include odd–even, mortal–immortal, visible–invisible, mobile–immobile, exhale–inhale, occupied–vacant and so on. A graded antonym, by contrast, refers to a lexical pair in which the opposite meanings of the two words describe opposite poles along a single axis and thus a continuous spectrum of meaning. Also known as antipodals for obvious reasons, examples include hot–cold, heavy–light, empty–full, young–old, early–late, etc. Last, relational antonyms are lexical pairings whose meanings are opposite only within the context of their relationship; examples include teacher–student, predator–prey, servant–master, doctor–patient, come–go and buy–sell. Here, we should also mention *incompatibles*, which are mutually exclusive members of a set that nonetheless lack complementary antonyms: red–blue, May–September, one–ten and so on.

Clearly therefore, Socrates's argument in the first part is *not* an argument from binary antonyms. Rather, exemplary pairings such as 'large–small' and 'weak–strong' take place along a single axis, making them *graded* antonyms. In the second part Socrates then further specifies that the paired antonyms are all *reversives*; that is to say, they consist of pairs of verbs denoting opposing processes in which one is the reverse of the other: 'to weaken' and 'to strengthen,' 'to become smaller' and 'to become larger.' Indeed, this relation of graded reversal is in fact the entirety of Socrates's argument from opposites, as we shall see. Staying with Socrates's first example, we can say that for something to become larger it must first have been smaller and for something to become smaller it must first have been larger, thus situating reciprocal processes of increase and decrease at work within the generative space of lexical polarity. Socrates, in other words, is attempting to play a zero-sum game with graded antonyms. As opposite poles along a single axis, however, the idealized pairing of large–small refers instead to an encapsulated continuum always in perfect balance insofar as any processual gains on one side of a central fulcrum produce an equal and opposite deficit on the other.

Rather than an argument for constitutive exclusion based upon mutually exclusive binary antonyms as seen previously in constructing the concept of 'true virtue,' for Socrates here generation or genesis is always a *relative* becoming. Largeness, in other words, does *not* come from smallness, just as weakness does *not* come from strength. Instead of production from opposition, there is only relative exchange: a becoming-larger-than a lesser grade of being-large, a becoming-weaker-than a lesser grade of being-weak. Socrates, we recall, explicitly counsels Cebes to take not just animals and plants into account, but 'all things which come to be'—an instruction immediately followed by a rapid-fire list of seemingly self-evident examples ending with the declaration that the argument is thus 'sufficiently established.' There is, however, only *one* pair of antonyms at work here, being and becoming, and only *one* reversive process, $x + y = 0$, this latter posing a very different form of 'zero-sum' game than the 'x *or* y' of binary encapsulation. Furthermore, it is in fact this very reduction that ultimately renders Socrates's argument applicable to *all* things, irrespective of whether an antonym can or cannot be determined (this latter being the case with incompatibles) or even if 'we do not have a name for the process' (71b). However, whereas for Socrates this constitutes sufficient proof of a universal process of becoming of each from its opposite, what he actually describes is the braid of spacetime as everywhere a process of becoming other than that which will have been.

And what of Socrates's favoured example? We recall that for Socrates the pairing asleep–awake and the reversive processes 'to go to sleep' and 'to wake up' exist 'in the same way' as the pairing dead–alive and the reversive processes of dying (or 'becoming-dead') and returning to life (or 'becoming-alive'). In contrast to the examples evinced in support of the first part of the argument, asleep–awake and dead–alive are in fact *binary* antonyms insofar as they compose pairs of antithetical, and thus mutually exclusive, terms: if one is asleep then by definition one is not awake; if one is dead then by definition one is not alive. Hence, with this move from graded to binary antonyms we already find a subtle drifting of terms at work behind the scenes, with the argument all the while remaining ostensibly 'founded' upon the claim from graded antonyms that everything comes into being from its opposite. So, just why is it that Socrates shifts his privileged examples from large–small in the first part to asleep–awake in the second? This question will prove critical. In the first instance, there exists a clear *comparative* relation between 'becoming-larger-than' and 'becoming-smaller-than' that Socrates requires in order to make his initial argument, after which he is then able to exploit the polysemy inherent to the concept of opposition so as to shift his focus to binary antonyms *as if* the argument from antithetical opposites has already been sufficiently proven.

Despite this bravura display of rhetorical trickery equal to any performed by the most celebrated of Sophist orators, however, Socrates now finds himself faced with a further problem. If he is to maintain the rhetorical illusion, then the same reversive processes that served to underwrite the choice of larger–smaller in the first part must also be found to be at work in the second, but things are far less clear-cut when dealing with binary rather than graded antonyms. Take mobile–immobile, for example: Socrates's argument requires the existence of the paired reversive processes 'becoming-mobile' and 'becoming-immobile.' However, the mutual exclusion inherent to binary terms renders these processes unworkable: in embarking upon the process of 'becoming-mobile' an immobile entity is *already* mobile, just as, in embarking upon the process of 'becoming-immobile' a mobile entity is *already* immobile. Ultimately, this goes a long way to explain Socrates' choice of asleep–awake as isomorphic to that of dead–alive. In contrast to such binary antonyms as mobile–immobile, it is all too easy to think of 'waking up' and 'going to sleep' as reversive processes taking place over time. Again, however, this is clearly a rhetorical ploy on Socrates's behalf, such vague notions having nothing to do with the either–or structure of the asleep–awake binary but serving only to enable an easy correlation with the dead–alive binary antonym due to the commonly perceived similarity of the states in question.

In summary, just as we habitually (if incorrectly) think of 'going to sleep' and 'waking up' as reversive processes and thus of the pairing asleep–awake as a graded antonym, so too we habitually (if incorrectly) think of dying (or 'becoming-dead') and being born (or 'becoming-alive') as reversive processes and thus of the pairing dead–alive as a graded antonym. Ultimately, Socrates plays on this common misperception in support of his claim to have sufficiently proven the existence of an indestructible human soul immune to the tyranny of temporal dissolution that holds sway over the entire material realm. In fact, such proofs rest upon little more than a common misconception regarding the existence of an analogous relation between sleep and death coupled with a wilful misapprehension of 'waking up,' 'going to sleep' and 'dying' as temporal processes taking place along a continuous spectrum of meaning. After this, Socrates is left needing only to fill in the missing process correlated to 'waking up'—that of 'coming back to life.'

Taking a brief backward step, we have previously seen that, in posing his argument for the existence of the human soul, Socrates first of all instructs Cebes not to confine himself to humanity or even to life in general, only to then very quickly and prematurely claim to have 'sufficiently established that *all things* come to be in this way, opposites from opposites' (*Phaedo*, 71a; italics added). Cast more simply, Socrates is thus claiming to have sufficiently proven that every thing that exists does so on the prior condition of its nonexistence. As we will see, however, this entails a number of unlikely conclusions in light of what follows, the most bizarre doubtless being the supposition of some kind of vitalist Socratic *cogito*, according to which everything that exists—from technical fabrications to vast armies and from mountain ranges to individual quanta—must, by the simple fact of their being, therefore possess a unique and eternal soul.

Of course, even the most cursory reader of Plato's dialogues will know that Socrates is most definitely *not* claiming any such thing. Nonetheless, this unconstrained miscegenation in breach of borders presumed secure reveals a highly symptomatic hesitation on the part of Socrates. Throughout the dialogue the referent of this phrase 'all things which come to be' shifts back and forth across the border erected between *all* beings and all *living* beings. At least initially, however, Socrates seems to resolve this ambiguity in favour of the former when he says of reversive processes that 'so too there is separation and combination, cooling and heating, and all such things . . . in fact it must be everywhere that they come to be from one another' (71b). At this point, Socrates is unwittingly positing a graded antonym with *being* and *nonbeing* as opposing poles along a single axis and continuous spectrum of meaning: existence (being) comes to be from nonexistence (nonbeing) and from nowhere else. Hence, given that the proof of the indestructibility of the soul rests upon the process of coming (back) into being from out of nonbeing, this proof must pertain equally to all things that come to be in this way, thus rendering the mere fact of existing sufficient proof of an immortal soul.

Unsurprisingly, however, this position does not survive a third and final iteration, wherein Socrates abruptly recasts the set of 'all things' as identical with the set of 'everything that partakes of life' (72c). Crucially, this unremarked shifting of ground both serves Socrates as the conclusion of his opening gambit and at the same time sets the (tweaked) terms for the argument to follow. Ultimately, as we shall see in the next section, it is this shifting of the stage from that of *being* to that of *life* that will thereafter enable Socrates to restrict possession of an immortal soul still further.

THE METAPHYSICS OF EXCLUSION

The initial impetus that led up to this point centred on the question of whether Socrates is in fact able to successfully escape the circular logic of Meno's original 'debater's argument' and, in so doing, safeguard philosophy at the very start by rescuing it from Sophist relativism. As yet, however, this argument still remains to be made. To this end, Socrates again falls back on the machinery of exclusion definitive of metaphysical discourse. However, just as the argument from graded antonyms both sets the scene and serves as a blind behind which Socrates is able to construct the argument from binary antonyms, so too the argument from exclusion requires this argument from opposites both to set the scene and, more importantly, to function as a blind behind which metaphysical exclusion can be most effectively mobilized.

In truth, the construction of sufficient proof with respect to the existence of an immortal human soul is not what concerns Socrates here. As in *Meno*, the question of the soul in *Phaedo* remains the reserve of priests and theologians rather than philosophers, and here Socrates merely borrows some of their authority in support of a claim that many of his contemporaries would have considered outlandish. Meno's 'trick' question, it is important to remember, does not concern the possible possession of a soul, but rather asks after the necessary conditions for the possession of *knowledge*.

Ironically, rather than a basis upon which the constitutive exclusions of metaphysics are to be built, Socrates's claim that all things come into being in the process of becoming other than what they will have been in fact threatens to undermine the ontological foundation of Platonism entirely. Hence, and just as in the *Meno*, Socrates is forced to abruptly shift ground while *at the same time* holding fast to the belief of having sufficiently proven the existence of the immortal human soul, a fabricated 'proof' the ultimate role of which is rather to safeguard both the possibility of truth and the proper domain of philosophical knowledge.

The shift from the argument from opposites to one from exclusion and from the immortality of the soul to the recollection of *a priori* knowledge is clearly signalled in *Phaedo* by Cebes's recollection—ostensibly for the benefit of Simmias—of the earlier dialogue between Socrates and Meno. For his part, Socrates has just announced the successful resolution of their initial inquiry, stating 'that this is very definitely the case and that we were not deceived when we agreed on this: coming to life again in truth exists, the living come to be from the dead, and the souls of the dead exist' (72d–e), whereupon Cebes immediately jumps in to declare that

> such is also the case if that theory is true that you are accustomed to mention frequently, that for us learning is no other than recollection. According to this,

we must at some previous time have learned what we now recollect. This is possible only if our soul existed somewhere before it took on this human shape. So according to this theory too, the soul is likely to be something immortal (72e–73a).

As is often the case in Plato's dialogues, Cebes here is clearly feeding this line to Socrates, calling on the latter to elaborate further about the role the immortal soul plays in the acquisition of knowledge. To this end, and with a clear reference to Meno's debater's argument, Socrates opens with a test of memory, arguing that in order for someone to recall anything to mind, they must have already known it beforehand. Moreover, sense perception not only recalls what is already known but can also bring to mind 'another thing of which the knowledge is not the same but different' (73c). The sight of a lyre, for example, might recall not only the knowledge of a lyre but also the knowledge of a particular person with whom the lyre is associated. A single stimulus, in other words, can recall from forgetfulness both knowledge of the thing perceived *and* knowledge of an entirely different thing associated with that first thing. It is from this initial, somewhat banal observation that Socrates thereafter attempts to define adequate knowledge as the correspondence of presentation with representation.

Focusing first on the knowledge of the same, that is, on intelligible concepts that directly correspond to the things being perceived, Socrates states that given such recollection one must 'of necessity also experience this: to consider whether the similarity to that which one recollects is deficient in any respect or complete' (74a). Here, Socrates seems to be suggesting that the 'experience' of knowledge recollection includes an inbuilt verification subroutine that, once recollection has taken place, thereafter immediately double checks the adequacy of its correspondence with the initial perceptual stimulus. While vague at best, these interrelated mechanics of correspondence, adequacy and verification nonetheless enable Socrates to shift the grounds of his argument, which he does through the introduction of the concept of 'the Equal itself.' First of all, says Socrates, 'there is something that is equal. I do not mean a stick equal to a stick or a stone to a stone, or anything of that kind, but something else beyond all these, the Equal itself' (74a). Moreover, he continues, whereas a given equivalence in nature is likely to bring to mind dissimilar associative equivalences—*viz*, staying with Socrates's example, the sound of a lyre may recall to mind a happy event for one person but only sorrow and loss for another—the 'equals themselves' can never appear *un*equal (74c). Here, Socrates is making two important points: first, that 'the Equal itself' and 'the Unequal itself' are mutually exclusive concepts; and second, that there exists a difference in *kind* between equal things and 'the Equal itself' despite our knowledge of the latter having ultimately been 'derived and grasped' from our perception of the former (74c).

What are we to make of this? Socrates, we recall, previously bases his argument from binary antonyms upon a proof that is in fact applicable only to graded antonyms. However, in explicit contradistinction to this claim for a continuous spectrum of meaning from which all things literally and figuratively began, Socrates here makes use of a very different form of opposition in order to posit as seemingly self-evident the basis of his transcendental idealism. Passing under the blinds of simple binarism, in other words, Socrates is now seeking to construct the transcendent ontological realm through its opposition to the everyday ontical world. Rather than a relation of mutually exclusive antithesis, however, the truth of the transcendental 'in-itself' is necessarily derived from the material examples it constitutes *as* excluded from its own domain of truth. This move entails some serious consequences. Most important, insofar as it maps the ontological–ontical relation directly onto the intelligible–sensible antonym, the latter now functions to set in place a judgement of *value* that is entirely absent from graded lexical antonyms such as hot–cold and big–small: well then, says Socrates,

> do we experience something like this in the case of equal sticks and the other equal objects we just mentioned? Do they seem to us to be equal in the same sense as what is Equal itself? Is there some deficiency in their being such as the Equal, or is there not? (74d–e).

Simmias is of course quick to confirm that yes, there is indeed a 'considerable deficiency' between the Equal itself and the endless variety of merely equal things that exist all around us.

We can summarize the Socratic argument from exclusion as follows: *the ideational concept is derived from a set of manifold entities from which it is retroactively excluded in the process of producing a deficiency*. In this case, to take Socrates's example, *Equality is deemed the essential truth of all equal things from which it is necessarily excluded*—simply put, metaphysics in a nutshell. However, if we are to follow the other, supposedly fundamental argument from opposites that brought us to this point, shouldn't knowledge of equality 'derive from' (knowledge of) inequality rather than from the ordering of examples perceived by the senses? What exactly is being argued here? Why this shift in the production of opposition?

In perceiving things *as* equal, states Socrates, we necessarily recall to mind the knowledge of Equality itself, knowledge that must then be brought to bear upon all those seemingly equal things that initially recalled that knowledge forth. According to Socrates, this circular logic warrants two conclusions: first, that insofar as they are compared with Equality itself, all equal things must therefore fall short of the ideality of Equality itself; and second, the very *re*cognition of this ontical inferiority or deficiency is itself sufficient proof of our having 'prior knowledge of that to which he says it is like, but deficiently so' (74e). Virtuous and virtuoso perhaps, the obvious circularity of the reasoning on display is in fact symptomatic of the problem of knowledge acquisition in general; the very same problem initially brought into focus for us by Meno's 'debater's argument'

Here, Socrates employs a phrase that strikes an ironic echo with the argument from opposites, claiming now that 'we also agree that this conception of ours derives from seeing or touching or some other sense perception, and cannot come into our mind in any other way' (75a). By this stage, the concept of equality is serving triple rhetorical duty: first, as the privileged example of binary opposition (equality–inequality); second, as the privileged example of ontological difference (equality in-itself–equal things); and third, as the ultimate arbiter of value insofar as it is the measure of equality, or rather of its absence, which determines sense perceptions as inferior to—that is, *unequal to*—the knowledge to which they give rise and which subsequently transcends them. As we shall see, the production of value through the absence of equivalence is absolutely crucial to the negotiation currently taking place around the exclusivity of the equal–unequal antonym. 'Our sense perceptions,' says Socrates, 'must surely make us realize that all that we perceive through them is striving to reach that which is Equal but falls short of it' (75b).

Upon reaching this juncture, we now find all three senses of equality being put to work in what is a decisive step not only for the dialogue, but also for the entire future of philosophy in the West, the impact of which is still being felt to this day. Having claimed that sense perceptions reveal the existence of intelligible concepts that retroactively transcend these same perceptions, Socrates reaches a fateful conclusion, stating that 'before we began to see or hear or otherwise perceive, we must have possessed knowledge of the Equal itself if we were about to refer our sense perceptions of equal objects to it, and realized that all of them were eager to be like it, but were inferior' (75b). This statement raises a number of important questions about origin, succession and causality that will only become more acute as the argument progresses.

Whereas in the preceding exchange all knowledge (in terms of transcendental concepts) is originally *derived from* the collection and collation of sense perceptions, Socrates is now claiming that transcendental knowledge is necessarily *prior* to sense perception as the latter's condition of possibility and, as such, outside of the finite realms of time and space. From here, it is a simple next step for Socrates to locate the first sense perception at the moment of birth and thus situate knowledge of the Equal itself—and, by extension, all knowledge of transcendental concepts and thus all knowledge as such—as necessarily gained prior to any given finite existence:

Our present argument is no more about the Equal than about the Beautiful itself, the Good itself, the Just, the Pious and, as I say, about all those things which we mark with the seal of 'what it is,' both when we are putting questions and answering them. So we must have acquired knowledge of them all before we were born (*Phaedo* 75c–d).

In short, Socrates is claiming here that the 'existence-before-existence' of transcendental knowledge necessarily follows from the conclusion of the argument from opposites.

THE UNIVERSAL EQUALITY OF
ADEQUATE KNOWLEDGE

We now reach the crux of the argument staged by Socrates first in *Meno* and then again in *Phaedo*. If we do indeed acquire knowledge before birth only to then lose that knowledge at birth as a corollary of acquiring sense perception, argues Socrates, then 'would not what we call learning be the recovery of our own knowledge, and we are right to call this recollection?' (75e). Simmias of course agrees, after which Socrates offers a somewhat convoluted summation of his argument thus far:

It was seen to be possible for someone to see or hear or otherwise perceive something, and by this to be put in mind of something else which he had forgotten and which is related to it by similarity or difference. One of two things follows, as I say: either we were born with the knowledge of it, and all of us know it throughout life, or those who later, we say, are learning, are only recollecting, and learning would be recollection (76a).

Most notable here is the ultimatum being offered to the hapless Simmias: given that sense perceptions have the potential to recall to mind something hitherto forgotten, says Socrates, then one of only two possible conclusions must follow: *either* we are born with essential knowledge and thereafter retain it throughout our entire lives, *or* essential knowledge is forfeit as a condition of birth but can be recovered through the process known as learning. After a quick acknowledgement that, yes, there are indeed any number of stupid people walking around, Simmias swiftly makes the expected choice. But why only these two possibilities? Nothing Socrates has said thus far refutes the conclusion that sense perceptions, for example, are collated on the basis of a common similarity subsequently identified with an arbitrary signifier—*re*cognition, in other words, rather than *re*collection.

That aside, we at last find ourselves right back where we started: with Meno's 'debater's argument.' If, like Simmias, we accept Socrates's claim that learning is the recollection of *a priori* knowledge that is otherwise forgotten at the moment of birth concurrent with our first sensory perception, the focus of our problematic becomes much sharper. In other words, insofar as the acquisition of knowledge is the recollection of that which was once known but has since been forgotten, our key question must now concern just *how* is it that we acquired this *a priori* knowledge in the first place—and this is Meno's argument in a nutshell: How is it possible to search for something you do not know at all? How can we search for knowledge without already knowing what we are looking for? And if you should by chance happen upon it, how will you ever know that this is the thing that you did not know? The importance of this 'debater's question' regarding the conditions of possibility for adequate knowledge cannot be overstated, and it is the formulation of an adequate response to this particular question that is at the forefront of Socrates's concerns throughout both *Meno* and *Phaedo*. However, whereas in *Meno* we find an initial hesitation on the part of Socrates as to whether this prior knowledge had previously been learned empirically over the course of multiple incarnations of the soul or if such knowledge is rather an essential *a priori* property, by the time of *Phaedo* any such doubt has clearly been excised: knowledge 'exists' in the form of *a priori* concepts that transcend the phenomenal realm, with the comparative inferiority of the latter serving as stimuli for the recalling to mind of superior intelligible knowledge.

So, having come all this way, just what is it about this relatively uncontroversial argument that is so momentous as to warrant so much of our time and attention even today? Tens of centuries later, Friedrich Nietzsche will identify the argument from exclusion as the definitive signature of metaphysics in the Western tradition. However, whereas Nietzsche correctly describes this signature as the *corruption* of reason, we must not forget that it is also and at the same time the originary *construction* of reason in the West. To better understand what is at stake here with respect to contemporary concepts of origin, succession and causality, we must again direct our attention to the rhetorical techniques employed by Socrates in the staging of his argument.

Most important for us here is the utilization of two closely related tropes of displacement. Socrates, as we know, defines adequate knowledge as the tropological correspondence of sensible presentation with intelligible representation. Moreover, while the former serves initially as the tenor to the latter's metaphorical vehicle, this relation is subsequently reversed, with sensible perception thereafter taking on the role of metaphorical vehicle to the tenor of the transcendental concept. Despite this, however, the fundamental trope of metaphysics being articulated here by Socrates is not in fact *metaphor*, but rather *metalepsis*.

First of all, the sensible and the intelligible must occupy discontinuous domains, as it is this discontinuity that ultimately makes every sense perception necessarily inadequate and thus inferior. It is, however, this same discontinuity of domains that renders their relation metaleptic rather than metaphoric. It is indicative of our problematic that metalepsis is specifically defined in rhetoric as an *abuse* of metaphor, in that it names a transgressive relation across fundamentally discrete levels or worlds, one that often utilizes unexpected causal linkage. At this point, the intelligible concept benefits from a further twist of negativity insofar as it is thereafter taken—or rather *mis*taken—to be the transcendental essence of the thing 'itself.' Whereas Socrates ostensibly defines learning as the process of recalling that which one has previously known but has since forgotten, what we instead discover at work here is in fact a *metaleptic reversal* of this process—succinctly described much later by philosopher Maurice Blanchot as the *forgetting of forgetting*: first, sense perceptions are forgotten in being subsumed to an empty concept, only for this first forgetting itself to be forgotten in the taking of this empty concept for an ideal value. Crucially, it is this operation of metalepsis that, behind the disguise of metaphorical correspondence, serves as the foundation upon which distinctions of value can ultimately be created. The much-vaunted 'truths of men' are, as Nietzsche puts it, merely 'illusions which we have forgotten are illusions' ('On Truth and Lies in the Nonmoral Sense,' 84). Dissimulation, in other words, is the very condition of reason.

With Meno's debater's argument now returned to the forefront of his concerns, it is but a simple and necessary step for Socrates at this point to attribute intelligence to the soul as it exists apart from the body and prior to its taking on of human form:

> So this is our position, Simmias? If those realities we are always talking about exist, the Beautiful and the Good and all that kind of reality, and we refer all the things we perceive to that reality, discovering that it existed before and is ours, and we compare these things with it, then, just as they exist, so our soul must exist before we are born. If these realities do not exist, then this argument is altogether futile (*Phaedo* 76d–e).

Only transcendental idealism, in other words, can save Socrates's argument—and Platonism generally—from abject futility. By this point, Simmias appears to be buckling under the Socratic onslaught, wanting nothing more than to tap out and let his tag team buddy Cebes take over for a while. Socrates, however, keeps pressing. Is it not in fact the case, he says again, 'that there is an equal necessity for those realities to exist, and for our souls to exist before we were born? If the former do not exist, neither do the latter?' (76e). Simmias can only concede defeat, agreeing almost desperately that, no, there can be no longer any 'possible doubt that it is equally necessary for both to exist'; that no, nothing is 'so evident to me personally as that all such things must certainly exist'; and that, yes, yes, 'sufficient proof of this has been given' (76e–77a).

SOCRATES THE SOPHIST

Having reached this point, there remains for Simmias and Cebes only one final point of possible contention: the survivability or otherwise of death. 'What is to prevent the soul coming to be and being constituted from some other source,' asks Simmias, 'existing before it enters a human body and then, having done so and departed from it, itself dying and being destroyed?' (77b). While flippant, we can reformulate this question as follows: How can we know for sure (and again, it concerns the possibility or otherwise of certain knowledge) that aliens do not parasitically animate our bodies from birth only to eventually perish along with the host organism? Socrates gently chides his interlocutors, telling them that the soul's survival of death has already been proven through the argument from opposites. 'If the soul exists before,' he argues, 'it must, as it comes to life and birth, come from nowhere else than death and being dead, so how could it avoid existing after death since it must be born again?' (77c). Once again, we find Socrates evading the question regarding the condition of possibility of adequate knowledge by circling back around to the argument from opposites.

According to the Socratic argument from opposites, as we know, everything that is comes into being from out of its graded opposite in a reversive process of exchange. To exist, in other words, is being composed in the constant mutability of becoming from being. Immediately after recalling this prior supporting 'proof,' however, the focus of Socrates's attention shifts radically, turning instead to the metaphor of the soul's dissolution and dispersion by the wind as a pretext for classifying the essential properties of the soul. Socrates begins this process by summarily excluding the composite and the mutable from the essential in order to thereafter attribute the immutable and the indivisible to the superior atemporal realm of the soul as a consequence of this prior exclusion, while at the same time relegating all things plastic and composite to the inferior sensible realm of mortal existence. From there, Socrates then loops back around again, recalling once more the supposedly 'proven' existence of 'the Equal itself, the Beautiful itself, each thing in itself, the real,' in order to further claim that all such forms 'remain the same and never in any way tolerate any change whatever' (78d). Having reached this point, the construction of transcendental idealism seemingly upon the back of the argument from opposites is almost complete, with only the exclusion of the entirety of existence from philosophical concern still remaining: despite there being so many such beautiful particulars, says Socrates, insofar as they 'never in any way remain the same as themselves or in relation to each other' everything that actually exists therefore does so 'in total contrast to those other realities' (78e).

For all intents and purposes, the definitive argument of metaphysics is now complete, with only a little a bit of mopping up here and there left to do. Whereas all that is perceived via the senses is mutable, concludes Socrates, such knowledge as is 'grasped only by the reasoning power of the mind' must therefore remain eternally the same (79a). As a result, he continues, there must therefore be 'two kinds of existences, the visible and the invisible,' with the invisible always remaining the same and the visible always changing (79a). Hence, the one kind of existence that gives rise to visible, finite and mutable bodies must have always already been excluded in order to constitute a second, superior kind of existence inhabited by invisible, immortal and immutable ideals:

> Consider then, Cebes, whether it follows from all that has been said that the soul is most like the divine, deathless, intelligible, uniform, indissoluble, always the same as itself, whereas the body is most like that which is human, mortal, multiform, unintelligible, soluble and never consistently the same. Have we anything else to say to show, my dear Cebes, that this is not the case? (80a–b)

Over and over again, we thus find the very same argument from exclusion in operation at the birth of what is now known as Western philosophy: just as 'Virtue itself' is constituted through the exclusion of ontical virtues, just as 'Equality itself' is constituted through the exclusion of ontical equalities, so too is 'Being itself' constituted through the exclusion of ontical beings.

So, having followed Socrates throughout all of these various tropes, reversives and turnarounds, has philosophy finally been able to put the debater's argument to rest? Just what, and where, is knowledge? And how is knowledge as attained? What determines such knowledge as adequate? Just how is wisdom attained? According to Socrates, it is only when liberated from the polluting influence of our grubby finite bodies that the soul ascends to the realm of the pure and immutable 'in itself.' In this perfect realm, the soul is 'in touch with things of the same kind, and its experience then is what is called wisdom' (79d).

This conclusion strikes a somewhat muffled note, not least from the ease of confluence and contamination across levels and domains otherwise posed as fundamentally opposed. However, while much has been and still remains to be written on the subject, this is not in fact our principal concern. Rather, we set out on this exegesis with the explicit aim of breaking free of our enchantment to a reactive and metaleptic logic of life, a critical endeavour at the heart of which is a clear understanding of the process from exclusion set in train here. As we have seen, the concatenation of arguments staged by Socrates in *Phaedo seems* perfectly reasonable, *seems* to conform to a clear and logical causality, but this apparent clarity of reasoning is itself something produced by Socrates's mastery of rhetorical technique. Ultimately, Socrates is here posing a second 'debater's argument' in order to appear to refute (and thus evade or circumvent) the 'debater's argument' previously posed by Meno. It is, in other words, *to illegitimately employ the artifice of sophistry in order to exclude the artifice of sophistry on the basis of illegitimacy.* Furthermore, this argument from exclusion as posed by Socrates with the aim of countering sophistry and cynicism *is itself the history of metaphysics.* Despite many and varied iterations over the centuries, the argument from exclusion ultimately serves but a single purpose: to safeguard the purity of a given realm from pollution or contamination and, *in one and the same process*, constitute that given realm *as* pure.

METAPHYSICAL BRUTALITY: THE
OWNING OF EXCLUSION

Meno, we recall, asks Socrates how it is that our knowledge of an object can escape the circularity of its positing and as such be shown to adequately correspond to that object. This question can be rephrased as follows: How can one know that what one *believes* to be true is in fact *actually* true? How can competing truth claims be verified as being either truly true or truly false? Hence, even at its outset philosophy is already being called upon to distinguish itself from both theology and what Quentin Meillassoux will, over two thousand years later, term 'fideism,' the doctrine according to which all competing truth claims are all equally valid insofar as there can be no external vantage from which judgements of value can be legitimately posed. As regards the former, it is thus ironic at best for Socrates to open his account by petitioning the support of priests and Bacchants—true believers all—before ultimately describing the recollection of knowledge as a process of ritual purging accompanied by absolute faith. Irony notwithstanding, however, only by initially grounding the realm of philosophy in faith does it thereafter become possible for Socrates to equate philosophy with purity in a move that can only ever end with the ritual cleansing of all bodily and worldly distractions from the realm of pure knowledge. It is thus symptomatic that the reasons given by Socrates as to why his argument should be favoured over that of Meno have nothing at all to do with the sufficient proofs and truth verifications that Socrates deems to be the proper remit of philosophy. Instead, we find only an imperative based entirely upon the perception of positive physiological and psychological traits: 'We must, therefore, not believe that debater's argument, for it would make us idle, and fainthearted men like to hear it, whereas my argument makes them energetic and keen on the search' (*Meno*, 81d–e).

Everything, as we now know only too well, begins with Meno's question: How can you know what you do not know already? Or, in other words, how do we safeguard truth and knowledge as properly the realm of philosophy? Socrates's response from constitutive exclusion is as simple as it is brutal: a given entity is first of all forgotten in being exchanged for an empty concept, and then this forgetting too is forgotten in the subsequent mistaking of this empty concept for the *a priori* essence of the thing whose place it simply holds—metaphysics in a nutshell. Things, however, do not end there. Simply put, the brutality of metaphysical exclusion always already breaches its attempted confinement within the idealistic realm of philosophy.

To understand this, it is imperative that we pay close attention to the broader context within which the argument is posed. We recall that Socrates, already labouring under a sentence of death, has been further tasked with the construction and legitimation of a domain of philosophical knowledge that, as the unique site of truth, is thus safeguarded from the polluting influence of self-serving cynics and rhetoricians. The key term here is *safeguard*. Indeed, the strategic function of the argument from constitutive exclusion is always one of safeguarding—be it of an area, a field, a property or a value—wherein the verb 'to safeguard' can be defined precisely as *a keeping safe by guarding against*. The argument from exclusion, in other words, constitutes a site of pure negation at the same time that it secures its borders against pollutants and contaminants—such 'contaminants' referring here to the incursion of those whose very exclusion founds and maintains the borders and barriers of a given property.

As with the verb 'safeguard,' the term 'property' in this context has likewise been chosen for its peculiar precision. We have already seen that the stakes of Meno's challenge to truth and knowledge far exceed the Platonic dialogues' initial concern with virtue, but we now discover that these same stakes in fact far exceed the general concerns of philosophy, knowledge and truth insofar as they further concern the production of value and the conservation of property, as well as that of ownership, profit and legality—all material contaminants from which Socrates ostensibly, if ironically, seeks to defend the newly immaterial domain of pure knowledge.

In order to safeguard *a priori* knowledge as the domain of philosophy, Socrates begins by constituting the soul upon the negation and exclusion of the body in a move that will ultimately lead to the constitution of intelligible truths upon the negation and exclusion of sensible matter. The inauguration and simultaneous salvation of philosophy in the West thus begins by depriving all things corporeal and physiological of any value and concludes by depriving of value all that has existed, does exist and will exist in the future. And what of everything in between these first and final posts? On the back of a single, apparently simple question concerning the conditions of possibility for knowledge, the construction from exclusion of an entire conceptual edifice is set in train:

> Look at it also this way: when the soul and the body are together, nature orders the one to be subject and to be ruled, and the other to rule and be master. Then again, which do you think is like the divine and which like the mortal? Do you not think that the nature of the divine is to rule and to lead, whereas it is that of the mortal to be ruled and be subject? . . . Consider then, Cebes, whether it follows from all that has been said that the soul is most like the divine, deathless, intelligible, uniform, indissoluble, always the same as itself, whereas the body is most like that which is human, mortal, multiform, unintelligible, soluble and never consistently the same (*Phaedo* 80a–b).

It is clear from this passage just how easily and rapidly the argument from constitutive exclusion exceeds its ostensible focus in order to legitimize and valorize—and therefore illegitimize and devalorize—a whole raft of seemingly unrelated concepts, concepts which are then collated in one of two mutually exclusive categories: 'to master' and 'to rule' on one side of the constitutional divide; 'to be mastered' and 'to be ruled' on the other. Hence, the value that accrues to empty conceptual ideals such as the essential, the intelligible and the atemporal; to the indivisible and the invisible; to the infinite, immutable, uniform and indissoluble, this value is wholly constituted through the ceaseless reiteration of the negation and exclusion *from* value of their antonymic others, *viz* the contingent, the composite and the temporal; the divisible and the visible; the finite, mutable, multiform and soluble; and the sensible, the empirical and the material. Equally clear in its negation of all things material, mutable and phenomenal is the fact that the price of safeguarding the possibility of knowledge far exceeds any possibility of payment. It incurs, in other words, a debt that can never be paid: the human names only the negation and exclusion from value of the animal, life names only the negation and exclusion from value of nonlife, and on it goes, the subject from the object, the master from the slave, the natural from the fabricated, the rational from the irrational.

The introduction here of an unpaid and unpayable debt is by no means incidental—what, after all, could be more grubbily material and inherently temporal than the relations of payment and debt? Ultimately, what Socrates safeguards in the movement from opposites to exclusion is not the possibility of *knowledge*, but rather the legitimacy of *ownership*. What is at stake is never truth but rather the structuring of power. Just as the polysemy of the term 'equality' makes it available for manipulation, so too the almost diz-zying polysemy of the term *property* gives of itself a considerable pliability of employment. What is property? What is a property?[3] For the sake of both brevity and clarity, the definitions of particular interest here can be roughly arrayed into three, somewhat independent groups. First, there is the concept of property (Greek *idion* and Latin *proprium*) that occupies such a preeminent position throughout the Western tradition, and according to which a property (also called an attribute) denotes either an essential or accidental predicate that is instantiated or exemplified in the individual to which it belongs. While properties may be universal or particular, primary or secondary, supervenient or emergent and so on, an essential property is such that if a given thing exists it necessarily instantiates or exemplifies that property. The second sense of property is construed more broadly in terms of *possession*. An *intrinsic* prop-erty, for example, refers to an inalienable possession of a given individual composed by internal (monadic) relations that are independent of all external relations and context. By contrast, an *extrinsic* property or attribute is instan-tiated or exemplified by an individual because of its relation to other things. This notion of property as either an inalienable or allocated possession serves to bridge the gap between philosophical and legal discourses. In the third and final case the concept of property is understood in the narrowly legal sense of *private* property (in contrast to common and collective properties), which presupposes a restricted system that allocates ownership of particular proper-ties to particular individuals to the exclusion of all others and of any detailed societal control.

As a consequence of this polysemy, the concept of property comes to signify *both* a value-neutral attribute *and* a contractually allocated posses-sion, *both* a definitive and inalienable predication *and* a commodity readily available for exchange. A property, in other words, is an attribute bestowed upon a material entity by God or Nature or Science or Chance *and* a privately bounded asset whose formal placeholding is constituted through the exclu-sion from that property of all others irrespective of need and enforceable by police order. In all the ways we understand it here, a *property* is that of a *placeholder*: it holds the place of that which is retroactively absented. And 'property' is itself a property, a placeholder. As with the property of equality, so too with the property of property wherein the empty ideal of 'Property itself' is similarly constituted through the exclusion of all ontical properties, with the latter thereafter relegated to the status of mere simulacra in contrast to the newly cleansed *idea* of property as purely itself and uncontaminated by material or materialist pollutants. And, of course, the sanctity and sanc-tuary of this ideal must thereafter be kept safe from all possible material contamination.

THE METAPHYSICS OF MORALS

Recalling our brief analysis in the introduction, we have seen how Leibniz's belated formulation of the principle of reason demands a universe of objects that, with the sole exception of the human animal, is fully comprehensible and thus wholly predictable. Furthermore, as a corollary of this fundamental determinism by calculable relations of cause and effect, time and temporal affects abruptly vanish from our mechanist universe. The rationale of calculation, in short, determines in their entirety the inhuman realms of matter, nature and artifice as *the condition of their existence*. Building upon this thesis, I aim to show in closing this chapter just how it is that the metaphysical argument from exclusion in fact serves to exclude the very *possibility* of ethics. In this, the notion of ability understood as an attainable practice or technique takes on a central role, acting closely in concert with the concepts of determinability, predictability and exchangeability.

Recalling once again the clichéd definition of insanity as doing the same thing over and over again and expecting a different result, the definition of sanity is presumably that of doing the same thing over and over again and expecting the same result. Sanity or insanity, in other words, is first and foremost a question of *causality*. Hence, it comes as no surprise that the process of classical reasoning ultimately inheres in a demonstrable ability to correctly predict the effect of a given cause in advance. The profound significance of this statement should not be overlooked: *to reason correctly is to know exactly what will happen in the future*. Similarly unsurprising therefore is that the counter logic of *in*sanity specifically concerns the expectation or anticipation of a breakdown of determined causal relationships. Put simply, you would have to be crazy to question the clearly self-evident law of cause and effect, of simple stimulus–response. Such is the pas de deux of metaphysical reason.

In accordance with the dance of metaphysics, the argument from exclusion and the argument for determinist causality are inseparable, marching in a perfectly coordinated lockstep throughout the time of philosophy in the West and in apparent ignorance of the fact that if the universe can indeed be calculated, that is to say, if *being* is in actual fact *being-determined*, then we would have neither need nor reason to construct a narrative of predictability. By contrast, it is precisely *because* unpredictability is a structural component of being that it becomes necessary to manufacture a simple, determinist causality, as only then does it thereafter become possible to safeguard purity and property—and thus ownership, exclusion and profit—into the future. As we know, this as yet somewhat vague concept of *safeguarding* serves a precise and fundamental function in the founding of philosophy in the West. Indeed, as a compound verb, 'to safeguard' names its own pas de deux insofar as it maintains its root words in the closest possible relationship, thus rendering inseparable the two activities of 'keeping safe' and 'guarding against' and, as such, shackling together the otherwise distinct concepts of safety and guardianship.

Just what are we to make of this conflation, perhaps even sublation, of two concepts into one? Is this a simple portmanteau or a complex dialectical synthesis? More precisely, how should we understand the role or function of this oddly phrased verb 'to safeguard'? First of all, its somewhat crude coupling of pre-existing concepts opens up a number of further readings: to safeguard is to guard safety, that is, to keep safety safe by keeping the unsafe at bay, and to safeguard is to maintain the safety and security of a given property and of property itself, to keep both it and safety itself inviolate, safe from incursion, to guard, defend and preserve the lines and limits of property. Such safeguarding, in other words, concerns the constitution and conservation of an oasis of conceptual purity through the very act of keeping itself safe. It concerns the vigilance and the violence of metaphysical humanism through the ceaseless reconstruction of its borders by which it defines its empty perfection. And, above all else, safeguarding describes the fabrication of value quite literally from nothing.

So, what role does causal sanity play when it comes to the safeguarding of ideals and properties alike? Put simply, insofar as the perception and affect of safety is dependent upon a perceived ability to correctly predict the future, causal sanity is the fundamental operator of the principle of reason. More specifically, the philosophical and political imaginary of 'safety' is founded upon a rigid conception of time in its classical sense as a succession of static presents. While the question of whether this vulgar conception of time can in fact ever be abandoned or overcome will have to wait until a later chapter, the metaphysical two-step of constitutive exclusion and mechanistic causality nonetheless remains the time of philosophy in the West insofar as it sanctions the ontologizing of substance and the de-ontologizing of temporality. What this means, in other words, is that ontological priority and purity is attributed to the present self-identical substance, whereas time is de-essentialized as accidental and derivative, a mere backdrop or setting for the privileged scene of presence. Furthermore, it is as a condition of this fundamental basis that it is thereafter deemed necessary to construct determinate moral programs in order to explicitly safeguard the fabricated unity and purity of a given populace. From its guarded beginnings in Plato's *Republic*, this will reach the atrocity of its summit in the decades leading up to the Second World War.[4]

It is worth repeating that it only ever *appears* necessary to safeguard the populace in such a manner. In contrast to such appearances, the structural condition of *ethical* possibility is rather one of profound *un*predictability, of an understanding of being as being fundamentally *un*safe. To understand this, it is in fact necessary that we *start from* the deconstruction of the metaphysical antonym living–nonliving, as well as the various correlates such as spirit–matter, *phusis–tekhne*, subject–object and being–thing. As noted in the opening of this chapter, it is a commonplace of posthumanist and new materialist discourse today to decry the human–animal binary while at the same time maintaining a constitutive operative distinction dividing living beings from nonliving things. Indeed, this simple opposition is not infrequently celebrated as proof of the overcoming of metaphysical humanism and anthropocentrism both. However, it was *also* pointed out that, just as deconstruction discloses the illegitimacy of the human–animal binary antonym, so too it necessarily discloses the illegitimacy of the normative structuring of simple ontological dualism in all of its myriad forms of exclusion. As such, if we are ever to break free of our engrained attachment to this normative logic of life, then we must first overcome our generalized anxiety about the speed and complexity of technological innovation today and tomorrow.

While this anxiety arises from out of a number of different sources, as we shall see in the next chapter, at its heart is the fear that life 'itself' is poised on the brink of being outstripped by its own machines and thus left without purpose. Since Aristotle, purpose—or the lack thereof—is what traditionally distinguishes life in general, and human life in particular, from that of mere things. Moreover, for a great many of us today the rise of the machines ultimately promises only the full and complete collapse of civil society. While not immediately evident perhaps, the reason for such pessimism, even fatalism, is not too difficult to understand insofar as the appearance of a secure ontological distinction between living beings and technological artefacts has for millennia served as the operative distinction upon which the foundations of our traditional discourses of morality and law are constructed. Longevity aside, however, this is a fundamental error with profoundly disturbing consequences. Indeed, millenarian polemics of fear are a staple of reactionary politics today, but their intimidation and coercion are all dependent upon a common failure to understand that a secure distinction between living beings and nonliving things not only never *has* existed, but that it also never *will* exist. Indeed, it is precisely *because* there can be no such ontological distinction that the operative distinction that traditionally founds our moral and legal apparatuses must be ultimately disclosed as paradoxical.

LIVING (WITH) ARTEFACTS

Given the central role typically accorded to the prospect of invasive biotechnological engineering within contemporary politics of fear, this claim can be best clarified by considering laboratory experiments involving biotechnological material. In this particular case, this paradoxicality is out front and centre insofar as the moral and legal justification of all such experiments depends in the last instance upon an unstated but nonetheless absolute distinction between living entities and nonliving objects. Indeed, it is the very obviousness of this compositional paradox that makes it so easy to overlook. As is well known, biotechnological beings are by definition fabricated syntheses of living *and* nonliving material, that is to say, fusions of singular forms of life that cannot be reproduced (*bios*) *and* compound forms of manufacture constructed from base matter and therefore infinitely reproducible (*tekhne*). Hence, taking a slightly more nuanced position, we can say that the *fabrication of legitimacy that allows for* the potential production and, indeed, *re*production of biotechnological beings is founded in the *first* instance upon explicitly contradictory premises: namely, that biotechnological bodies are simultaneously *both* hugely complex singular lifeforms *and* simplistic mechanical gadgets no different from a wind-up clockwork toy. Be it as biological technicity or engineered life or indeed any of the many formal composites, biotechnology at once names both its possibility and its impossibility—that of a necessary commensurability composed of profoundly incommensurable parts.

While experimental bio/tech offers perhaps the most immediately visible example, it is important to recognize that this manifest contradiction is in fact infinitely more commonplace and extensive. Stated as simply as possible, *the deconstruction of the living–nonliving binary is at once the impossibility of reliable prediction*. Every present configuration of particles, in other words, every manifest metastable system and every form of organized being *also*, by the simple fact of enduring in being, simultaneously instantiates the potential for profoundly unpredictable iterations in the future. As such, every metastable system *is* the manifest potential of *multi*stable futures, that is to say, of future metastable forms that are radically incommensurable and thus unthinkable based upon formal configurations in the present. Hence, to begin again *following* the deconstruction of the living–nonliving antonym means that, when it comes to 'mere' objects, we must reconsider our naïve supposition concerning causal determinism.[5] Furthermore, as we shall see going forward, it is for this reason too that technological evolution itself must ultimately disallow its own continuance on the basis of a traditional separation of natural beings and technological artefacts and, in the process, disclose ethical concern as a formative condition of technological being.

Staying for the moment with the production of legitimacy that serves to establish biotechnological experimentation as morally and legally acceptable to both scientists and the general populace alike, we discover that not only does this apparent legitimacy rest upon a fundamental inconsistency, but also that this inconsistency is absolutely necessary for the production of its legitimacy. In other words, it is *only* insofar as it is constituted upon a foundation of profound contradiction that such experimentation is ultimately able to happily sidestep the issue of ethics altogether. How it works is in fact very simple: it is only insofar as a given entity is categorized *as an object* and therefore deemed to be *non*living that scientists can pre-emptively dismiss any and all ethical questions arising out of their research—a pre-emptive dismissal that is in turn predicated upon the assumption that, when it comes to dealing with inanimate objects, all effects into the future can be unerringly predicted in the present in accordance with the simple calculus of determinist cause and effect. Life is tricky; it raises all sorts of complex ethical concerns. Dealing with *lifeless* beings, by contrast, is deemed mere child's play, all such objects being mechanistically determined and therefore under our absolute control. In short, the potential *risk* of biotech experiments aimed at exploiting surplus value locked up within singular forms of life can only ever be ethically justified on condition that these singular lifeforms are *simultaneously* construed as lifeless fabrications—hence the oxymoron bio*engineering*—and this despite the fact that the practically limitless potential promised by such experiments inheres entirely in their being singular forms of life and not at all in the mundane predictability of their alleged clockwork construction.

Lifeforce, entelechy, *élan vital*—if it is anywhere at all then it is likely to reside with the promissory structure of the *will*. Life, in other words, is presumed to be an attribute, effect or function of an alchemical *causal* structure that ultimately transmutes forms of base leaden matter [*hyle*] into the precious gold of vital biological material [*bios, zoe*]. As we shall see in the next chapter, if Plato's *Phaedo* marks the inauguration of the metaphysical tradition in the West and Nietzsche's *Twilight of the Idols* [*Götzen-Dämmerung*] marks the noontime of its necessary secularization, then its fundamental thesis can only be that of Aristotle's *Physics* [*Phusike akroasis*]. It is with Aristotle that Life and Will are first cast as synonymous, with Aristotle that willing as intentional and purposeful action is decreed to be the exclusive property of life, and with Aristotle that being alive means to possess ends that transcend the immediate demands of presence. Exclusion from property, as we know, constitutes a crucial step and an equally crucial negation in the two-step definitive of Western metaphysics, and it is Aristotle who formally rationalizes and ratifies exclusion by way of what are today the long-held truisms of the law of noncontradiction and the law of the excluded middle.

Contrary to this entrenched tradition, however, the perceived *potential* of biotechnology moving into the future allows us to clearly identify just what, if anything, remains of ethical choice today, insofar as it explodes the myth of linear causality considered as fully determining in the case of any entity we care to classify as lifeless, that is to say, as lacking a life*force* and thus *less than* a living form of being irrespective of whatever such a force might, or might not, be imagined to exist and to consist. Instead, contemporary notions of living technologies and technological lifeforms mean that we are now obligated—philosophically, ethically and politically—to recognise that the future effects of animate and inanimate causes alike can by definition never be predicted with *absolute* surety. Furthermore, all of this perfectly accords with a post-Darwinian understanding of evolution as a cyclic material process of reiteration at every level of complexity, with selection for mutation being necessarily nonlinear insofar as innovation depends upon strong mutual interactions and feedback between components constituted through the transmissible memory of changes linked to a given environment.

So, what exactly does this all mean for us today? What difference does it really make? The answer is as simple as it is unremarkable: it changes everything. Beyond the resurgent illusions of vitalism today, beyond the manifold delusions of safety constructed exclusively upon an ideology and a politics of exclusion, contingency is thus disclosed in this way as the structure of being itself. Moreover, rather than demonstrating a lack or absence of an ethical dimension, this *a priori* inscription of a potential to give rise to profoundly unforeseen and unforeseeable forms as the condition of every possible material presencing in fact marks absolute ethical *necessity*, as we shall see. First and foremost, it follows from this constitutive potential for nonlinearity that any predictions into the future founded upon present or habitual states of being are *necessarily* subject to possible error given the unpredictability that is the condition of all emergent forms of being. It is, in other words, *a priori* impossible to predict with absolute surety the future emergence of a novel existent, be that a biological mutation or a technological innovation.

Clearly this raises extremely serious questions about both the legitimacy and the usefulness of any decisions being made today on the back of predicted futures that erroneously assume the absolute determinability of all such things unthinkingly deemed to lack the alchemical privilege definitive of life. Indeed, it is a particular irony that what defines our universe as lifeless and thus predictable into the future is the fact of its being *without* a future insofar as its 'future' has already been contained and fully prescribed by its past. And of course—and here we turn full circle—*to be without a future* is precisely the definition of causal sanity as well as the condition of the adequation of knowledge as decreed by the principle of reason.

THE NEW ETHICAL CONDITION

Stated in the baldest of terms, the modus operandi of classical causality—what I am calling causal sanity—is *instrumentalization*. This is already clear in the synonymous description of determinist causality as mechanistic, that is, as concerning forces and movements over time (mechanics) and as concerning fully determinable instruments (mechanisms). Despite this unambiguity, it nonetheless remains extremely difficult for a great many people to accept the proposition that *it is only with the collapse of the simple ontological distinction between 'life' and its absence that relations of unfettered instrumentalization cease to be possible.* The reason for this manifest difficulty is one of simple common sense, which dictates that being recognized *as* a living being—or, better still, being *interpellated* (and thus constituted) *as* a living being in the sense philosopher Louis Althusser gives to this term—in fact serves as what is likely the only but nonetheless best protection against the basest forms of exploitation. To be judged as a bona fide lifeform, in other words, is to be judged worthy of minimum ethical consideration with respect to their particular being in the world. After all, one of the very first things we are taught as children is that one must never treat fellow living beings in the same instrumental manner that defines our interactions with objects—a self-accredited practice that, despite being disabused a billion times over, is still used today in beleaguered attempts to prop up the collapsing citadel of humanist moralism.

The distinction between the two positions is thus as simple as it is stark: on one side, it is only the interpellation and categorization as a living and thus singular being that constitutes an entity as deserving of *a priori* ethical consideration and, on the other, that it is rather the *destruction* of this same constitutive exclusion dividing life from lifeless and organism from automatism that is a necessary prior condition of ethical possibility. Despite the prevalent politics and theologies of fear seeking to put a halt to biotechnological innovation, what the evolution of technology evidences so vividly is *not* the breakdown of moral structure, *not* the imminent collapse of law and order, but rather *the priority of its own ethical dimension.* Yes, the evolution of biotechnological innovation into the future has a central role to play in the collapse of all moral programmes hitherto but, rather than marking the end of ethics, constitutes instead the long-overdue announcing of its commencement.

Staying with the new ethical condition as manifest in contemporary biotechnologies, it is important for us to recognize that any truly novel form of genetically engineered being—should such a form ever emerge into being—will inevitably lack the *relative* stability of form that comes with the iteration of genetic patterns over tens of millions of years. Moreover, as we know, even given the relative stability of 'natural' forms established over countless eons, this in no way precludes the possibility of an unthinkable transformation at another point in time. In lacking the probabilistic legitimacy provided by countless prior reiterations of form constituted through the transmissible memory of changes linked to a given environment, practices aimed at the production of potentially unforeseen and unforeseeable forms of engineered being must therefore rely instead upon the very *un*naturalness of such forms—that is to say, upon their *artificial construction*—in order to construct a legitimizing narrative of safety and control. In other words, it is only insofar as the products of bioengineering—now and in the future—are conceived as artfully fabricated instruments that allow us to lay claim to sufficient knowledge regarding effects into the future of their enduring presence in being. Once again, the contradiction is clear—the extravagant potential for profit that today drives biotechnology resides entirely within its singular biology and not at all with its mechanistic reproduction other than that required for commodification.

In summary, the cultural acceptability of biotechnologies broadly construed is founded upon an assumed ability to predict with absolute surety the movement of recombinative events far into the future—to unerringly predict, in short, the constitutively unpredictable. This systemic error then gets further compounded insofar as it forcibly channels our thinking on the subject along a single track concerning the reliability or otherwise of this or that particular prediction. The perception of risks arising from bioengineering practices and the consequent biotechnological products, in other words, is thereafter focused exclusively upon the reliability of 'scientific' prediction while at the same time protecting its practitioners and commoditizers from individual accountability. Ultimately, what the presumptions of sane, scientific rationality serve to ensure is only their continuing failure to recognise that the very notion of reliable prediction, like that of a fully determined universe upon which it is founded, is nothing more than a myth. More importantly, if there are to be any futures beyond imagining—if, in other words, the future is to *be*—this systemic failure of recognition must be urgently and profoundly redressed.

The simple distinction that excludes lifeless things from living beings thus serves to ground two intimately related assumptions: first, insofar as an entity is deemed to be lifeless it is thereby excluded *a priori* from ethical consideration in being definitively recast as a mere tool in service to the ends of life; and second, insofar as an entity is deemed to be lifeless it is therefore determined *a priori* by simple calculations of cause and effect, thus allowing for all of its future intra- and interactions to be unerringly predicted in advance. These two assumptions serve as keystones in the formation of what Heidegger terms 'the world picture,' according to which the absence of a perceived ethical dimension in relation to the exercise of technoscientific knowledge depends upon a fundamental view of nature as being essentially an external supply depot from which privileged human groupings can take without restriction or consequence in support of their ends irrespective of what such ends may consist. Ultimately, this reductive conception of externality results in a wildly skewed vision of the world that preserves inequality, facilitates commodification and exploitation and supports injustice—such is the sway of the Western metaphysical world picture under which everything and everyone continues to labour.

That said, it is critical that we understand that the perceived encroachment of technology into the once imagined sacrosanct domain of biological life today does nothing to challenge this world picture but seeks only to incorporate certain *other* lifeforms—both actual and potential—within its vast stockpile of technologies. As Heidegger argues, this construction of the relationship of humanity to the world as that of a 'standing reserve' [*Bestand*] is fundamental to the world picture proposed by modern science and by the principle of reason upon which such scientific rationality depends. The modern world picture, as Heidegger writes, is constructed precisely upon the entrapment of nature as 'a coherence of forces calculable in advance.'[6]

The concepts of determinability and predictability both suppose an active ability or capacity and both infer and defer to the possibility of *calculating in advance*. However, to lay claim to such a precognitive ability is to already reduce the external world to the status of an undifferentiated mass in which any given part is essentially indistinguishable from any other. It demands, in other words, the instrumentalizing of an excluded outside. Furthermore, this absolute exchangeability of parts is not only definitive of instrumentalization, but is also the prior condition of commodification. This is not by chance—the world picture of Heidegger's standing reserve is the picture of our modern, rationalized and postindustrialized world under the aegis of capitalist relations of production. It should thus come as no surprise that what contemporary innovations in the field of biotechnology reveal is that it is the potential value as a *commodity*, or the absence thereof, which ultimately determines whether an entity is to be counted as a purposeful living being and thus deserving of ethical concern, or as merely an object and thus prohibited by definition from making any such claim whatsoever. All of this, however, serves to maintain an incalculably dangerous delusion: that a baseless attribution of objecthood can serve as a guarantee of future safety.

The irony of this position is not immediately evident, but only becomes clear once we take seriously the question of what happens when the absolute distinction between living beings and nonliving objects can no longer hold, as only then does it become possible to leave behind our spurious theological fantasies of exceptionalism on the one hand and an equally obnoxious reduction of life to commodifiable nonlife on the other. Stated as simply and starkly as possible, it is only by deconstructing the monumental exclusion that divides life from lifeless and biology from artifice that instrumentalization then *ceases* to be possible.

No doubt many readers will remain reluctant to commit themselves to what appears, at first glance at least, to be such a dangerous path. And yes, to embark upon such a course is *by definition* not without risk. That said, however, the recognition of just this risk is exactly what is so urgently needed today in order to challenge the denial at once prevalent and convenient as to the inherent riskiness of our every decision, *a denial that rather enables such risks to be taken at the same time as fundamentally refusing to acknowledge their possibility*. At stake here are the fundamental philosophical concepts of beinghood and thinghood, of subject and object. As such, we should not be surprised to see these questions increasingly becoming the site of intense ontological, social, economic, political and ethical dispute. As the very matter of foundational collapse, these sites and these bodies contest the future or otherwise of the future, and they do so *not without risk*. And it is because they are not without risk that we still have the chance of a future.

Chapter 2

Ends of Nature

The Question Concerning Posthuman Technology

In the previous chapter it was argued that if we are to ever to move beyond our hubristic fantasies of self-accredited exception that rest on the props of reductionist classification in primary service to the reproduction of surplus value, it is necessary first of all to move beyond the ultimately untenable ontological distinction aimed at establishing absolute separation between living beings and nonliving objects. Building on this discussion, in this chapter I argue that the deconstruction of the organic–inorganic, animate–inanimate and nature–technics binaries makes possible the disclosure of the event previously obscured by the machinations of traditional reason. To do so, we leave behind the originary safeguarding of Western philosophy and turn our attention instead to its consolidation in the work of Aristotle, and most notably in the *Physics* [*Phusike akroasis*] which, in the pre-*Kehre* paper 'On the Essence and Concept of φυσις [*phusis*] in Aristotle's *Physics* B, 1' (1939), Martin Heidegger emphatically describes as '*the hidden, and therefore never adequately studied, foundational book of Western philosophy*' (185, italics in original).

While the Socratic argument from exclusion constitutes the modus operandi of metaphysics, Aristotle's *Physics* lays out its fundamental treatise insofar as it deems *willing* to be synonymous with *living* and, in so doing, makes possible the process of instrumentalization that will ultimately determine the essence of our technological modernity. Philosophy, as Heidegger argues in his reading of the Heraclitean fragments, "in its essence, is so primordially Occidental that it bears the ground of the history of the Occident. From out of this ground alone, technology has arisen. There is only an Occidental technology. It is the consequence of 'Philosophy' and nothing else" (*Heraclitus: The Inception of Occidental Thinking*, 3). In *The Principle of Reason*, Heidegger follows this same intimate braiding of philosophy, instrumentality and technology albeit from the opposite direction when he states:

> Modern technology pushes toward the greatest possible perfection. Perfection is based on the thoroughgoing calculability of objects. The calculability of objects presupposes the unqualified validity of the *principium rationis*. It is in this way that the authority characteristic of the principle of reason determines the essence of the modern, technological age (121).

The question that guides Heidegger's engagement with technology in general, and his reading of Aristotle's *Physics* in particular, is deceptively simple: What is the instrumental itself? To begin to answer this question, it is necessary to understand exactly how instrumentality is assembled and what this means for our accounting of causation. Wherever instrumentality reigns, as Heidegger argues in *The Question Concerning Technology*, there reigns causality and, in formulating this co-incidence as fundamental to thought, situates and at once obscures Aristotle's *Physics* as a foundational text of Western philosophy. Ultimately, Aristotle here determines just what can and, more importantly, can*not* be counted as a purposeful living body deserving of ethical consideration. Based entirely on mutually exclusive forms of causation, however, what for the most part remains hidden (and thus inadequately studied) is the fact that this fundamental division of competing causalities serves to maintain to this day an incalculably dangerous delusion: *viz*, that an unfounded attribution of objecthood can guarantee our future safety. But what if we suppose, as Heidegger suggests, that causality is indeed 'veiled in darkness with respect to what it is' (*The Question Concerning Technology*, 6)? What happens then? The answer does not concern what happens, but rather what *no longer* happens: in deconstructing the metaphysical exclusions of matter from life, artifice from biology and technics from nature, it is the very process of instrumentalization that is no longer possible.

ENDS OF NATURE

Things start to go awry for us, writes Heidegger, with the translation of the Greek term φυσις [*phusis*] as the Latin term *natura*. From this initial misstep and continuing all the way to our postindustrial present, 'nature' thus becomes 'the fundamental word that designates essential relations that Western historical humanity has to beings, both to itself and to beings other than itself' ('On the Essence and Concept of φυσις,' 183). Paradoxically, however, this long prevalent concept of 'nature' in fact derives its normative force from the dual role it occupies. First of all, the *domain* of nature is negatively described by way of an interlinking series of exclusionary antonyms: nature and grace, nature and history, nature and spirit and so forth. At the same time and in the same way, however, we *also* speak of "the 'nature' of spirit, the 'nature' of history, and the 'nature' of the human being" (183). In this second sense 'nature' refers not to a natural realm, territory or jurisdiction, but rather serves as the *definition* of nature 'itself.' When we speak of the 'nature' of things, writes Heidegger, "we mean *what* things are in their 'possibility' and *how* they are, regardless of whether and to what degree they 'actually' are" (183). In short, the nature *of* things, *of* every thing, names the irreparable divorce of the essential from the empirical. As such, the actual domain or territory accorded to 'nature' through the orchestrated exclusion of its opposites ultimately gets downgraded in status to that of a contingent empirical realm, having been stripped of its specific value by the universality of its being. In other words, the exclusionary nature *of* nature in turn begets a further dichotomy in which Nature as essence is constituted through the exclusion of nature as empirical domain, and in accordance with which the *truth* of Nature is always already withdrawn from the *realm* of nature. Stated more precisely, we can thus say that *the concept of nature attributes absolute jurisdiction to itself through the exclusion of itself as naturally contingent.*

By this stage such means and machinations will likely be all too familiar insofar as this constitutive exclusion of nature from Nature mirrors perfectly the Socratic constitutive exclusion of virtue from Virtue with which we began and which is, as we know, the definitive operation of metaphysics. And knowing this, we are thus better able to understand Heidegger's claim that, no matter the scope and sense attributed to the concept of nature over the centuries and squabbles of Western philosophy, the word 'nature' in every case "contains an interpretation of beings as a whole, even when 'nature' seems to be meant as only one term in a dichotomy" (184). In this latter case, continues Heidegger, 'nature' is never just one of two equal terms but rather "'essentially' holds the position of priority, inasmuch as the other terms are always and primarily differentiated by contrast with—and therefore are determined by—*nature*" (184). Moreover, as we have seen, this primary exclusion from the essential still holds even when, and perhaps even especially when, 'nature' comes to occupy both opposing poles.

The claim that every concept of nature carries within itself an interpretation of beings as a whole should certainly give us pause. As Heidegger writes, "[t]he systematic articulation of the truth at any given time 'about' beings as a whole is called 'metaphysics'" (185). Moreover, it is not required of this 'systematic articulation' that it be explicitly expressed in the form of a system—indeed, the concept of nature rather gains a great deal of its normative force from its *not* being expressly articulated. Metaphysics, continues Heidegger, "is that knowledge wherein Western historical humanity preserves the truth of its relations to beings as a whole and the truth about those beings themselves. In a quite essential sense, meta-physics is 'physics,' i.e., knowledge of *phusis* [*episteme phusikē*]" (185). It is this thoroughgoing enmeshing of nature, truth and knowledge that leads Heidegger in the first place to describe Aristotle's *Physics* as the hidden yet foundational work of Western philosophy. It is also the reason why rigorous critical engagement with the ends of nature in Aristotle's *Physics* remains to this day a prerequisite both for our having of a future and for the future of ethics. As Heidegger puts it,

> if we consider that this fundamental word of Western metaphysics harbors within itself decisions about the truth of beings; if we recall that today the truth about beings as a whole has become entirely questionable; moreover, if we suspect that the essence of truth therefore remains thoroughly in dispute; and finally if we know that all this is grounded in the history of the interpretations of the essence of φύσις [*phusis*], then we stand outside the merely historical interests that philosophy might have in the 'history of a concept.' Then we experience, although from afar, the nearness of future decisions (185).

What might this mean, to *experience from afar the nearness* of future decisions? Of what are 'future decisions' composed, if indeed they can be said to 'be' anything at all? *We who will then experience from afar the nearness of future decisions*—not by chance, this phrase of Heidegger's offers up a dizzying array of possible readings. Before we get to that, however, it is helpful first of all to address the antecedent serialization in the passage above. Composed of four temporally or causally linked 'ifs,' the sequence proceeds as follows: first, *if* we are to accept that any given concept of 'nature' contains within itself the various culturally specific decisions that constitute the truth of its relations to beings as a whole; and second, *if* we accept that the truth about beings as a whole is therefore a consequence of cultural contingency, we must also accept that what we recognize today as the truth about beings as a whole must also lack any necessary foundation. Third, *if* we accept that our particular truth about beings as a whole is devoid of foundation, then we must cease naively clinging to the last scraps of our deluded secular faith as to the possible existence and/or articulation of universal truth. Finally, *if* we accept that all of this is grounded in historical interpretations of nature and, moreover, that this is all contained within our contemporary concept of nature, then this entire sequence wraps back around itself, closing the circle of disenchantment in situating ourselves for the first time outside of the obscure confines of historical bias.

In finding ourselves uniquely situated in this way within a potential line of flight *from* human history that only now becomes possible for the first time *in* human history, argues Heidegger, it thus becomes possible for us to experience for the first time and from afar the nearness of future decisions. At first glance, this claim may well appear as yet one more of any number of similar claims that together compose the history of Western philosophy. This, however, is not that. Rather, Heidegger here is laying claim to something that not only *has* never happened previously, but which also *could* never have happened until now. *If* the sequence of required antecedent conditions is met, he argues, *then* philosophy necessarily becomes something profoundly other to the entirety of metaphysics hitherto, and does so insofar as it arrives ultimately at its own freedom from the tyrannical bias of situated historical interests. With Heidegger's reading of Aristotle's *phusis* and in what is almost a parody of the constitutive exclusion definitive of Socratic transcendental idealism, philosophy thus at last attains its originally ahistorical conception of nature as the truth of beings as a whole and, as such, *arrives in the form of its own freedom from itself and thus from nature as conceptual containment*.

END OF NATURE

In summary, Heidegger argues that, as a consequence of our contemporary historical situatedness, a previously unthinkable form of explicitly postmetaphysical philosophy emerges into being for the first time in history. As such, the antecedent causal sequence is itself the cause of which contemporary philosophy with its new conception of nature is the effect. Furthermore, it is this work of temporal and causal economies that for the first time in history makes possible an entirely novel experience of nearness from afar to future decisions. But just what kind of temporal and causal determination is in effect here? As we shall see, such questions of time and necessity will ultimately take us to the heart of Heidegger's reading of Aristotle.

Before that, however, given the announcing of philosophy's liberation from its confinement hitherto within the vicious ideological circles of metaphysical nature within the first few pages of 'On the Essence and Concept,' we must first of all ask ourselves if perhaps Heidegger has in fact *already* entrapped himself within a circle from which there can be no escape. What he describes here is the origin and ordering of an ahistorical and thus fundamentally disinterested philosophical standpoint that arises out of a necessarily contingent temporal and causal process. Both historicity and historiography are, in short, the time, place and condition of our liberation from the binds and blinds of our finite history and finite nature. At the very least, such determining causality is far from simple, far from *reasonable*.

So, while neither simple nor in a strict sense reasonable, this strange causal and temporal movement with its determining of the undeterminable is nonetheless the foundation upon which is built all that follows here. As Heidegger argues, a new thinking of 'nature' will have been heralded or announced *by means of* the old word 'nature,' and that which is not yet nature will only become possible by the way of, and on the basis of, 'old' nature. We shall address this paradoxical transformation at length in chapter 4 by way of a reading of Jacques Derrida's 'event-machine,' wherein Derrida invokes a profound homonymic disparity between old and new concepts of 'thought' that are at once identical *and* exclusive, always the same *and* radically otherwise. Staying here with Heidegger, we ultimately find the same movement at play wherein *nature* (as *phusis*) names that which can no longer be thought *and* that which remains impossible to think, that which validates antecedence as it invalidates novelty *and* that which validates the future as it invalidates the past. All of this, however, must wait until a later chapter. For now, it still remains for us to follow Heidegger in asking just what it means to 'experience, although from afar, the nearness of future decisions' ('On the Essence,' 185).

First of all, it is important to note here that Heidegger is describing a *relation*, and that this relation is itself last in line along a string of determining causes. Second, this relation marks the emergence of both a posthistorical nature and a postmetaphysical philosophy. It is therefore as a consequence of the various machinations undergone across millennia by the concept of nature that we are somehow simultaneously given to experience our senses of both remoteness and proximity to such decisions that as yet will not have taken place. Leaving aside the preliminary steps sketched out above, we are left with two distinct transitions and transformations: one going *from* the harboured decisions of Western metaphysics *to* the future decisions of posthistorical nature, and another going from a *position* of distance to a transformative *experience* of nearness. Hence, if we are to recognize the herald of philosophy's liberation from historical bias, we must address ourselves to these very different and complex causal mechanisms.

At this stage, however, we still have a great many more questions than answers—questions that can be loosely grouped together according to their principal concern. What, first of all, is the *ontological status* of these 'future decisions'? Are such decisions essentially of the future and therefore ahistorical? Is the future itself ahistorical or atemporal? Second, what of the novel *experience* of proximity at a distance? Is this necessarily ahistorical? How might the affective experience of a new form of relation to the future impact individual experience understood by definition to be contextually contingent, and what becomes of the concept of 'distanced relation' as a result of this new experience? Third, is the experience of distanced proximity perhaps *constitutive*—be that as a cause, process or mechanism—of future decisions? Or is it perhaps the 'sense' of the emergent algorithm of nature itself? Fourth, to *what* or *whose future* do such decisions pertain? Does the very concept of decision already presume a willing, intentional subject, or are such decisions autonomous events? And how do they come to be determined, if indeed they are? Finally, what becomes of *causality* itself? What of the concepts of determinism and indeterminacy, of immediacy, priority and mediation? How are we to get from (harboured) decisions to (future) decisions, from (metaphysical) nature to (philosophical) nature, and from (presently) distanced to (proximally) distanced? Are future decisions simply those that come *to* us *from* the future and if so, how? And why? And, in the end, does it even matter?

The answers to some if not all of these questions, suggests Heidegger, are to be found within Aristotle's *Physics*. Key to Heidegger's reading is the distinction that Aristotle makes between φυσει-beings ('living' or 'natural' [*phusei*] beings) and φυσις [*phusis*] itself. Whereas the former *are* in the state of movedness, argues Aristotle, *phusis itself* is the αρχη [*arkhe*]—that is, the origin and ordering—of that movedness. From this, writes Heidegger, 'we may readily conclude that the character of φυσις [*phusis*] as origin and ordering will be adequately determined only when we achieve an essential insight into that *for which* φυσις [*phusis*] is the origin and *over which* it is the ordering power: κινησις [*kinesis*]' (207). It is clear from this that the concept of 'movedness' plays a crucial role in determining the traditional concepts of life and nature within Western philosophy.

According to Aristotle, every form of being constituted by nature—that is, each of those beings that are what they are and how they are from *phusis*—has 'within itself a principle [*arkhe*] of movedness and of rest, and where movedness and rest are specified sometimes with regard to place, sometimes with regard to growth and diminution, other times with regard to alteration' (*Physics* 192b12–15, translation modified). Further clarifying this relation between movedness as *principle* or *cause* of *physei*-being and movedness as the *state* of *physei*-being, Heidegger notes:

> *Arkhe* means, at one and the same time, beginning and control. On a broader and therefore lower scale we can say: origin and ordering. In order to express the unity that oscillates between the two, we can translate *arkhe* as originating ordering and as ordering origin. The unity of these two is *essential*. And this concept of *arkhe* gives a more definite content to the word αιτιον [*aition*] (cause) ('On the Essence,' 189).

Before going further with this question of causation, however, it is important at this stage to introduce here one further Aristotelian concept, that of *number* [*arithmos*], and to do so specifically in relation to what Catherine Malabou in *Before Tomorrow: Epigenesis and Rationality* (2014) describes as 'the difference and juncture of the before and the after' (133).

THE TIME OF AGGREGATION

Addressing the concept of correlationism as formulated by philosopher Quentin Meillassoux in *After Finitude: An Essay on the Necessity of Contingency* (2008), Malabou is quick to point out that Heidegger would 'certainly have drawn attention to the error that comes of the constant confusion between correlation and articulation in *After Finitude*, a confusion that the reading of Aristotle prohibits specifically' (*Before Tomorrow*, 133).[1] *Articulation*, writes Malabou, names 'the neutral synthesis that holds together the moments of time,' whereas *correlation* refers instead to 'the synthesis that holds together subjectivity (or *psyche*) and time' (133). Just because the two syntheses are themselves linked, she continues, this 'does not mean that they are reducible to one another' (133). Indeed, this distinction ultimately proves crucial insofar as it reveals that the practice of dating is thus 'never intrinsically mathematical' (133). But just what does this mean—surely a date is simply a number arrived at by way of simple arithmetic? Well, yes. And no.

On this point Malabou invites us to recall the 'famous definition of time' proposed in Aristotle's *Physics*: 'For this is what time is: a number [*arithmos*] of change in respect of before and after' (219b1 cit. Malabou, 133). In her gloss of the opening lines of section 219b, Malabou closely follows Rémi Brague in focusing her critical attention on the precise meaning and subsequent role of the concept of *arithmos*.[2] First of all, she writes, time serves to distinguish before from after in exactly the same way that we 'establish the distance from point A to point B on a trajectory' and, as such, it is clear that time is a type of *number* [*arithmos*] (133). Less clear, however, is how we are to understand the concept of 'number' in this context insofar as *arithmos* also has a *pre*-arithmetic meaning in which 'it refers to a structure, an assembly. In this sense, it is very close to *harmonia*. Thus, *arithmos* refers *less to a number than to a structure organized by numbers*' (133, italics added). As such, continues Malabou, a more accurate translation of *arithmos* is that of 'articulation': a shift that has profound consequences when it comes to our understanding of Aristotle's definition of time, the translation of which now reads, 'For this is what time is: the before and after articulation [*arithmos*] of movement.' Time, in other words, is the *articulated synthesis of movement*. *Arithmos*, writes Malabou, is therefore 'not what enables counting, but rather what a collection must have to be a collection. Not an aggregate, but again, rather, an order and a structure of conjuncture. . . . That which is numbered in time is thus articulation, in other words, the difference and juncture of the before and the after' (133). As we shall see, this distinction is absolutely fundamental if we are to move beyond the confines of residual metaphysics maintained by the living–nonliving dichotomy.

Of particular interest for us here is the corollary distinction that Malabou makes between an *ordering structure* on the one hand and *aggregation* on the other. On this point, however, we must first understand just what is at stake in decoupling the very different syntheses of correlation and articulation. As we have seen, Aristotle's concept of *arithmos* as articulation refers only to the holding together of *disparate moments of time*, whereas the correlationist synthesis refers instead to the holding together of *time and subjectivity or psyche*. In other words, the synthetic articulation of the before and after is entirely independent of an ordering subject and, as such, constitutes an entirely neutral function that both precedes and exceeds biological consciousness. As Malabou puts it, '[t]he fact that there is movement, and therefore time, in the soul does not mean that time is essentially psychic' (133). More importantly, as we shall see, this privileging of machinic function over biological bias, while counterintuitive, is in fact and at once the *condition* of creative teleological purposiveness and the *im*possibility of a mechanistic or 'technical' aggregation of matter. The world, as Heidegger writes, is indeed 'shifting out of joint—if indeed it ever was *in* joint—and the question arises whether modern man's planning, even if it be worldwide, can ever create a world order' ('Essence and Concept,' 185). In other words, whereas the triumphant domination of modern technology ultimately rests upon an absolutization of ordering instrumentality, it is technology *itself* that ultimately renders this triumph merely a mirage, albeit an ordering mirage on a planetary scale.

By way of an excellent close reading of Paragraph 27 in Kant's *Critique of Pure Reason*, Malabou argues in *Before Tomorrow* that the figure of *epigenesis* is in fact the 'sensible presentation' of *arithmos* as articulation insofar as it 'assumes the co-implication of all the moments of time, without granting any privilege to either the past or the sudden emergence of a present' (134). With this we are returned to Heidegger's reading of Aristotle, insofar as Malabou argues that it is 'entirely possible' to read epigenesis as a figure of the movement that in *On Time and Being* Heidegger terms *reichen*, meaning the 'mutually giving to one another of future, past and present' (*On Time and Being*, 14; cit. Malabou 134). Never one to forsake clarity for the sake of brevity, Heidegger in 'On the Essence and Concept of *Φυσις*' describes this strange causal movement as follows:

> *Φυσις* [*Phusis*] is a 'going' in the sense of a goingforth toward a going-forth, and in this sense it is indeed a going *back* into itself; i.e., the *self* to which it returns remains a going-forth. *The merely spatial image of a circle is essentially inadequate* [italics added] because this going-forth that goes back into itself

precisely lets something go forth from which and to which the going-forth is
in each instance on the way. This essence of φυσις [*phusis*] as κινησις [*kinesis*]
is fulfilled only by the kind of movedness that μορφη [form: *morphe*] is (224).

This final sentence bears reiterating: *the essence of nature as movement is
fulfilled only by the kind of movedness that form is*. It is this kind or way
of 'movedness that form is' that will preoccupy us for the remainder of this
section and will, after what has been an admittedly protracted detour, return
us to what for Heidegger is the transformative experience of both remoteness
and proximity to future decisions given to us through a new and definitively
contemporary concept of nature.

HERE AND NOW AND FOR THE FIRST
TIME IN HUMAN HISTORY

Just what, and how, is form as movedness? As we have seen, Western metaphysics arrives in the form of its own freedom from itself and thus *from
nature* as conceptual containment and *into nature* as being as such—is this
the kind of movedness that form is? Or is its movedness that of the 'other'
philosophy that escapes its trappings through the work of homonymic flight
alluded to above? Or is it something else, some other work of causal insanity
or figural paradox? Morphological unreason, as we shall see, is the darkly
veiled *id* of causality. Such is the name of the challenge posed to the instrumental reason of the ego by the dense and real *peut-être*.

Independent of specific context, 'causality' always describes a relation
that precedes its description. By contrast, the relation that concerns us here
and now is more precisely one of *articulation*, which can be understood in
two distinct senses: first, articulation is synonymous with causation insofar
as it names the description of a mechanical relation that precedes it; and second, articulation names the temporal process through which all possible and
impossible entities emerge into being. And crucially, writes Heidegger, we
too are uniquely articulated within human history insofar as, here and now
and for the first time in that history, it becomes possible to articulate—in
both senses—a potential line of flight from human history and to a new and
originally ahistorical conception of nature as the truth of beings as a whole.
Furthermore, it is insofar as we are temporal and historically determined bodies that it becomes possible here and now and for the first time in history to
articulate the movement from the harboured decisions of Western metaphysics and toward the future decisions of posthistorical nature, and from a position of distance to a transformative experience of nearness. It is unsurprising,
therefore, that the need for an entirely novel articulation of being—that

is, here and now and for the first time in history—has increasingly moved centre stage in otherwise diverse contemporary articulations of Continental philosophy as, for example, in texts by Catherine Malabou, Jacques Derrida, Quentin Meillassoux, Bruno Latour, Michel Serres and Claire Colebrook, to name just a few.

While we will address in detail the articulation of novel emergence in Derrida and Meillassoux in the 'mad times' of chapter 4, it is useful at this stage to briefly convey a sense of this articulation in the work of some of those other thinkers named above, all of whom occupy key positions in what follows. In her reading of Kant's *Critique of Pure Reason* in *Before Tomorrow*, Malabou argues that all prior readings of Kant up to this point in history "express a symptomatic indecision between 'before' and 'after'" that is the 'flagrant mark' of the instability of the transcendental itself and which betrays our failing thus far to think the figure of epigenesis as a possible line of flight beyond both the rigid prior accord of preformation and the 'magical animation of the inorganic' (113). That said, however, the figure of epigenesis does not simply memorialize the site of a fundamental indecision with respect to the definition of reason. Epigenesis, argues Malabou, takes place exactly at the 'articulation' or 'trigger point' between pure concepts and their implementation in experience and as such the figure of epigenesis thus describes the reciprocity of interference and transformation that animates both old and new in the 'process of bringing the fusion of times to fruition' (158). Rather than a creation myth that forever awaits redemption through the subsequent recovery of its genetic past, epigenesis instead 'names a dynamic, creative and self-forming relation,' ultimately giving rise to 'the embryo of a specific temporality' (158). As such, writes Malabou, the newly articulated figure of epigenesis ultimately makes available here and now and for the first time in human history the 'generative force proper to thought' (25).

For Colebrook too, we currently occupy for the first time in history an explicit articulation of historical fracture. In 'Posthuman Humanities' (2014), she identifies a 'definite historical sense and teleology' along which and according to which our various objects of the humanities are composed, objects such as language, literature and, indeed, "'Man' itself" (176). Consolidated throughout human history, continues Colebrook, this teleology necessarily presumes an emergence *from* life in two distinct and contradictory senses: first, as emergence from life insofar as the latter constitutes the ground of the former; and second, as emergence from life understood as an absolute separation of the former from the latter.[3] By contrast, however, Colebrook follows Michel Serres in arguing that henceforth we must cease to sequester the human away from life in this manner so as to 'destroy the history of man in favor of a history of bodies . . . and an emphasis on *sense*' (176). Both Serres and Colebrook, in other words, similarly identify a potential line of flight from human history for the first time in human history, one that takes place only by way of a profound 'new sense of *sense* and a new sense of history' (177).[4] This profoundly novel sense of sense, writes Colebrook, "would not be *meaning* or the way in which the world is for 'us' but would open out onto a broader domain of interaction and relations (as well as that which is devoid of relation and connection)" (176). As we shall see in chapter 4, this focus on a history of bodies coupled with a new emphasis on a reworked sense of 'sense' has very clear parallels with the philosophical projects of both Meillassoux and Derrida insofar as the attribution of the ability to *make* sense—and thus a capacity to be affected—traditionally serves to ground the event–machine antinomy with which both thinkers take issue. For the moment, however, it suffices here to note that for Colebrook too it is only here and now and for the first time in history that it has become possible—and maybe even neces- sary—to inhabit an inhuman approach to knowledge that moves us beyond the history of life and toward an entirely novel articulation of being.

Even with such a brief overview, it is nonetheless clear that all of these thinkers are, in diverse ways and from different beginnings, attempting to articulate a new relation of movedness that was literally unthinkable before now. This articulation, this movedness, as Heidegger tells us above, is such that the 'merely spatial image of a circle is essentially inadequate' insofar as its physical essence as kinesis 'is fulfilled only by the kind of movedness that form [*morphe*] is' ('On the Essence and Concept,' 224). And this new articulation, this other movedness, renders experience monstrous and there- fore transformative—the experience, in other words, of proximity from afar to future decisions. Our question then, is still the same: Just what kinds of spatial, temporal and causal determinations are in effect here?

THE PRESENT ABSENCE

In referring to the fundamental inadequacy of the spatial image of a circle when it comes to articulating a specifically morphological kind of moved- ness, Heidegger here signals the principal targets of his critique of Aristotelian ontology. Above all else, Heidegger seeks to challenge the long dominant conception of time as circular that has its foundation in the conjunction of χρονος [*khronos*] with the σφαιρα [*sphaira*] first formulated by Aristotle. As he notes in *Being and Time* (1927), while the extraordinary success and lon- gevity of Aristotelian ontology is well known, 'the kind of effect it has had, the path it has taken, even its limitations, have hitherto been as obscure as the Fact itself has been familiar' (500, n.xxx). Moreover, as a key step along the way toward conceptual clarification we are required to consider further the functioning of the concept of *number* as *arithmos* [αριθμος] in Aristotle's definition of time, as briefly touched upon above.

Put simply, the kind of movedness that form is cannot be adequately described either by the figure of the circle or by any spatial trope or combination thereof. As movedness, in other words, forms of being are therefore irreducible to ordered patterns or sequences of points in space. Instead, the kind of movedness that form *is* is, as Malabou writes, an ordering and structuring articulation of 'the difference and juncture of the before and the after' (*Before Tomorrow*, 133). Malabou, we recall, describes this same movedness through the figure of epigenesis, a figure which she argues is entirely compatible with the movement termed *reichen* by Heidegger and defined as the mutual giving of one to another of future, past and present and without any prioritizing or privileging of one term over any other. Form, in other words, is an ordering articulating of time. Hence, as Derrida points out in a key early reading of Heidegger's existential analytic, not only is 'the formulation of temporality to be delivered from the traditional concepts that govern . . . the history of ontology from Aristotle to Bergson, but also the possibility of this vulgar conceptualization [of time] is to be taken into account.'[5] Just how, in other words, is the 'vulgar'—that is, circular and spatial—conceptualization of time even possible? Exactly how did this happen? And what happens when this vulgar conception of time is recognized for what it is, and thus its impact and implications become available to thought for the first time in history? According to Heidegger therefore, traditional ontology 'can be destroyed only by repeating and interrogating its relation to the problem of time' (Derrida, '*Ousia* and *Grammē*,' 31).

Building upon the Socratic argument from exclusion, the fundamental relation of nature and time as formulated in Aristotle's *Physics* ultimately comes to guide all subsequent interpretations in the Western philosophical tradition. Insofar as nature [*phusis*] has its essence in the state of movedness [*kinesis*], the fundamental question to be addressed by physics thus becomes one of defining the essence of movement. Indeed, as Heidegger suggests, it has today become 'merely a truism to say that the processes of nature are processes of movement' ('On the Essence and Concept,' 186). Nonetheless, prior to Aristotle the conception of movedness as the fundamental mode of being remained literally unthinkable. That said, however, the essential movedness of nature that form is inevitably gives rise to an infinitely regressive aporetic as described initially by Aristotle in Book IV of the *Physics*, where it follows from the positing of two questions concerning time: 'First, does [time] belong to the class of things that exist or to that of things that do not exist? Then secondly, what is its nature [*phusis*]?' (217b). With these questions, Aristotle introduces two fundamental stumbling blocks along the way to a proper understanding of temporality—the first of which concerns the divisibility or otherwise of time into parts [*meros*] and the second the time or otherwise of the now [*nun*]—stumbling blocks that in fact constitute the very *form* of time as that of 'vulgar' time, that is to say, as the form in which time ultimately 'cannot not be given' (Derrida, '*Ousia* and *Grammē*,' 39).

Aristotle begins Paragraph 10 of Book IV as follows:

> One part of time has been and is not, while the other is going to be and is not yet. Yet time—both infinite time and any time you like to take—is made up of these. One would naturally suppose that what is made up of things which do not exist could have no share in reality. Further, if a divisible thing is to exist, it is necessary that, when it exists, all or some of its parts must exist. But of time some parts have been, while others are going to be, and no part of it is, though it is divisible. For the 'now' is not a part: a part is a measure of the whole, which must be made up of parts. Time, on the other hand, is not held to be made up of 'nows.' Again, the 'now' which seems to bound the past and the future—does it always remain one and the same or is it always other and other? It is hard to say (218a).

While the paradox of eternity—that is, of infinite time and, indeed, of 'any time you like to take'—will have to await its proper place in the discussion of immediacy that follows here and in more detail in the next chapter, we must consider first the articulation of parts and wholes with respect to the nature or *phusis* of time as traditionally conceived from Aristotle to Bergson. More specifically, is the forming of time a form of presence or a formative absence, that is, a form of substance or a formative supplementarity? Is it the nature or *phusis* of time to be of the one and the same or of the always other and other?

What, then, are the parts of time? And of what might time as the whole of those parts be composed or persist? This first question seems simple enough: one part of time, writes Aristotle, is that which has been and is *no longer*, and another part is that which is going to be but is *not yet*, with the part of time that is the present instant [*nun*] being somehow sandwiched between prior and future parts. Here, as Derrida writes, Aristotle is 'giving in' to that which is as obvious as it is unavoidable, namely

> that time is, that time has as its essence, the *nun*. . . . The *nun* is the form from which time cannot ever depart, the form in which it cannot not be given; and yet the *nun*, in a certain sense, is not. If one thinks time on the basis of the now, one must conclude that it is not. The now is given simultaneously as that which is *no longer* and that which is *not yet*. It is what it is not, and is not what it is. . . . Thereby time is *composed* of nonbeings. Now, that which bears within it a certain *no-thing*, that which accommodates nothingness, cannot participate in presence, in substance, in *beingness* itself [*ousia*]. This first phase of the *aporia*

involves thinking time in its divisibility. Time is divisible into parts, and yet none of its parts, no now, is *in the present*' ('*Ousia* and *Grammē*,' 39–40)

So, if we accept that time is indeed composed of parts none of which actually exist in the present, then what can be inferred as to the *nature*, the *phusis*, of time? Ostensibly in the hope of perhaps gaining a better grasp on the ontological elusiveness of time, Aristotle in the second phase of the aporetic proposes instead the inverse hypothesis, i.e., that the 'now' is *not* in fact a part of time. No fool of course, Aristotle knows exactly where this opposing formulation will take us. What, then, becomes of time should we accept that it is not in fact composed of nows, that the now has no part to play in time? Appearances notwithstanding, this question in a strict sense remains unthinkable, and necessarily so. If time is *not* a composite of parts, then time is always and everywhere *one and the same*, that is to say, time describes an indivisible being that can allow of no discrimination. As self-present and self-presencing, time thus destroys itself in posing itself as an undifferentiated and thus eternally unchanging present being.

Hence, no matter which side we take as regards the Aristotelian aporetic—time is composed of parts or time is not composed of parts—the answer is ultimately the same: time *is* that which *is not*. What is more, there is no way out from this aporia, no dialectical sublation or third way, for the simple fact that nonpresence can only be thought either in the form of presence or else as a modalization of presence. The past and the future, as Derrida puts it, 'are always determined as past presents or as future presents' ('*Ousia* and *Grammē*,' 34). However, what makes this of particular interest for the thesis being developed here is that, in both phases of the aporetic, time is ultimately proscribed from enduring or presencing in being for reasons of *immediacy* and *simultaneity*. Staying with Derrida's bravura close reading, he notes:

> If time, in the first hypothesis of the aporia, appears not to take part in pure *ousia* as such, it is that it is made of nows (time's parts), and that several nows cannot: (1) either follow each other by immediately destroying one another, for in this case there would be no time; (2) or follow each other by destroying each other in a not immediately consecutive way, for in this case the intervallic nows would be simultaneous, and again there would be no time; (3) or remain (in) the same now, for in this case things that occur at intervals of ten thousand years would be *together*, *at the same time*, which is absurd. It is this absurdity, denounced in the self-evidence of the 'at the same time,' that constitutes the aporia as aporia ('*Ousia* and *Grammē*,' 56).

At the same time: this shorthand phrase thus describes the self-evidencing of immediacy and simultaneity by way of which time always already comes to denounce itself as absurd. Moreover, as noted above, the concepts of immediacy and simultaneity are inextricably bound up with the supreme theological concept of *timeless presence* on the one hand and, on the other, with *being-timeless* as *being-mindless*, that is to say, all beings deemed to be instinctive, reactive, nonpurposive, nondesirous, automated, fabricated, technological and machinic. The absolute sovereignty constitutive of theological fancies the world over thus betrays only the wishful thinking of the medieval alchemist attempting in vain to produce perfection from out of base and debased material.

THE MOMENT OF MAGIC

Centred on concepts of proximity and distance and of adequation and representation, however, instantaneity and simultaneity in fact serve jointly to produce a very different form of magic. They are, in other words, pressed into largely unwitting service of a triumphant hylomorphism based upon a restricted and reductive thinking of causation. As we saw with the discussion of Sagan and Schneider's idiosyncratic use of the hyphen in the introduction, it is the apparent simultaneity in space and time of a supplemental form of being with that which it supplements that bestows upon transitional and transformative movements an apparent magic. Immediacy, in other words, is indistinguishable from magic insofar as it describes a formal dislocation in space but not in time, or a formal dislocation in time but not in space. Put simply, magic describes the collapse of all traditionally accepted rules of causality.

On this point, there remains an important coda to Sagan and Schneider's account of Taylor flow vortices as expressing '*near*-instantaneous' processes of transformation. Despite the suggestion of conflict perhaps betrayed by the hyphenated prefix, it is the historical weight of scientific truth that ultimately causes Sagan and Schneider to believe neither their eyes nor the accumulated data. In accordance with scientific method, 'data' refers only to a preliminary material resource that can only make sense upon its supplementary organization in the form of scientific 'truth.' Truth, in other words, names the form through which the nonsense of a given material *has been made* to *make sense*. For Sagan and Schneider, however, this segregation of formal scientific truth from passive material repository serves only as an ideological blind from behind which it becomes impossible to acknowledge the challenges posed to our habitual conceptions of time and space by the strange spontaneity and simultaneity definitive of novel emergence in(to) being.

Whatever its form may become in time, new formal events cannot exist in any previously recognizable form and, as such, cannot exist for thought. In other words, *any truly novel form of being must come into being over time and without precedent*, and as such cannot be made to make sense. Whatever form the new takes in time, the possibility of its emergence into being must be always impossible *prior to* its factual emergence into being, thus marking newly emergent forms of being as fundamentally *material, unpredictable* and *irreversible* and, as such, posing serious questions to our traditional concepts of temporality and causality and to their functioning with respect to configurations of matter generally. It is to some of these questions that our analysis of the 'movedness that form is' will hopefully provide a response.

ARTICULATING THE MOVEDNESS THAT FORM IS

As we know, Heidegger argues that, if we are ever to recognize the herald of philosophy's liberation from its constraining historical bias as evidenced in the thought of Sagan and Schneider above, it is necessary first of all to displace the determinist conception of nature as *phusis* as formulated so decisively by Aristotle. To this end, Heidegger seeks to articulate a new relation of movedness that, in taking us from the harboured decisions of Western metaphysics to the future decisions of posthistorical nature and from a position of distance to an experience of nearness, radically reworks the articulation and organization of all possible forms of being.

Returning to his reading of Aristotle's *Physics*, Heidegger makes the important point that Aristotle's notion of αιτιον [*aition*] is not at all reducible to a simple mechanism of cause and effect. *Aition*, he argues, concerns instead 'that which is responsible for the fact that a being is *what* it is' ('On the Essence and Concept,' 188). Such a *responsibility*, he clarifies further, "does not have the character of causation in the sense of a 'causally' efficient actualizing. . . . Cause as the origin [*Ur-sache*] must be understood here literally as the originary [*Ur-tümliche*], that which constitutes the thingness of a thing. 'Causality' is only a derivative way of being an origin" (188). *Aition*, in other words, describes that which is responsible for, and as such originarily constitutive of, the very thingness of a thing. By contrast, simple mechanistic causality will only come to hold sway in such devastating fashion much later, having as its condition a conception of what Heidegger calls the 'stable' as a 'standing over against' in the manner of an *object*, with Heidegger arguing further that "something 'standing over against' [*Gegenstand*]" is in fact the proper translation of the word 'object' (188–189). From this, of course, it inevitably follows that beings 'can be experienced as objects only where human beings have become subjects, those who experience their fundamental relation to beings as the objectification—understood as mastery—of what is encountered' (189). Other beings can become objects, in other words, only when human beings *deem themselves* to be subjects and, as such, subjects of a perverse and all-pervading ontological privilege.

While the ideological deafness that comes of causal objectification will prove fundamental to Heidegger's subsequent post-*kehre* texts addressing questions of technology and scientific rationality, to understand this we must first clarify what *distinguishes* the three key concepts in Heidegger's reading of Aristotle, and how it is that these three concepts *come together* in the production of 'the movedness [*kinesis*] that form [*morphe*] is': namely, *aition* [αιτιον]; *phusis* [φυσις]; and *arkhe* [αρχη]. Even with all we have learned already about *aition* and *phusis*, this task remains far from simple. Heidegger, we recall, defines *aition* as that which is 'responsible for the fact that a being is *what* it is' and which, as such, bestows or takes on form by way of a relation that is other, and more, than one of simple cause and effect. Almost in the same breath, however, Heidegger then defines *phusis* as 'what is responsible for the fact that the stable has a unique kind of standing-on-its-own' (189). With little seeming to distinguish between these two definitions, however, it is only with the introduction of the third term *arkhe* that it becomes possible to articulate as distinct their two forms of responsibility.

To this end, Heidegger turns to Book II of Aristotle's *Physics*, citing what for him offers a 'more clearly delineated' account of the concept of *phusis*:

> Indeed each of these beings [that are *what* they are and *how* they are from *phusis*] has in itself the originating ordering (*arkhe*) of its movedness and its standing still (rest), where movedness and rest are meant sometimes with regard to place, sometimes with regard to growth and diminution, other times with regard to alteration (change) (Aristotle, *Physics*, 192b13–15; cit. Heidegger, 'On the Essence and Concept,' 189).[6]

Here—and this point is crucial for Heidegger—'in place of αιτιον [*aition*] and αιτια [*aitia*] we find explicitly the word αρχη [*arkhe*]' (189). At first glance, this clarification would seem to offer very little, suggesting only a synonymous replacement of *aition* by *arkhe*. That said, however, we in fact find here a subtle shift of meaning regarding its relation to *phusis*. *Insofar as* beings are *what and how they are* from *phusis*, they must in some way have within their *phusis*-being an originary mechanism whose *a priori* function it is to impose formal order upon the relations of movedness and rest that uniquely compose each and every given *phusis*-being. *Arkhe*, in short, describes the originary ordering of movedness that form *is*. Put another way, as the originary ordering of continuity and change in the movedness that is one form of *phusis*-being to that of a differing form of movedness, *arkhe* describes the *a priori* inscription within a given form of *phusis*-being of its history of constitutive relations both internal and external. It is this 'originating ordering' constitutive of the *form* of *phusis-being* that Heidegger seeks to put in place of *aition* as that which is responsible for the factual thingness of a given being. Rather than simple synonymous exchange, however, *arkhe* is for Heidegger the *mechanism* of *aition*, is the function by way of which *aition* takes responsibility for the fact that a being is what it is in fact. *Arkhe*, he concludes, 'means, at one and the same time, beginning and control. On a broader and therefore lower scale we can say: origin and ordering. In order to express the unity that oscillates between the two, we can translate αρχη [*arkhe*] as originating ordering and as ordering origin. The unity of these two is *essential*' (189).

It is at this point in the *Physics*, argues Heidegger, that Aristotle 'defines φυσις [*phusis*] as αρχη χινησεως [*arkhe kinesos*]' (190). To be from *phusis*, in other words, is to be an originarily ordered form of movedness and rest. Furthermore, continues Heidegger, Aristotle is also quick to point out that the concept of movedness cannot be restricted to simple changes of place— i.e., locomotion—but rather must include all of the various forms of movedness. Regarding Aristotle's stated examples of growth and diminution and alteration and locomotion, however, Heidegger is equally quick to point out that the kinds of movedness offered by Aristotle are 'merely enumerated, i.e., they are not differentiated according to any explicit respect, nor grounded in any such differentiation' (190). Moreover, he continues, not only is this 'mere enumeration' incomplete, but it also overlooks precisely the one kind of movedness 'that will be crucial for determining the essence of φυσις [*phusis*]' (190).

So just what, according to Heidegger, is this special kind of movedness that, while missed out by Aristotle, nonetheless describes the fundamental character of all these other kinds of movedness? Consider, he writes, the running fox and the autumnal tree: running, the fox changes her place but not her colour, which remains unchanged; with the change of seasons, the tree's leaves are moved one way, becoming withered and dry, and also in another way, changing colour from green to yellow, whilst all the while the tree remains in place and thus *un*moved. Something that moves, in other words, may do so in several differing ways, all the while remaining simultaneously at rest and unchanged in others. Insofar as we perceive "these overlapping 'appearances' as types of movedness," writes Heidegger, we also perceive as common to all such appearances—as unchanged across all phenomenal apparitions, in other words—'their fundamental character, which Aristotle fixes in the word and the concept μεταβολη [*metabole*]. Every instance of movedness is a change from something (εχ τινος [*ek tinos*]) into something (εισ τι [*eis ti*])' (191). While at first glance this conclusion may well seem banal in the extreme, Heidegger is introducing here what might be called the 'essential core' of his own thinking: "[T]he essential core of what the *Greeks* meant in thinking μεταβολη [*metabole*] is attained only by observing that in a change [*Umschlag*] something heretofore hidden and absent comes into appearance. (In German: '*Aus-schlag*' [the breaking out of, e.g., a blossom] and '*Durchschlag*' [breaking through so as to appear on the other side])" (191). Stripped of its varied appearances—that is to say, at its most fundamental and profound—the movedness that form is, in other words, is that by which something that heretofore can*not* have being breaks out of or breaks through *into* being, and as such appears *in* being for the first time.

We can now summarize the argument thus far as follows: in contrast to the lifeless fabrications of technical and cultural objects or, in other words, all entities deemed to be *from* nature, *from phusis*, are as such only insofar as they have both within their being and as the condition of their being an originarily ordering form of movedness [*arkhe kinesos*] premised upon the concept of change as *metabole*. Hence, writes Heidegger, we must stop thinking about movement primarily as a change of place and instead 'learn to see how for the Greeks movement as a mode of *being* has the character of emerging into presencing. Φυσις [*Phusis*] is αρχη χινησεως [*arkhe kinesoes*], origin and ordering of change, such that each thing that changes has this ordering within itself' (191). As yet, however, it still remains for us to consider just how it is that natural beings come to be formed differently in being than all other forms of being. Just how is it, in other words, that 'the character of emerging into presencing' confers upon all entities deemed 'natural'—that is to say, upon living, biological beings—a privileged form of existence?

FORM IS *PHUSIS* TO A GREATER DEGREE

It is very clear that, within the presentation, withholding or withdrawal of the privileged status of 'being natural' there resides a quite extraordinary normative power. Furthermore, this power comes not at all from there being an essential nature of nature, but rather from its impossibility. In other words, it is only *because* nature is an indistinct and undefined property or condition that it becomes possible to present, withhold or even withdraw from individuals and groups alike the status of natural-being [*phusei*-being]. As can be clearly seen in the recounting of the convoluted biography of extremophiles which closes this chapter, it is rather the *absence* of essential nature that makes the cynical manipulation of life possible in the first place.

Turning his attention to the emergence into form [*morphe*] specific to beings from nature [*phusis*], Heidegger argues that *morphe* 'is the placing into the appearance; i.e., it is κινησις [*kinesis*] itself, the changing of the appropriate as a breaking out of its appropriateness' (219). He then further clarifies this as follows:

Μορφη [*morphe*] is *φυσις* [*phusis*] 'to a greater degree,' but not because it supposedly is 'form' that has subordinate to it a 'matter' that it molds. Rather, as
the placing into the appearance, *μορφη* [*morphe*] surpasses the orderable (*υλη*
[*ule*]) insofar as *μορφη* [*morphe*] is the presencing of the appropriateness of that
which is appropriate, and consequently, in terms of presencing, is more original
('On the Essence and Concept,' 220).

Here, Heidegger states explicitly that the placing into form as *morphe* does
not concern the subordination of a material resource [*ule*] to the given form
that moulds it, as is the case with hylomorphism which, as noted previously,
is founded upon a restricted and reductive thinking of causation. Rather,
continues Heidegger, by learning to 'see' in the way of the early Greeks, we
therefore get to sidestep two thousand years of reductive thought that has
ultimately led to the domination of modern technology built upon the absolutization of an ordering instrumentality. This 'other' thinking of *morphe*,
however, is not *phusis* 'to a greater degree' because it offers an alternative but
nonetheless equally definitive account of the form–matter relation, but rather
describes a prior and profoundly excessive form that surpasses the orderable
in being insofar as its placing into the appearance, as *kinesis* or *movedness*,
concerns the presencing of that which is, or is not, *appropriate*.

Forms of being from nature are thus said to exist 'to a greater degree'
in contrast to such forms of being deemed *not* from nature, but this is not
because natural forms *are*, in some undefined yet nonetheless fundamental—
that is, *vital*—way, '*better*' than other, nonnatural ways of organizing material
resources. Whereas vitalism presumes an absolute distinction between forms
of life and forms in which life is deemed to be absent, Heidegger here speaks
instead of forms of being that differ not in *kind* but in *degree* and, more precisely, in their greater degree of being: forms from *phusis* simply *exist* more,
they *are* more, than forms from elsewhere than *phusis*. Finally, that which
marks out such a form as existing more—that is to say, both *being more* and
possessing *more being*—is its movedness, its constitutive *kinesis* that is to
be always already reiterated differently as the very condition of placing into
appearance. As simply as possible therefore, *phusei*-being is the presencing
of form [*morphe*] to a greater degree through the differing *of* itself *from* itself
[*metabole*] that constitutes the prior condition of its manifest being. Hence,
argues Heidegger, what is *appropriate* to the presencing of *phusei*-being 'is'
difference, 'is' change, that of transformative appropriation as *morphe* of 'the
appropriateness of that which is appropriate' (219). As the constant iteration
of its own prior condition, to be from nature is thus to be *always already
breaking through and thus breaking out of the form appropriate to its being*.
Such, for Heidegger, is the originary movedness that (*living*) form is.

HEIDEGGER'S CHALLENGE

Of course, it goes without saying that that tiny parenthetical coda quite literally changes everything. Symptomatic of that change is the logical contradiction that arises from the claim that natural forms, by reason of their possessing a greater *degree* of being than all other forms, are uniquely situated in being and thus different in *kind* and *not* in degree as a result. From Aristotle to Heidegger, in other words, the self-allocation of ontological privilege remains unmoved. More importantly, however, this change without change that marks both the distance and the proximity of Heidegger to Aristotle is also the site of the twofold challenge posed by Heidegger to our modern conception of mechanistic nature.

There is no doubt, writes Heidegger, that "a good deal of time has yet to pass before we learn to see that the idea of 'organism' and of the 'organic' is a purely modem, mechanistic-technological concept, according to which 'growing things' [φυςει οντα (*phusei onta*)] are interpreted as artifacts [ποιουμενα (*poionmena*)] that make themselves" (195). This then speaks to the first part of our challenge as that of learning anew how to see the 'idea' of the organism and the organic. At this point, however, Heidegger continues to maintain that as far as artefacts are concerned "the origin of the making is 'outside' the thing made. Viewed from the perspective of the artifact, the αρχη [*arkhe*] always and only appears as something 'in addition'" (195). Here, Heidegger discloses the second part of the challenge as concerning the concept of 'artifactual' being, which is to say, technical being as being from *tekhne* rather than *phusis*.

It is my contention here that sufficient time—and thought—has now passed for us to be able to respond at least in part to this twofold challenge. That said, however, we should not be surprised to find this response ends up moving in a very different, even antagonistic direction to that supposed by Heidegger—indeed, in suggesting that 'a good deal of time has yet to pass' before such changes become possible, Heidegger himself is already signalling as necessary a movement beyond the sociohistorical constraints to which all thought is subject. According to Heidegger, the rethinking of the artefactual viewpoint that results from our learning to see the organism and the organic as 'purely modem, mechanistic-technological concepts' is necessary in order to 'avoid misunderstanding φυσις [*phusis*] as a kind of *self-producing* and the φυςει οντα [*phusei onta*: being from *phusis*] merely as a special kind of artifact' (195). The passage of a good deal of time, however, ultimately turns Heidegger's viewpoint through 180 degrees and turns instead to a seeing and a thinking anew of artefacts as much as organisms, and to our learning anew how to perceive the technological as much as the organic. Furthermore,

this 'other' turn (or *kehre*) brings Heidegger's thinking into productive relation with Gilbert Simondon's thesis *On the Mode of Existence of Technical
Objects*, first published in 1958.

While a detailed reticulation of Heidegger with Simondon must await the
discussion of technical genesis in the conclusion, we are nonetheless able to
offer a brief sketch as to its orientation. Heidegger, we recall, maintains that,
in order to avoid misunderstanding *phusis* such as defines the contemporary
era, we must *learn to see* both the organism and the organic anew. By contrast, Simondon argues that, in order to avoid misunderstanding *technics* such
as defines contemporary culture, we must *learn to see* technical ensembles
anew. As we shall see, these mirrored orientations in fact comprise two sides
of the same coin, one that seeks to break out of our contemporary normative
numbness and into 'genuine awareness' otherwise occluded by habitual repetition that ultimately erases such awareness of structures and operations with
'the stereotypy of adapted gestures' (Simondon, *On the Mode*, 18).

Before that, however, it still remains for us to follow Heidegger's reasoning
just a little further so as to gain a clear picture of exactly what is at stake here.
For this, we must understand the challenge initially posed by Heidegger to
the instrumental or cybernetic conception of being as *enframing* [*Gestell*] that
currently orders our relation to nonhuman others. Recalling once again the
epigraph with which we began, Heidegger characterizes modern technology
as a push toward the greatest possible perfection. While seemingly uncontroversial, this point in fact takes us to the heart of the misunderstanding upon
which modern technology is premised, in that its operative concept of perfection is 'based on the thoroughgoing calculability of objects. The calculability
of objects presupposes the unqualified validity of the *principium rationis*.
It is in this way that the authority characteristic of the principle of reason
determines the essence of the modern, technological age' (*The Principle
of Reason*, 121). The *validity* and thus *authority* of reason, in other words,
depends upon the assumption that all objects are thoroughly deterministic
forms of being and as such entirely calculable over time and in both directions. In short, the governing power of reason is premised upon an infallible
ability to predict the future and, as such, the principle of reason withdraws
once more into the theological realm of miracles and magic.

ON HOW NOT TO OVERLOOK THAT WHICH IS SO
FAR OFF AS TO BE NEARER THAN EVERYTHING

Prior to shifting focus toward genetic and epigenetic ordering in the next
chapter, it just remains for us to briefly consider the time of *proof* before then

concluding this chapter with the cautionary tale of the extremophile, whose revisionist biography ultimately gives the lie to the pervasive but incalculably dangerous belief that an unfounded attribution of objecthood can somehow serve to guarantee our future safety.

In the previous section, the principle of reason is shown in fact to depend upon a supernatural ability to foresee the future, so we should perhaps not be too surprised to discover that the identification of *life* in turn depends upon the possession of a magic eye. Returning to the *Physics*, Heidegger ostensibly seeks to test Aristotle's assertion at the beginning of Book Two that any attempt to prove '*that phusis* exists' is quite simply absurd (193a2–6). But, asks Heidegger, why shouldn't we take this task seriously? Surely it is the case, he continues, that without "a prior proof *that* something like φυσις [*phusis*] 'is,' all explanations about φυσις [*phusis*] remain pointless" ('On the Essence,' 201). Of course, readers of Heidegger will doubtless recognize the ironic undertone in the phrasing of this opening gambit, similar in style to the Socratic stingray. With seeming wide-eyed innocence, he thus suggests that we do indeed attempt just such a proof. Ah, but wait, interjects Heidegger, immediately interrupting himself, in that case we would *also* 'have to suppose that φυσις [*phusis*] *is not*, or at least that it is not yet proven in its Being and as Being' (201). As such, any attempt at constructing such a proof cannot therefore make reference *to phusis*, insofar as 'phusis' is precisely that which the existence of which is yet to be proven. With this in mind, writes Heidegger, 'how could we ever find or point to something like φυσις οντα [*phusis onta*], growing things—animals, for example—the very things by means of which the Being of φυσις [*phusis*] is supposed to be proven?' (201). Here, then, Heidegger supports Aristotle's charge of absurdity by pointing to the logical contradiction at the core of all attempts aimed at such a proof. In other words, the attempt to prove the existence of *phusis* is already absurd because of an inherent *temporal* paradox that renders all such attempts inconsistent and as such contrary to the principle of reason. Hence, the proof that *phusis* exists is 'impossible because it must already refer to the Being of φυσις [*phusis*], and precisely for that reason this kind of proof is always superfluous' (201). What are we to make of this sudden appeal by Heidegger to the precepts of principled reason? What is really at work in this paradoxical priority constitutive here of the *time* of proof?

For his part Heidegger is quick to move past such concerns, stating that 'already by its first step it attests of itself that its project is unnecessary. In fact the whole undertaking is ridiculous' (201). This most unequivocal of dismissals, however, is not without its own problems of causal linearity. The being of *phusis* and *phusis* as being, argues Heidegger, 'remain unprovable because φυσις [*phusis*] does not need a proof, for wherever a being from φυσις [*phusis*] stands in the open, φυσις [*phusis*] has already shown itself and stands in view' (201). But does this reasoned proof of the necessary lack of proof not in fact depend upon the same paradox of priority that was cause for dismissal of the initial attempt aiming to prove the existence of *phusis*? The paradox that always already invalidates every attempt at proving the existence of *phusis* is, in other words, the very *same* paradox that ultimately proves that *phusis* does, in fact, exist. Indeed, the vertigo to which such questions give rise is symptomatic of the temporal and causal paradox they attempt to describe. However, if we do not wish to simply maintain the blinds put in place by Aristotle and then by Heidegger after him, it is necessary for us to address ourselves to the actual paradox instead.

Again, both Heidegger and Aristotle emphatically decry such an approach to be the height of intellectual folly, an uncommon forcefulness which of itself should suffice to arouse intellectual curiosity. What, in other words, is being obscured by the stridency of such dismissals? Indeed, Heidegger does not stop here, but goes on to say of those who demand and attempt such a proof that 'one can at best draw their attention to the fact that they do not see *the very thing* that they already see, that they have no eye for what already stands in view for them' (201). To *try* to prove that *phusis* exists is thus to be blind to the *fact* that *phusis* exists, just as to ask for such a proof is rather proof only of a being in a state of perpetual blindness to that which otherwise lies in plain sight before their eyes. *Phusis*, lifeforce, *élan vitale*, *Geist*, *zoē* and *bios*: we thus need only to presuppose its existence in order to be able thereafter to see it. Reason once again succeeds in finding only what it has itself hidden.

AN EYE FOR MAGIC

At this point, things take an even more baffling turn. This eye for life, writes Heidegger, 'does not belong to everyone' (201). Such an eye, he continues, is not only for what one sees but also 'for what one already has in view when one sees what one sees' (201). At first glance, it might seem that Heidegger is here proposing a legitimate argument from phenomenology that sense perception is necessarily *ap*perception, insofar as sensibility can never describe pure perception but is rather always an iterative process of *re*cognition. This, however, is not at all the point being made. Rather, for Heidegger this eye is the eye for the *essential*, an ability that is possessed only by the privileged few and for the sole purpose of differentiating between living and nonliving forms of being on behalf of the eyeless masses. *This* eye, he writes, 'has the ability to differentiate what appears of and by itself and comes into the open

according to its own essence, from what does not appear of and by itself'
(201). In the same way that 'history' appears antecedently in all historical
occurrences and as 'art' does in all artworks, writes Heidegger, so too does
'life' appear antecedently in all living things, but this nonetheless is only
'seen with the greatest difficulty, is grasped very seldomly, is almost always
falsified into a mere addendum, and for these reasons simply overlooked'
(201).[7] For Heidegger, the failure of the masses in this regard is 'of course' to
be expected: 'Of course, not everyone needs to explicitly hold in view what
is already seen in all experience, but only those who make *a claim to deciding*, or even to asking, about nature, history, art, human beings, or beings as a
whole' (201–202, italics added). In the light of Nietzsche's genealogical critique, this amounts to nothing less than the creation of a new priesthood who
are alone deemed capable of interpreting the world and, as such, to decide
for their blind and senseless flock exactly what should and should not count
as ends and exactly what should and should not count as merely means to
those ends. A new priesthood, in short, perfectly engineered so as to officiate
over the modern, technological era otherwise condemned by Heidegger as
hell-bent on global catastrophe.

That said, however, it is no surprise to discover such a claim at work in
Heidegger's account, the reason for which is simple: there can be no humanist,
anthropocentric or vitalist standpoint that does not ultimately have recourse to
the supernatural, theological realm. To state this more baldly, in laying claim
to a fundamental humanism as constitutive of the Dasein, Heidegger is ultimately left with no other choice than to restage the metaphysical two-step as
described in the previous chapter. Once again, we find 'lifeforce' or *phusis*
now posited as a pure ontological concept constituted through the exclusion
of all material or bodily economies of exchange—'art' as the pure antecedent
constitutively excluded from all actual forms of art, 'history' as the pure antecedent constitutively excluded from all forms of historical occurrence and,
ultimately, 'life' as the pure antecedent constitutively excluded from all forms
of life. Hence, the same metaphysical mechanic that begins with Socratic virtue and which, for Heidegger, reaches first its apogee with Leibniz's supreme
principle and then its alleged *Destruktion* at the hands of Heidegger himself,
thus returns yet one more time and with the same operative ideology intact: as
the pure *a priori* constitutive of all forms of life deemed to exist as such, 'life'
is thereafter figured as a pure, and thus purely empty, ontological concept
from which all worldly forms of existence are necessarily excluded. "In order
not to overlook what is nearest yet likewise farthest, we must stand above the
obvious and the 'factual'" (202). Based upon an unreasonable act of faith and
with its unaccountable limits dictated by a coterie of self-appointed priests,
the acquisition of Heidegger's magical eye for life ultimately nullifies any
and all designated forms of life.

In an echo of Socrates's attempt in the *Phaedo* to dismiss the material and bodily realms as productive only of 'illusory appearances' lacking soundness and truth and fit only for slaves (69b), the concept of *blindness* functions here both as a neutral phenomenological state definitive of the human masses *and* as a metaphorical defect that renders those same masses inferior to—and thus in need of—a Heideggerian coterie of soi-disant interpreters tasked with dispelling all such visual phantoms to which the masses are necessarily subject. Lost in a darkness illuminated only by illusion, it is only the magic eye of the self-styled visionary that keeps us from falling prey to delusion. And thus, by way of the simple Socratic two-step, the production of ownership and control continues without pause.

Even more important, however, is that the same obscure magic upon which all humanist, anthropocentric or vitalist ideologies depend is in fact the very *same* magic that ultimately allows relations of instrumentality to continue unperturbed by ethical concerns and with no regard for futures in the making—as can clearly be seen in the new and yet timeless history of extremophiles that still remains to be written. Above all else, the story the extremophile tells is one of extraordinary human hubris giving rise to a severely misguided notion of safety that serves to put every form of being at risk.

EXTREMOPHILES: FABRICATED HISTORIES AND CONTESTED FUTURES

Despite this reactionary failing, we should not forget that at the crux of Heidegger's later thought is the urgent demand that we rethink the contemporary order of reason that reductively determines our postindustrial world as nothing other than a stockpile of resources awaiting instrumentalization. It is with this in mind that extremophiles offer both a limit case and a cautionary tale.[8] The imaginary magic eye that allows the select few to claim for themselves alone the capacity for judgment and, as such, the capacity to accredit, withhold or retract from others the categorical status of being *natural*, that is, as 'growing things' [*phusei onta*]—*living* beings, in short—shows clearly the extraordinary normative power at work within our everyday conceptions of life and nature, of the biological and the organic, and of the organism and the machine. Extremophiles, by contrast, are rather manifestations of the *absence* of essential nature that paradoxically makes the cynical manipulation of life possible in the first place.

In brief, 'extremophile' is a blanket term attributed to any form of being who, by virtue of being able to synthesize protective extremolytes, thrives (as opposed to survives) within an environment previously considered too extreme to support life—environments such as those with very high or very

low temperatures or that exist at extreme pressure, or with drastic concentrations of salt, toxic gases and/or heavy metals, or with high levels of atomic
radiation or which are strongly acidic or alkaline. Hence, as the set of specific
forms of being capable of living, thriving and evolving within the most inhos-
pitable of environs, it is clear that the concept of the extremophile only makes
sense on the basis of their being classified *as* living. Upon being transported
within the sterile walls of the laboratory, however, this clear and definitive
ontological status abruptly loses all definition, becoming uncertain and,
above all else, categorically *in*distinct. Crucially, this shift into ontological
indistinction is neither a category error nor a simple mistake requiring recti-
fication. Rather, this rendering indistinct within the laboratory of that which
elsewhere is ontologically distinct marks the machinery and machinations of
instrumental reason at work.

The potential value of extremophiles for technoscience today inheres in
their extraordinary ability to *live* and to *evolve* in places that were previously
presumed incapable of supporting life. The perception of the potential *usefulness* of extremophiles is based, in other words, upon the fact that they are *living*
beings whose evolutionary adaptivity promises to fundamentally rewrite the
(human) future. At the same time, however, this practically limitless potential
can only be unlocked within a laboratory setting, at which point everything
gets a bit tricky. As living beings, extremophiles are, at least theoretically,
automatically the subject of ethical concerns—concerns that inevitably and
severely hamstring the dreams of technoscience. In other words, the potential
usefulness of extremophiles can only be unlocked once they are withdrawn
from the realm of ethical culpability and made *available for use* as lifeless
artefacts and thus merely means without ends of their own. Hence, in the
illegitimate shift from living-in-the-wild to object-in-the-laboratory, extremophiles are recast as a simple resource, as new, fully determined objects to be
used and abused without any concern for the hindering encumbrance of ethics. By way of nothing more than a reclassification of status, extremophiles
are henceforth determined as mere objects whose every relation and evolutionary pathway moving into the future are entirely predictable on the basis of
simple cause and effect. Despite being unthinkable and incalculable until only
very recently, our relations with extremophiles are nonetheless guaranteed as
fully under our control and thus 100 per cent safe going forward on the basis
of nothing more than a simple shift in classification.

Brushing such nominal considerations aside, technoscience quickly got
to work on fabricating extremophiles in the laboratory with the aim of putting them to work on dissolving—literally—various planetary restrictions
that currently stymie the expansion that is the modus operandi of global
capitalism. Extremophiles are thus being engineered to thrive upon a diet of
pollutants that range from nuclear waste, oil spills, discarded plastics, and

contaminants in the water table, to the vast lagoons of faeces expelled from the enormous, windowless blocks that are factory farms and CAFOs. After all, the story goes, what point in living forever if the world is to perish any minute? The success of this project, however, depends entirely upon the impeccable behaviour of its test subjects, that is to say, upon extremophiles being always and everywhere predictable. But unfortunately in this regard, extremophiles are in fact wildly *un*predictable. Indeed, their economic potential is premised upon just this fundamental unpredictability—the *same* unpredictability, moreover, that poses an explicit challenge to the conception of nature that otherwise serves to ground the exploitation of extremophiles in the first place.

If we are to begin to come to terms with just what, exactly, this defining nonlinearity means for our predictions of the future—an imperative task given just how much is routinely wagered upon their accuracy, and how dangerously misplaced is the faith upon which it is based—it is incumbent upon us first of all to recognize that every definition of life proposed hitherto has been profoundly overturned by the novel ways and forms of beings known today as extremophiles. Prior to the late 1970s, a rare consensus had long reigned among the sciences as to the two conditions that must precede the emergence of any lifeform whatsoever: namely, sunlight and a calorific food supply. As a result, it was self-evident that, upon exploration, the light-less ocean depths would prove utterly devoid of life. This, however, turned out to be far from the case. When technology finally caught up with what it transpired were completely misplaced assumptions, biologists discovered hydrothermal vents on the ocean floor that, spouting boiling water out into the cold ocean, produce differential gradients capable of fuelling the evolution of various, densely populated ecosystems. In fact, it soon became clear that what was for so long taken to be the definitive category of 'life' actually contains only a fraction of the total number of Earth's inhabitants. Among these vast populations, as Nigel Calder writes in *Magic Universe: A Grand Tour of Modern Science* (2005), extremophiles were, and continue to be, primary producers, having evolved the remarkable capacity to utilize 'dissolved minerals and gases to power their own biochemistry' (293).

Furthermore, adding insult to injury, not only did the entirety of 'life' in human terms turn out to be but a minor subset occupying the fringes of an almost infinitely diverse array of existence, but it also quickly became clear that extremophiles had claim to a phylogenetic lineage that stretched way back to well before the supposed time of 'life' and, even more shocking, some of those same arche-fossil extremophiles likely still exist alongside us today. As Sagan and Schneider explain in the preface to *Into the Cool*,

> the very origins of life can be traced to the energy flows of an energetic universe, most likely on a hot pockmarked Earth of molten iron, bubbling with sulfur and hissing with steam. . . . Deep in the chemical cycles of present-day bacteria are metabolic pathways, chemical traces repeating, with variation, the steps by which matter came to life. . . . Recent discoveries of deep-sea ecosystems feeding not on light or food but on chemical energy suggest an origin of life, paradoxically but poetically, in fire and brimstone (xii–xiii).

Of particular interest for us here is Sagan and Schneider's failed attempt to reconstruct an ontological distinction separating living beings from nonliving fabrications that takes into account the existence of extremophiles. Inevitably, as we shall see, their claim about a revised but nonetheless determinable origin of life ultimately has recourse to a pairing of premises that are in fact fundamentally incompatible.

THE COPYING MACHINE AT THE ORIGIN OF LIFE

For Sagan and Schneider, the innovation of life in the form of extremophiles is a result of their having 'probably evolved' into 'the earliest natural copying machines' (xii). This point is crucial: *before it is anything else, life is a copying machine*, a technological artefact that, having adapted through reiterated mutations in order to record and reiterate patterns and codes, has *evolved* (Sagan and Schneider's word) the capability to produce copies of itself—to reproduce, in other words. Indeed, Sagan and Schneider insist on this particular point: 'Life,' they write, 'must be regarded, at the deepest level, as a matter as much of energy transformation as of genetic replication' (xiii). This, however, is also a copying *machine* of a very different order—of Aristotle, of Kant, and perhaps of Derrida above all. Despite being a copying machine before it is anything, or anything living at least, Sagan and Schneider nonetheless attempt to once again bestow upon life an exceptional status on the basis that only living beings bear their own immanence of intelligibility, which is to say, only living beings are the effect of their own cause. And, as such, what happens in Aristotle, in Kant, and above all in Derrida inevitably repeats itself in Sagan and Schneider, extremophiles notwithstanding.

While Derrida's concepts of the trace and the event-machine will be engaged at length in the chapters to follow, for the moment, and serving as a brief introduction, let us stay with the two irreconcilable premises that not only ground Sagan and Schneider's argument for a determinable origin of life, but which in fact underwrite *all* such claims regarding a determinable origin of life: (1) *life emerges as a distinct ontological category*, and (2) *life is dependent upon machinic repetition*. On the one hand, then, the first living being must somehow show itself as being fundamentally—i.e., onto-logically—different from every previously existing entity, meaning that the genesis of life is *the* creative event that, by definition, could have been neither predicted nor predicated on the basis of linear causality. Hence, life as *invention* in the strict sense, as *creation*, is necessarily *non*linear. On the other hand, however, the 'first' form of life, the original Adam so to speak, can only ever be just one more reproduction of what already is—unless, that is, one wishes to fall back upon theological folly. As such, every attempt at distinction relies upon a completely arbitrary stopping point in what is in fact a ceaseless process of reiteration—of repetition-with-variation—that both precedes and succeeds any notional logic or location of 'origin.' Life, there-fore, merely reproduces nonlife—continuum as opposed to simple difference.

Extremophiles are artefacts and fossils, technologies and machines, but they are also consumers, engineers, producers, reproducers and much more. In simply being, the dream of building barricades that will keep the living safe and free from contamination is revealed as cynical sophistry, both mechanism of control and theatre of the absurd. Not least, thinking with extremophiles means contesting the thoroughly entrenched narrative construing techno-logical progress as one more promise to the future. Today, staggering sums of money and time are being spent on experiments aimed at reengineering extremophiles, either in part or in whole, in the hope, as Raj Kumar and Ajeet Singh write, of being able 'to counter diseases and disorders [in humans] induced as a result of harsh environments.'[9] Tellingly, in the course of a single paragraph Kumar and Singh describe the ability to thrive under extreme con-ditions as both an 'in-built machinery' *and* 'a variety of ingenious strategies for survival' ('Smart Therapeutics from Extremophiles,' 390). Here again, we find the same indecision marking the juncture of the living and the nonliving and of the natural and the technical: extremophiles are *either* living beings that take their place amid fluid and evolving intra- and inter-relations within a given milieu, *or* they are simple mechanisms no different from clockwork mice—mere objects, in other words, and thus commodities to be exploited. Extremophiles, however, are both *and* neither at the same time, reciprocally shaping and being shaped by the thresholds they inhabit.

Unsurprisingly then, extremophile bodies are increasingly becoming the site of intense ontological, social, economic, ethical and political contesta-tion. Central to this is of course their extraordinary ability to synthesize extremolytes in such a way as to protect macromolecules and cells from external damage, with the result that extremophiles are most often perceived as nothing other than the promise of human protection: a promise to protect against UV damage, or against radiation damage or blast damage, or perhaps even against the damage of *time itself* and so render the human animal body of the future practically immortal, as is already the case with a number of distinct species of extremophile. Potentially harbouring within their body chemistry the twin grails of both *more life* and *more death*, it is therefore hardly surprising that for many years scientists have been very active in the search for extremolytes 'in the wild' (so to speak), as well as within the labs of genetic and genomic engineering.

That said, however, the worlds of wild animals and the abstracted realities of their domesticated kin are not at all the same. They neither carry the same weight nor do they share the same possible futures. Whereas extremophiles evolved their extraordinary abilities over countless eons, technoscience is now approaching the point of being able to fabricate extremophiles, or partial extremophiles, from whole cloth. As such, laboratory-engineered extremophiles raise the absolute breakdown of traditional distinctions between life and nonlife to a further, dizzying degree. At the very least, the engineering of extremophiles promises a radical rewrite not only of what it means to be human or even what it means to be living, but what it might mean to be *biological*. Technology, fabricated being, and living object, the engineered extremophile embodies the paradoxical: at once an entirely novel construction, the repository of a billion years of evolution, and the promise of extraordinary transformation—human into superhuman perhaps, or else into something no longer human, perhaps not even living in the sense that life presupposes death. What *is* clear, however, is that the question of ethics must be radically resituated as a result. In wagering Earth, it has long been time to stop fleeing the world for the deathly quiet of one delusion or another.

Hitherto, the purview of ethics concerns itself primarily with issues of safety, economics and control, at the centre of which lies a bolstering of faith in the security of a living–nonliving dichotomy. On its own, this statement will likely be met with scepticism at least. Considering the ethics of extremophiles, however, we quickly discover that it matters not at all in fact whether they have been around for a billion years or else have just now been fabricated in a laboratory somewhere. Rather, when dealing with extremophiles both wild and tame, historical and ahistorical, past and future, the sole ethical concern in the present is being seen to be able to guarantee absolutely the safety of such entities going into the future following their recasting as mere means in the form of new technical objects. The process by which such a guarantee of safety is established is simplicity itself: one need only ascribe object status to a given being and thus, *as if by magic*, render that being fully determinable and therefore compelled to interact within a given environment in an entirely predictable, linear fashion.

Putting the question of ethics quite literally to one side, however, those extremophiles considered so valuable to the potential development of engineering technologies in the future are the very same extremophiles who more so than perhaps any other being interrupt the traditional living–nonliving dichotomy and, in so doing, give the lie to the myth of linear causality as fully determining in the case of any entity classified as an inanimate object. Should it ever become possible in the future to engineer new extremophiles from scratch then, just like their most ancient of kin, they too must adapt themselves to the pressures of hitherto inconceivable selection gradients and, again like their ancient kin, just how these new adaptive relations might play out over time simply cannot be foreseen or even predicted. Simply put, the structural unforeseeability of evolutionary processes, rather than demonstrating the natural *absence* of any ethical dimension, is instead the mark of its absolute necessity. The necessary nonlinearity of being makes it impossible to predict what ways of being are likely to emerge in the futures of technical evolution. Moreover, this must therefore be true of *every* technological process. Put another way, by recognizing that potential future effects of inanimate causes can similarly never be accurately predicted, technical evolution simultaneously discloses the ethical dimension at the core of its being—and this in spite of its assumed absence being the reason why technical evolution has hitherto gone largely unchecked. Furthermore, given that it is the evolution *of* technology itself that ultimately discloses *to* itself the priority of its ethical dimension, it thereafter becomes impossible to deny the fabrications of technology a central role in what amounts to the collapse of all ethical programs based upon an abyssal separation of natural beings from technological artefacts. To think with extremophiles is, in other words, to radically resituate the place of ethics today and into the future.

ETHICS BY CONVENTION

While the uncanny ethics of technical evolution that ultimately disavows its own exploitation will be addressed in detail in the following chapters, for the moment we shall restrict our consideration to the process by way of which ethical decisions are conventionally reached. Above all else, it is clear that acceptance of the nonlinearity of being renders massively problematic any and all decisions being made today on the basis of what are presumed to be reliable predictions into the future given that they depend upon an ordered society of fully determined 'things' the futures of which are wholly contained within the past. This is not to say, of course, that the sciences, and technoscience in particular, are unaware of the immense risks they are running should their predictions prove to be fundamentally unreliable. Indeed, warnings to that effect proliferate exponentially whenever concerns are raised about extremophiles and about bioengineering technologies in general. More specifically, it is widely recognized that, since genetically engineered entities lack the relative stability that comes from the evolution of genetic patterns, one requires, *first of all and above all*, a fully reliable prediction regarding future recombinative events. The problem, however, remains the same, insofar as the solution is always perceived as a need for increased reliability, and thus for a more complete knowledge of the present context in terms of the totality of simple cause and effect. What such scientific rationality *fails* to recognize, however, is that the very notion of reliable prediction, just like that of a deterministic universe that founds it, is necessarily a myth—a failure of recognition that, if there are to be futures beyond imagining, needs urgent redress today.

In 'Life in the Fast Lane: An Introduction to Genomics Risks' (2005), Michael Tyshenko and William Leiss acknowledge that scientific researchers are largely "unconcerned with the gap between things that 'can be done' and 'will be done,' placing science innovation as a technical exercise apart from any ethical concerns" (n.p.). This lack of concern is simply unacceptable, however, once scientific determinism no longer holds. As we have already seen, since Aristotle at least, living beings have been conceived as ontologically distinct from fabricated artefacts by virtue of being 'natural,' and thus we should not be at all surprised to discover that a certain concept of nature still underwrites the instrumental approach to 'simple' objects that today maintains the separation of technical exercise from ethical concern. The absence of an ethical dimension that allows for a largely unheeded technical innovation depends upon the 'fundamental notion that the world of nature is essentially a field in which human ingenuity can be exercised without restriction.' This concept of nature, a vision of the world and the vast majority of its inhabitants as a storage facility—what Heidegger calls the 'standing reserve' [*Bestand*]—stocked with ready-to-hand instruments both fabricated and 'natural,' continues to function in a contradictory manner across a variety of levels. As we have seen, beings deemed to be biological organisms and thus deserving of our ethical concern in one time and place need only be reconfigured as objects at another time and place in order for any ethical concerns to simply vanish into thin air in concert with demotion to the status of simple means—a process of instrumentalization that, as a process, presupposes both a biological-technological continuum *and* an absolute biological-technological separation.

In *The Question Concerning Technology*, Heidegger argues that a technological artefact is never simply a tool but rather constitutes a *way* or a *mode* of *revealing*. The particular mode of revealing that rules so imperiously over modern technology subjects all beings to the steamroller that is the universal equivalent form of value. As Karl Marx writes in the indispensable opening chapter of *Das Kapital* (1867), this 'money commodity' serves the specific social function of transforming our shared and partial worlds of beings into a world of uniform commodities, flattening all specific differences and singular values in the production of a world of available 'things' that can be directly and universally exchanged for any other (*Capital* vol. 1, 162).[10] In the process of commodification, in other words, all existent specificity is lost, reworked into indistinguishable parts of the undifferentiated order that a small subset of humanity decrees makes up its outside, and which are thereafter available to be combined and recombined, arranged and rearranged, stored, displaced, replaced, redistributed and regulated in a mode of revealing that never rests. Crucially, argues Heidegger, modern science is the herald of this 'ordering attitude' because its 'way of representing pursues and entraps nature as a *calculable coherence* of forces' (*The Question Concerning Technology*, 21). It is in the face of just this ordering attitude that urgent questions concerning causal accountability still struggle to be heard.

When it comes to future and emergent technologies, our gravest fears are reserved for a future possessed by unforeseen and unwanted recombination events. We have been warned, for example, that genetic and genomic engineering technologies will 'inevitably' give rise to *unintended* effects due to 'altered metabolism, altered brain functions or unforeseen gene actions, insertions and recombination events' (Tyshenko and Leiss). But this same warning necessarily applies even to seemingly minor technologies. A single gene alteration targeting weight loss, for example, will inevitably 'affect a number of other interrelated metabolic pathway genes; many enzyme pathways are interconnected both up and down-regulating other genes by feedback loops' (ibid.). As a site of intense anxiety in regards to our global future, it can only be hoped—and not without enormous irony—that biotechnology itself will herald the end of the world viewed as an undifferentiated stockpiling.

Rather than a storage facility warehousing an aggregation of lifeless and uniformly exchangeable objects, the worlds of the future are *necessarily* unforeseeable insofar as nonlinearity is a condition of being itself, which is to say, existing is both radical innovation *and* machinic repetition at once. Just as physicist and philosopher Arkady Plotnitsky writes of the wave-particle paradox that makes up the quantum postulate, the paradox of invention and repetition similarly serves to constitute an 'interactive ensemble or matrix' that feedbacks in 'a mutual inhibition and a complementary asynthesis' that is never a unified presence in the present, but is instead the production of effects without classical causes (*Complementarity*, 69).

Chapter 3

Ends of the Future

Contingency and the Life of Machines

Following Heidegger—here and now and for the first time in human history—it becomes possible to plot a line of flight from out of that history and therefore out from under the harboured decisions that serve as the props of Western metaphysics. It is the chance, uniquely ours, of an authentically original possibility that Heidegger argues is the chance of a future other than that which a presumption of determinism brings into being. In disarticulating the imperialism of instrumentality, we thus find the articulation of novel emergence increasingly coming to occupy centre stage in the thought of a number of key thinkers at work within the contemporary Continental tradition. While a detailed engagement with the work of Jacques Derrida and Quentin Meillassoux must await the next chapter, we will focus here on the structuring of articulation and emergence in the recent work of Claire Colebrook and Catherine Malabou, facilitating in turn a reworking of *machinality* as the intrusion of an accidental, parasitical and mutilating element always already at work in the process of automation.

We recall that in 'Posthuman Humanities' (2014), Colebrook identifies a 'definite historical sense and teleology' according to which the various objects of the humanities are composed—objects including "language, literature and, indeed, 'Man' itself" (176). Consolidated throughout human history, this definitive teleology is ultimately founded upon two distinct and contradictory premises: first, that life is the constitutive condition of emergence, and second, that life and its original conditions for emergence are necessarily divided by an absolute and thus unbridgeable disjunct. Indeed, we have already encountered this defining and definitive historical sense and teleology in a number of places in the preceding chapters, most notably in the version proposed by Dorian Sagan and Eric Schneider.

Sagan and Schneider, we recall, attempt to reinscribe an absolute ontological distinction between living bodies and lifeless artefacts that could take into account the fact that extremophiles do indeed exist. To do so, however, they have no other option but to propose a revised but still determinable origin of life constructed upon a pair of fundamentally irreconcilable claims—no option simply because all such claims for a determinable (rather than theological) origin of life ultimately depend upon this same pairing of incompatible claims. One is that right at its origin the emergence of life is the coming into being of and as a distinct ontological category, and another is that the possibility of an original and thus determinable emergence of life *from out of* nonlife is therefore dependent upon machinic repetition and a general continuum of existence that disallows any such ontological fracture. Indeed, it is not by chance that religions the world over are founded first and foremost upon the myth of magical genesis.

While there are differences between these two versions of life's originary paradox, by considering them in concert we are better able to understand its function as that of sanctioning and/or vetoing the validity of *precedence*. In the first formulation, emergence is reserved in a strict sense for the production and reproduction of *living* beings, that is to say, only 'growing' things are deemed to 'emerge' consequent on 'natural' processes. Life, in short, is the necessary precedent of emergence. At the same time, this proprietary claim to emergence is only possible insofar as 'life' denotes a distinct ontological category: *only* living beings emerge because only life *can* emerge. However, if life does indeed compose a distinct ontological category, then it follows that living beings cannot have emerged within a world that prior to that emergence was entirely devoid of life: only life *can* emerge and thus life itself cannot *have* emerged insofar as its originary emergence lacks the necessary precedent of life. The necessary condition for life's emergence is thus necessarily absent, arriving instead only *after* life has already come into being. Here, it is clear that the paradox that the production of a determinable origin of life invariably gives rise to issues of temporal, logical and causal precedence. Returning to Sagan and Schneider, we find the same paradox of precedence at work insofar as the original emergence of life is the coming into being of that which is both new and ontologically distinct and thus without prior relations in being: life, quite literally, must emerge without precedent, that is, unprecedented in the instant of its emergence. And yet unless we are willing to accept divine intervention or seeding by aliens, the world that exists prior to life's arriving into being must also be the *a priori* condition of life's possibility.

Beyond squabbles about the times of life, there are far more important reasons for dwelling at such length on the paradox of life's emergence, insofar as it discloses the universal paradox of *originality*, of the *event*, which thus ceases to be a property or a capacity reserved for the living alone. Unprecedented emergence, in other words, describes *invention* in the most rigorous sense of the term, that is, the impossible emergence into being of that which is without precedent and thus absolutely distinct. By definition, invention is nonlinear—it is, in a strict sense, an *event*.

HERE AND NOW AND FOR THE FIRST TIME IN HUMAN HISTORY: SERRES AND COLEBROOK

As we have seen with Sagan and Schneider, while the imperialism of the principle of reason in the form of the 'scientific method' serves to guarantee both the objectivity and the repeatability of scientific truths, it can also serve as a blind behind which challenges posed to certain habitual concepts inevitably pass by unseen and unheard. Central among these is the conception of the external world as a meaningless material repository that can only *make sense* by way of its supplementary organization as a form of scientific 'truth.' Truth, in other words, names the form through which the nonsense of a given material *has been made to make sense*. In light of the strange spontaneity and simultaneity definitive of novel emergence, however, this veil of normativity can no longer be maintained—this is what it means to be here and now and for the first time in human history. It is this same light that leads Colebrook to declare it necessary to productively destroy the currently dominant form of the concept of the humanities 'as critical and interdisciplinary' so as to put in its place a 'new sense of *sense* and a new sense of history' ('Posthuman Humanities,' 184, 177). For Colebrook too, we occupy an explicit articulation of historical fracture.

While it is precisely *because* of the overwhelming contemporary investment in the notion of interdisciplinarity that her argument will doubtless strike many in the first instance as conservative and even reactionary, this call for destruction 'in a productive manner' is a necessary sidestep along the way to breaking down the blinds put in place in accordance with a definite historical sense and teleology that can no longer be maintained. Here, Colebrook follows philosopher Michel Serres in stressing the need to 'destroy the history of man in favor of a history of bodies (where bodies would include technological objects, words, languages, animals, polities, cities and images) and an emphasis on *sense*' (176). With clear parallels to the philosophical projects of Meillassoux and Derrida to be examined in the next chapter, this need for a new history and for a new sense of sense is already long overdue. As Serres puts it in the brief preface to *Branches* [*Rameaux*] published in 2020:

> At serious risk, we have to invent new relations between humans and the totality of what conditions life: the inert planet, the climate, living species, visible things and invisible things, sciences and technologies, the global community, morality and politics, education and health—We are leaving our world for other worlds,

possible ones, and will have to abandon a hundred passions, ideas, customs and norms brought about by our narrow historical duration (n.p.).

Once meaning can no longer be confined to the way in which the world is for 'us,' writes Colebrook, a new sense of sense becomes possible, one that opens out on a far broader domain of 'interaction and relations (as well as that which is devoid of relation and connection)' ('Posthuman Humanities,' 176). As a critical corollary of this move, it no longer suffices for us to approach the problems of history and sense with the sole aim of '*extend*[*ing*] the life of the humanities by melding it with a single interdisciplinary domain of which the sciences would also be a part' (176). By contrast, argues Colebrook, to think beyond the limits of life instead requires 'an *inhuman* (rather than post-human) approach to knowledge' that would 'intensify certain dimensions of the humanities only by destroying certain majoritarian, anthropomorphic or dominant components' (176).

Colebrook then further clarifies this point, arguing that it is 'precisely the expansion of a disciplinary tendency beyond its *human* form' that inevitably brings about the destruction of 'a certain model of inter-disciplinarity' (177). Hence:

> If one could think of concepts, affects and functions *not* as practices grounded in a self-maintaining human life, then one would not only have to rethink the supposed self-evident good of *inter*-disciplinarity and the unity of the humanities, but also the future and survival of disciplines and the dominant image of the (now highly humanized) humanities. Such a future would not assume the value of *living on* in its current form, either of humanity or the humanities, and it would abandon such assumed values precisely because of what we might refer to—after Serres—as climate change (177).

It is worth pausing here, just for a moment, just before the future: '*Such a future would not assume the value of living on in its current form, either of humanity or the humanities.*' With this we return once more to the nub of the argument being posed here and throughout, only this time we return to the physicians of ancient Greece by way of Lucretius's defence of the atomistic philosophy of Epicurus. Here, Colebrook seeks to follow Serres in imparting a far more radical sense to the term *climate* by recalling its etymological roots *clinamen* and *clima*, the former from the Latin *clīnāre*, meaning to incline, and the latter from the ancient Greek κλιμα or *klíma*, meaning a region or zone of latitude from which we later get the word 'climate.' To 'imagine the radical sense of climate, from *clima* and inclination,' writes Colebrook, is to imagine 'the inflection that yields a certain patterning of what surrounds us' (177). Such a move, she continues, has serious implications for just how we go about making sense both now and in the future insofar as it puts into question both the human *and* the posthuman basis of thinking so prevalent in the humanities today, 'especially when the posthuman has been a return of the human into one single life with one single inclination, that of ongoing self-maintenance' (177). This latter point is particularly important for two reasons. First, it marks as imperative the need for scholars within the humanities to take a critical distance from what today is largely a triumphal discourse built around the defining role of *autopoiesis*—a role predicated upon the conflation of infinite lives to a single life. Second, for Colebrook the corresponding conflation of all inclinations to one single inclination describes the peerless triumph of global capitalism that we know today as the Anthropocene.

While it will be necessary to return to the highly problematic concepts of both autopoiesis and autoaffectivity in the following chapters, it is important at this stage to limit our critical focus to what for Colebrook is 'a more positive—which is to say, destructive—approach to thinking beyond the interdisciplinarity of the humanities' (177). To facilitate this, we turn now to Serres's signature concept of *parasitism*.

THE AUTOMATON AND ITS PARASITES

Just as evidence of relations of symbiosis and cooperation have increasingly come to displace the old ideological construct that decrees the realm of nature as a war of one against all, the host–parasite [*hôte–parasite*] relation as evinced by Serres in *The Parasite* (1982) explicitly displaces the attendant generalization of the predator-prey relation that habitually paints the realm of nature as 'red in tooth and claw.' The stakes of this move are hard to overstate, heralding as it does a profound transmutation of valence. As Colebrook puts it, a generalized parasitism "entails several consequences for humanism, posthumanism and the 'disciplines' that might be adequate to thinking the inhuman" (178). Notable among these many consequences, she continues, is that by abandoning the predator–prey system we must also 'abandon the concept of the good and just relation' (178). No longer can humanity excuse its exploitative relation to the world around it on the grounds of reciprocal exchange—the parasitic relation, as Serres makes clear, *only ever moves in one direction*. There could be, as Colebrook writes, 'no *good* humanity of reasonable predatory use that might be morally distinguished from a parasitic humanity that would be nothing more than a consumer or digester of energies not its own' (178).

Stepping back for a moment, the ordering of bodies on the basis of a generalized predator–prey relation brings along with it a number of unstated presumptions. Most notably, it presumes the prior existence of unified organisms with the capacity *to choose the mode of their relations* to their external milieu along a continuum ranging from equable exchange at one pole to cynical destruction at the other. Similarly, the predator–prey relation too maintains an absolute distinction between the living and the inanimate, with 'merely material' entities precluded from inclusion at any point along this relational spectrum. Machines, in other words, can never be truly predatory, as predation presupposes a willing subject, nor can a fabricated entity ever truly become prey insofar as this presupposes a pre-existent relation. Moreover, the roles of both predator and prey also demand a certain degree of spontaneity insofar as their interrelation presumes the ability to respond to sudden changes in the immediate environs. As Jacques Derrida puts it so well in 'Typewriter Ribbon: Limited Ink (2)' (1998), the 'automaticity of the inorganic machine is not the spontaneity attributed to organic life' (72). The life of the machine remains one of profound anaesthesia: indifferent, senseless and unfeeling, lacking orientation and desire.

So what becomes of these presumptions once the predator–prey relation comes to be supplanted by a general host–parasite relation? Can a machine ever truly host a parasite? Can a fabricated entity—mechanism, instrument, commodity, algorithm, self-reinforcing network—truly inhabit a relation of parasitical consumption? And just what, exactly, constitutes the possible criteria by which an emergent processual structure might be defined as either fabricated or otherwise in the first place? As we shall see, the host–parasite relation goes far beyond a willingness to nominally include certain privileged metastable systems such as whirlpools and hurricanes within an expanded category of living beings. In a parasitical relation, writes Serres, the 'relation of the guest is no longer simple. Giving or receiving . . . goes through a black box. I don't know what happens in there, but it functions like an automatic corrector. There is no exchange, nor will there be one. Abuse appears before use' (*The Parasite*, 7).

The introduction here of the complicating role of the guest into the host–parasite relation depends upon a well-known peculiarity of the original language that does not carry over into English: in French, the homonym *hôte* refers both to the 'host' (*hôte*) *and* to the 'guest' (*hôte*)—a paradoxical identity that Serres plays with throughout *The Parasite*, with both meanings rendered always implicit and not infrequently explicit. In a similar vein, it is important too to remember that, in French, *le parasite* also bears a third sense of *static* or *noise* in addition to those of biological and social parasite already present in English. So what does Serres mean when he claims that the relation of the guest (*hôte*) is 'no longer simple'? *Before all else*, he writes, *is a black box*. The relation of host (*hôte*) and parasite clearly describes a specific relation of giving and receiving in which the host is always the giver and the parasite always the receiver in a relation of giving and receiving that only ever goes in one direction and thus offers no possibility of exchange, be it just or otherwise. Furthermore, Serres continues, the irreversible relation of the parasitical encounter or event necessarily takes place by way of a 'black box' that, in the manner of an automatic 'corrector,' ensures that abuse precedes any and all use. As we shall see, it is this 'black boxing' of the host–parasite relation that ultimately renders the role of the guest (*hôte*) no longer simple.

The black box, as we know, refers to a strongbox recorder installed in aircraft cockpits that, in the event of an accident or attack resulting in the destruction of the craft, makes possible the subsequent recovery of all data leading up to and including the destructive event itself. Employed figuratively by Serres, 'black boxing' thus refers to an event of parasitical giving and receiving, the sense of which can only ever be recovered after the fact. The *sense* of an event, in other words, is only ever the aftermath and the supplement of a parasitical relation that is 'true of all beings,' and which has already withdrawn from all possible sense. Furthermore, this black boxing of a systems-wide parasitism *installs both machinery and machination at the core of every event*. By definition, there can be no living survivors to bear witness to an event understood as always both tragic and traumatic. The black box, in other words, *already* defers the event *before* it even happens. It marks the event as necessarily belated insofar as it serves to reconstruct exactly what such an event *will have been*—the event, that is, defers to its own absence in the supplementary form of the future perfect tense.

In fact, the black box is a *fabrication after the fact* in both senses: it fabricates the future—that other which will have been—only insofar as it is itself a fabrication. This recalls to mind Edwin Schrodinger's famous thought experiment illustrative of Niels Bohr's quantum postulate, wherein another 'black' box obscures and, in so doing, withdraws from being the event of a parasitical relation that only ever *will have been* between a cat and a radioactive isotope. The system constructed here, writes Serres, 'beginning with a production, temporarily placed in a black box, is parasitic in a cascade. But the cascade orders knowledge itself, of man and of life, making us change our terminology without changing the subject' (*The Parasite*, 5). Indeed, in a strict sense black boxes are everywhere and nowhere: the parasitic relation, he continues, is 'the atomic form of our relations. Let us try to face it head-on, like death, like the sun. We are all attacked, together' (8). In her excellent reading of Serres, Claire Colebrook offers the following summary:

[I]f *the relation* of parasitism, and its capacity to displace the illusion of predator-prey relations, is general, then what parasitism discloses are irreducible differences and singularities that require highly discerned cuts and judgments. Whereas a predator would be a vaguely self-sufficient body, capable of

maintaining itself and using some other body as means of sustenance, the parasite would have no existence other than that of supplementarity ('Posthuman
Humanities,' 177–178).

In short, the originary relation of parasite and host describes a ceaseless process of expropriation and consumption of energies from an external position
and irreversibly oriented in one direction only. Such, writes Colebrook, is the
general nature of *distinction* and thus *being itself.* At this point, however, it
is crucial for us to *not* overlook the *second* processual relation that in concert
with the parasitism of the first composes this general relation of being: *viz*,
the relation of *guest to host* [*hôte à hôte*]. The host, argues Serres, is never
simply *preyed upon*:

> Gifted in some fashion, the one eating next to [*para*-site], soon eating at the
> expense of, always eats the same thing, the host, and this eternal host gives over
> and over, constantly, till he breaks, even till death, drugged, enchanted, fasci-
> nated. The host is not a prey, for he offers and continues to give. Not a prey, but
> the host. The other one is not a predator but a parasite. Would you say that the
> mother's breast is the child's prey? It is more or less the child's home. But this
> relation is of the simplest sort; there is none simpler or easier: it always goes in
> the same direction. The same one is the host; the same one takes and eats; there
> is no change of direction. This is true of all beings (*The Parasite*, 7).

Despite Serres's opening gambit in the above passage, one should be particularly cautious when it comes to describing the relation of guest to host [*hôte
à hôte*] in terms of *gifting*. Just as the mother's breast cannot be thought of
as the child's prey, neither can the breast be thought of in a strict sense as a
gift received by the child. Rather, as Serres explains, the mother's breast both
hosts the child and is host to the child in such a manner as to 'more or less'
compose the child's *home*. Furthermore, the host eternally and invariably
hosts the guest in an *ecstatic* relation described here as 'drugged, enchanted,
fascinated.' Even at this stage, it is clear that the unequal and irreversible
relations of guest to host [*hôte à hôte*] and host to guest [*hôte à hôte*] that
compose a parasitical encounter cannot be adequately accounted for in terms
of the gift economy as traditionally conceived. Similarly, it is important to
distance such thinking absolutely from the empty justifications offered by
apologists for animal exploitation based on a purported 'gifting' of the animal
body to his or her own slaughter—a baseless justification for a manifestly
unjust predation that the parasitic relation renders dumb in every sense.
     The inextricability of host, guest and parasite instead makes possible the
formal articulation of organized beings as *metastable composites* of otherwise ceaseless processes, at the centre of which is a complex layering of
eternity, contingency and automaticity; of ecstasy, noise and interference; of

prior abuse that already disallows every possible form of exchange; and of an irreversible linear orientation that paradoxically installs nonlinearity as the necessary condition of all beings. And if that isn't enough to deal with, this articulation *of* being and *as* being necessarily takes place within a black box to which we, as metastable organizations and thus 'of being,' are always already denied access. As we shall see, however, things become somewhat simpler once we understand that, just as with Schrödinger's black boxing of life and death, Serres's analogy of the aircraft black box is nothing more nor less than an obligatory placeholder for the breakdown of the normative principle of reason.

The parasite, first of all, is not *simply* a predator, which is to say that while all predators belong to a subset of the universal set of all parasites, the function of the parasite is by no means reducible to that of simple predation. The parasite eternally consumes that which the host offers at its own expense and with no possibility whatsoever of even the most meagre recompense, either at the time or at some point in the future. The role of the host, in other words, is to endlessly give its self over to the parasite and to receive absolutely nothing in return: the host can take no pleasure, gain no benefit, nor can it change or be changed in any way, now and in the future, as a consequence of being abused by the parasite, insofar as this would mark instead a relation of exchange. As neither gift nor exchange, just how are we to make sense of this baffling relation, one that explicitly goes against our ingrained evolutionary narratives based on universal relations of competition and dominance?

STATIC ECSTASY: ABUSE BEFORE USE

Before everything, there is a black-boxed process of automatic correction that always already determines the impossibility of exchange. Abuse, in other words, precedes use insofar as the latter always presupposes some form of exchange. And this, writes Serres, 'is true of all beings' (*The Parasite*, 7). Furthermore, it is precisely *because* this is true of all beings that there can therefore be no relation *simpler*, that is, there can be no cause, relation or condition prior to this 'atomic form' of the host–guest–parasite relation. What is essential, argues Serres, 'is neither the image nor the deep meaning, neither the representation nor its hall of mirrored reflections, but the system of relations . . . through story or science, social science or biological science, just one relation appears, the simple, irreversible arrow' (8). Crucially, he continues, the parasite occupies a 'somewhat fuzzy spot' pulled all at once between the three nodal points of 'an abusive guest, an unavoidable animal, a break in a message' (8)—this latter, we recall, referring to the additional sense of the parasite as static or noise only found in French.

While we must defer engagement with what Serres describes as the parasitic *cascade* until the discussion of thermodynamic systems in a later chapter, at this stage we are able nonetheless to address a number of key concerns raised by Serres's account of originary parasitism, at the heart of which is a preoccupation with the condition of possibility of *novel* production, which he claims serves to distance his thought from the current posthumanist 'illness' that seeks instead to celebrate 'the engulfing of the new in the *duplicata*, the engulfing of intelligence in the pleasure [*jouissance*] of the homogeneous' (4). This explicitly recalls both the homogenizing tendency of instrumental reason in general and more specifically what for Colebrook is the homogenizing tendency of much of today's posthumanist discourse, insofar as it reduces what are infinitely diverse ways and inclinations of being to just one way of being with but a single inclination indistinguishable from the inclination toward instrumentality characteristic of global capitalism.

Unlike reproduction, writes Serres, production is always rare, unexpected and improbable and, *as such*, 'it overflows with information and is always immediately parasited' (4). Production, in other words, describes a system of relations founded upon the *immediate* parasiting of such information that overflows its banks and limits hitherto. Hence, production is not reproduction but rather the production of the real that necessarily exceeds reproduction and, as such, is always already withdrawn from being insofar as it is immediately being-parasited. In short, the production of the real is simultaneously immediate *and* the impossibility of immediacy. The parasite, in other words, is the manifestation or expression of *originary supplementarity*: '[I]t is on the side, next to, shifted; it is not on the thing, but on its relation. It has relations, as they say, and makes a system of them. It is always mediate and never immediate' (38–39).

Enchanted, drugged, fascinated, the host hosts the parasitic supplement in giving of its self eternally to this strangest of guests, and does so in a manner that has already rendered recompense or exchange impossible. Most important here, the parasitical relation of guest to host [*hôte à hôte*] has nothing whatsoever to do with any simplistic metaphysical division aimed at shoring up and safeguarding a privileged category of living beings, and similarly nothing whatsoever to do with the instrumental exploitation of resources that is ultimately based upon this unsupportable division and to which Heidegger gives the name *Gestell*. Life, like immediacy, simply does not stand up to scrutiny. Following on from her critique of the prevailing posthumanist bias that unwittingly returns the human to centre stage, Colebrook argues that in order to engage productively with the radical sense of climate change after Serres, it is imperative that we cease thinking of concepts, affects and functions as 'practices grounded in a self-maintaining human life' ('Posthuman Humanities,' 177). Rather, she continues, if we are ever to take the first step along the broken, nonlinear and unpredictable path toward the future, it is incumbent upon us all that we accept the simple fact that life in general, and humanity in particular, *is and must be* parasitic. Put as bluntly as possible, life does not enter into the equation other than belatedly in the form of an ideological illusion after the fact.

As always already a *consuming* body, argues Serres, a body is the production of a complex reticulated system of relations composed of stations and paths that can be formally described on the basis of the 'formation and distribution of the lines, paths, and stations, their borders, edges, and forms' (*The Parasite*, 11). As always already a *parasitic* body, however, this systemic production of the consuming body is already at risk of interference and interception. One must, writes Serres, 'write as well of the interceptions, of the accidents in the flow along the way between stations—of changes and metamorphoses. . . . There are escapes and losses, obstacles and opacities' (11). Parasitical consumption, in other words, 'is quite simply the system itself' and which, as the prior condition of a body's standing in being, necessarily takes its place by way of a black-boxed process of automatic correction on 'the dark side of the system. . . . This constant is a law' (12). So what exactly does this mean for a future of climate change?

First, and most importantly, it means that a pathological expropriation and rapacious consumption without recompense of external resources is *neither accidental nor unique to* the system of postindustrial humanity, and that to think otherwise is yet one more example of anthropocentric hubris. As a result, climate change can neither be reversed (expropriation only ever moves in one direction), nor redeemed (there can be no exchange), nor nullified through a more mindful husbandry of resources in the future (climate change is not a uniquely human responsibility but rather the workings of universal law). While at first glance this may seem to support the denial of global warming offered up by conservative apologists, the two positions are in fact mutually exclusive. Whereas the apologist rhetoric serves only to close off *the* future, it is by making sense of parasitical production that we stand any chance of *a* future. As Colebrook writes:

> Climate change would be the condition of human organicism in general: for there would be no climate, only *clinamen,* an inclination, deviancy or parasitism that creates a supplemental body (of man) who would then retroactively imagine that he has an environment, a *klima,* for which he ought to have been more mindful. But if this places humanity as one aspect of a general parasitism, then it is also the case that 'man' occurs as a specific inclination or deviation, and it would be the task of thinking to examine each parasitic swerve (human and non-human) according to its own differential ('Posthuman Humanities,' 178–179).

To illustrate this point, Serres offers dozens of examples of parasitic systems ranging from the orbits of satellites and the circulation of raw materials to the irreversible pathways of money and the vagaries of philosophical theory. Colebrook, however, restricts her own account to two principal examples of supplementary bodies: namely, mathematical and poetic systems of relations. In both cases, she argues, parasitical interruption occurs in the deflection from 'living praxis' in the becoming of a formalized supplemental system about which it only then becomes possible to articulate 'the geneses of formalization and ideality' (179). Here, Colebrook deliberately employs the problematic notion of 'living praxis' to illustrate the irreversibility of relations of expropriation as well as to highlight the twofold folly that presumes first of all that the existence of a given system presupposes the *prior* existence of that system in its original form and, second, that it is both possible and desirable to *return* a given system of relations to its original form. Stated once again, parasitism never goes in two directions—there can be neither change nor exchange.

Given that *all* systems, *all* bodies—which is to say, *all* organized forms of being—are always already parasited, Colebrook is thus able to isolate an axiomatic principle as it relates to systems of relations: 'A system develops its own laws of survival irrespective of its host' (179). So, what does this mean for us here? First of all, a given system develops new laws of enduring stations and paths in a relation that is at once *on* and *to the side of* its host. Notable here is the slight shift in nomenclature in my reading of Colebrook, replacing 'survival' with 'endurance' in a move that, just as with 'living praxis,' is important given the etymological rooting of survival in the French term *survivre*, which translates directly into English as 'on-life' or 'living-on' [*sur-vivre*]. Second, a system *produces its own laws* of parasited being through the ceaseless expropriation and consumption of energies not its own, but which are in fact given by a host in thrall to its system. In contrast to systemic *re*production, the production of a system's *own* laws is the production of a new—that is, profoundly unexpected and essentially unpredictable—relation of guest to host (*hôte à hôte*). Third, the process of production is necessarily black boxed *because* the automatic process of production *is* the corrective production of causal insanity, obscured by static that is both the noise of the system and the system itself. In thrall to the *re*production of the present, the host always already gives and gives way to the parasitic other and is, in the process, consumed in order to endure as profoundly other both on and to the side of that system. In this way, as we shall see, parasitic production names that which philosopher Quentin Meillassoux describes in 'Time without Becoming' as 'a very special possibility, which is not a formal possible, but a real and dense possible' ('27).

POWER AND THE PARASITE

Returning to the many and varied machinations of metaphysics that begin with Socrates and a vain attempt to banish the spectre of sophistic relativism, we have seen how the argument from exclusion ultimately serves but a single purpose: that of safeguarding the fantasized purity of a given realm from pollution or contamination and, as such, retroactively constituting that realm *as* pure. By contrast, parasited bodies inhabit a world of prior *incompossibility*. What this means, as Colebrook explains, is that not only 'is each inclination or deviation an opening and disruption of a quite specific or singular differential—a quite singular creation of a field—it occurs always as disruption of other differentials and relations. The emphasis on parasitism and pollution precludes any nostalgia or restoration' ('Posthuman Humanities,' 180). Hence, the *a priori* parasitism constitutive of metastable systems is at once the impossibility of both the metaphysical 'as such' *and* of the banal posthumanist version of Lovelock's Gaia hypothesis that presumes the prior ordering of a natural and symbiotic whole that is subsequently and variously expressed in the form of every living being.[1] Abuse, let us not forget, is what makes 'making-use' possible in the first place: 'in the beginning is defilement' (180).

Consequently, the sense of climate change following Serres and Colebrook imposes a very different set of requirements. Not only, writes Colebrook, would 'man' now have to *"recognize his natural milieu, but that the very concepts of milieu, environment and climate in their singular sense would have to be rendered obsolete if nature also 'contracts.' Nature also has its inflections, worlds, multiplicities and differentials"* (181, italics in original). Once again, I find Colebrook's invocation here of 'nature' and the 'natural' to be particularly problematic insofar as it severely restricts the scope of her critique, blunting its edge by imposing unnecessary and groundless limits. That said, however, in light of her work as a whole Colebrook may well be making use of these and other, similarly weighted terms for explicitly strategic reasons, akin both to the political machinations based around the reiterative 'queering' of habitual terms of exclusion, as well as to the homonymic manoeuvring from 'thought' to 'thought' in Derrida's accounting of the event-machine that will be the focus of our next chapter. Indeed, further evidence of just such an approach is to be found in Colebrook's concluding remarks, wherein she maintains the untenability of any political imaginary that installs nature as both foundation and fundament. More important for us here is Colebrook's point that we can no longer 'imagine a grounding or ideal (even inaccessible) nature that is lost in the creation of technical systems' (181). As a result, the concepts of both 'nature' and 'natural contract' are radically transformed:

> The 'contract' of the natural contract is therefore not a signature (an act of the hand, inscribing a blank surface) but a contraction (the introduction of a noise or pollutant that ramifies throughout the open whole). . . . The world is a monadology, an infinitely divisible chaos in which smaller and smaller differentials will enable subtler and subtler relations and encounters—so that there is no nature in general outside or beyond the multiplicity of contractions (181).

With this sense or state of nature in mind, writes Colebrook, Serres leads the call for a *futural* concept of humanity that, rather than reflecting 'upon man as he is or has been,' would instead 'require and enable an interrogation into humanity as inclination' (184). Such futural thinking, she continues, becomes ever more urgent in our late-capitalist era that we now know as the Anthropocene, insofar as this marks our having crossed a new threshold wherein a *general* parasitic system has now become 'capable of infecting or polluting every other line of system or parasitism' (184). The system of postindustrial capitalism, in other words, has attained such a level of entropic generality that it 'now precludes the dynamisms, systems and disturbances of anything outside its own terrain' (183). This of course returns us to a fundamental concern that today, and perhaps more than ever, is still too often overlooked by some of the more optimistic and at times even triumphal declarations of posthumanist intent. In short, any rigorous critical engagement with posthumanist theory cannot simply refuse to engage with the critique of systemic late-stage capitalism, insofar as the latter is predicated upon the exploitation of surplus value that can only be legitimized through the instrumentalization that is at the heart of commodification.

Colebrook lays out the stakes of this issue with distinctive clarity: How is it possible, she writes, 'that in a life or earth that is nothing other than a multiplicity of inclinations and parasitisms one specific line or disturbance has taken over the whole, at the very expense of its own tendency?' (184). Something like humanity, in other words, 'has been rendered possible and effective not because of knowledge as recognition but because of a general polluting and parasitic power that has overtaken the locality of systems and relative disturbances' (182). At the same time, however, this general pollution that is the instrumentalization definitive of the Anthropocene *also* makes available—here and now for the first time in *human* history—a new way of thinking about a positively destructive 'humanities.' Such thinking, argues Colebrook, would not therefore be *post*human but rather *in*human, 'precisely because the creation of the single system or axiom where work and production overcode all other relations, including supposedly environmental or ecological imperatives of survival and adaptation, would need to be annihilated to give way to differentials along a different axis' (182).

THE HOST AS HOSTAGE TO ITS FUTURE

So, how and where, here and now in thrall to the Anthropocene, inclined and inclining toward the homogeneity of the instrumental, are we to find ourselves today? And what, then, of tomorrow? For Heidegger, Serres and Colebrook alike, we occupy a place *before* tomorrow that, uniquely ours and for the first time in history, is the chance of a future other than that which the presumption of determinism brings into being. It is through the power of the instrumental, of the determinable, that humanity makes itself 'capable of the mastery of the world in the sense of a systematic world-domination' (Heidegger, 'On the Essence,' 183). When Heidegger describes modem humanity as seeming to be 'rushing headlong toward this goal of *producing itself technologically*' (197), he describes what we know today as the Anthropocene, marking the completion of the modern world picture that at the time of Heidegger's writing is still in process.

This distinction has important consequences for how we should read Heidegger's analysis of technology, at the core of which is the belief that it is still possible for us to reorient, or at least halt, the headlong rush toward the completion of the modern epoch. For us today, however, no such belief is possible; as such, we can no longer afford the empty comfort that comes from thinking otherwise. Hence, to read Heidegger on technology today is akin to deciphering an apocalyptic warning that will always have arrived too late. Should the modern epoch be allowed to arrive at its end, writes Heidegger, humanity "will have exploded itself, i.e., *its essence* qua *subjectivity*, into thin air, into a region where the absolutely meaningless is valued as the one and only 'meaning' and where preserving this value appears as the human 'domination' of the globe" (197). This warning clearly accords with the process that has already arrived at its end as the Anthropocene, and which Colebrook identifies as a 'general polluting and parasitic power' that has taken over the whole at the expense of its own tendency ('Posthuman Humanities,' 182). So what has happened, and what still needs to happen, if we are to have a chance of a future that is otherwise and, moreover, to be at home in that future?

To begin to answer this question, we must return to what Colebrook describes as

> another counter-logic of artifice that is not quite counter to life, not quite imma-
> nent to life, but that is perhaps best thought of as a destructive and inhuman
> force within figurations of artifice. Rather than think of life as a force of infinite
> becoming and creativity, the post-apocalyptic milieu of the twenty-first century
> allows us to entertain the unbecoming forces that refused the ever-more-complex
> systems of life 2.0 ('All Life Is Artificial Life,' 1).

Uniquely situated, here and now, in a post-Heideggerian, post-apocalyptic milieu, the chance of a future otherwise than that which is presently presented rests with the contrary logic of artificial figuration. This point simply cannot be overstated. More specifically, this chance of a future is the chance of an inhuman force constitutive of such figurations, which installs as its condition a fundamental ethics of technological innovation. Before considering in more detail this 'something like' a formal power that, according to Colebrook, opens the present on to a nonliving future, it still remains for us to summarize—and hopefully further clarify—the critical foundation of Serres's general parasitism insofar as it underpins the move away from 'something like' humanity and toward that which is, more or less, a child's home.

Let us begin again by recapping several key points regarding the parasitic relation that takes its place on the relation of host to guest [*hôte à hôte*]. First of all, for something to *be*, that is, for something to endure in being, it *will have been* formed by way of a black-boxed process of automatic correction that always already determines the impossibility of exchange. And second, this *a priori* impossibility of exchange inscribes the irreversibility of the arrow of time as a necessary corollary of the process that intercedes parasitically between linear input and nonlinear output. But what are we to make of—or, rather, what *can* we make of—such processes and incompossible inclinations that, constitutive of metastable systems, are nonetheless forever closed off behind an impassable screen of time and being? An interactive matrix producing effects without classical causes, the black box records the necessity of the prior breakdown of meaning into noise, sense into static—a systemic interference that, *becoming without sense*, cannot be made sense of other than as what it *will have been* in its future sense. The host of the parasite is thus hostage to its future.

As prior to time and thus excluded from being, the host must thus remain forever in thrall to its abusive guest and, in so doing, sustain its second order of relation with the parasite. This, however, gives rise to a further temporal or chronological paradox: prior to time as the condition of being, the processual relation of host to guest [*hôte à hôte*] must therefore be eternal, yet it is *also* the case that the host, enchanted beyond all measure by its guest, gives of itself without limit and ultimately so unto its own destruction. But how is this possible? In what fashion or form can that which is eternal ever be destroyed? To answer this question, we must consider further the intersecting roles played by eternity, automaticity and contingency in the articulation of general parasitism. In this, the law of the conservation of energy provides a useful analogy: as an open processual structure, the cyclic networks of energy flow compose an eternal and infinitely complex system and yet, as clearly evidenced by the increase of entropy as described by the second law of thermodynamics, the manifest processual *forms* of this mesh of energy flow tend toward expenditure unto dissolution and thus toward the transformation of manifest forms of being. Here, it is helpful to recall Sagan and Schneider's point that deep in the chemical cycles of present-day bacteria 'are metabolic pathways, chemical traces repeating, with variation, the steps by which matter came to life' (*Into the Cool*, xii–xiii).

At this stage, we can begin to sketch out a very preliminary diagram of the force, causal directions, and nodes of matter-energy whose functioning in concert ultimately articulates an ontology that is at once posthumanist and parasitic:

1. *Iteration* as general structuring force of manifest being.
2. *Retentions* and *protentions* as compassable orientations of determining past cause and undetermined futural cause.
3. *Recuperation* (or conservation), *recombination* (or innovation) and *dissolution* (or destruction) as the three nodal attractors of material plasticity.

While there still remains a great deal of work to be done in order to flesh out what are now just bare bones, we can nonetheless offer some initial remarks that will hopefully help to orient this thesis going forward. First and foremost, iteration describes time and movement without any human or cognitive or organic or living privilege. As Derrida argued so long ago, the iterative trace is the becoming space of time and the becoming time of space, by which we mean that iteration is movement in time, is enduring and mutating, and the placing and holding and changing of position in space. Put as simply as possible, iteration is the spacing of time and of enduring in space. As such, iteration organizes movement in two temporal directions at once, that is, from past to future-present (retentions) and from future to present-past (protentions). Finally, it is important to note that, insofar as they are attractors, the nodal points of recuperation, recombination and dissolution therefore cannot exist either individually or in composite form, but rather constitute asymptotic limit points *toward which* all forms of being tend but which can never be materialized. Once again, a useful analogy of this relation and correlation can be found in the discourse of thermodynamics, wherein recuperation, recombination and dissolution can be taken as abstract idealizations of the endpoints toward which the mesh of *negentropic* and *entropic* processes always tends. While these attractors are necessarily situated outside of time and thus inexistent, they nonetheless function in such a manner as to introduce static interference at the structural level of being.

A CHILD'S HOME, MORE OR LESS

Returning to the noise constitutive of Serres's general parasitism, systems work simply because they do *not* work. Indeed, this is the ground upon which all else is built:

> Nonfunctioning remains essential for functioning. And that can be formalized. Given, two stations and a channel. They exchange messages. If the relation succeeds, if it is perfect, optimum, and immediate; it disappears as a relation. If it is there, if it exists, that means that it failed. It is only mediation. Relation is nonrelation. And that is what the parasite is. The channel carries the flow, but it cannot disappear as a channel, and it brakes (breaks) the flow, more or less (*The Parasite*, 79).

If a system works faultlessly, argues Serres, it can no longer be a system of relations, simply because faultless exchange precludes all possibility of mediation and as such vanishes into the impossibility of immediacy. Hence, for a system to *be*, it must have already undergone systemic failure as the *a priori* condition of its becoming. Fallibility, in other words, is the condition of possibility of being and becoming and at once the impossibility of their separation. Put simply, noise both *makes* and *marks* every system of relations from the most simple to the unfathomably complex as fallible before it can be anything at all. Abuse precedes use, and parasitism is everywhere and nowhere:

> This is the paradox of the parasite. It is very simple but has great import. The parasite is the essence of relation. It is necessary for the relation and ineluctable by the overturning of the force that tries to exclude it. But this relation is nonrelation. The parasite is being and nonbeing at the same time. Not being and nonbeing that are the names (or the nonnames) of stations; but arrow and nonarrow, relation and nonrelation. Hence its metamorphoses and the difficulty we have in defining it (79).

Interesting in light of our earlier discussion tracing the inauguration of Western metaphysics to the *agora* of ancient Greece and the already failed attempt by Socrates to safeguard philosophy from the pollutants of sophistry, Serres too has recourse to this same scene and to the prior interruption of its bivalent reason. Whereas ancient ontology depends upon the pure and simple relation, he writes, 'the *Sophist* and the *Statesman* are inside the functioning of the *Dialogues*. . . . Or rather, the sophist and the politician (the statesman) are interceptors of every relation in general; they are the relation itself' (79). As well as helping to clarify the relative position of the parasite as that which *preys upon* the host to guest [*hôte à hôte*] relation as its necessary third, both the sophist and the politician serve here as figural embodiments of noise that already interrupt the general systems of reason and polity and in so doing make possible the system both as a being-in-the-world and as an organized entity subject to transformation over the time of its being. A system without noise of its being is a system which, in its immediate perfection, can never be anything other than what it is. Sovereign in its perfection, in other words, such a system would be without relation and as such withdrawn from possible being. Exchange, in short, is possible only if a relation is instituted. Furthermore, insofar as noise is the condition of a system becoming otherwise than what is, it thus follows that the noise of a system can only be supplanted *by* noise. Fomenting (ex)change, the sophist brings forth a new iteration of the system upon which the sophist has already been at work.

Again, there are clear—and by now expected—parallels between the parasitical processes described by Serres and those formalized by contemporary proponents of far from equilibrium thermodynamics. Moving between the sociological and physical sciences, writes Serres, the discourse remains the same: '[N]oise is the fall into disorder and the beginning of an order' (79). Not at 'the center of everything like a sonorous echo,' noise rather takes place 'on the edges of messages, at the birth of noises' (67). Noise, in other words, is a liminal function twice over: on the edges both of *sense* and of *noise* itself.[2] At this point, Serres takes a further, critical step that raises the stakes considerably. The erratic path traced by noise at the very edges of being, he writes, *'follows the paths of invention exactly'* (67, italics added). At the edges of all that exists, in other words, the liminal movement of noise is ordered by paths of invention that both precede it and are traced by it. Noise, in short, is the mark of invention and marks invention as a process of erratic pathing having already taken place at the very limits of being.

Noise is the sound of systemic instability and the *a priori* impossibility of insular perfection as being without relation. A component functions increasingly as part of a particular system the less it perceives noise and the more it represses noise: 'All dogmatism lives on this division, be it blind or decided' (68). Systems change state and states change phase, writes Serres, but equilibrium remains an ideal that, outside of time, can never be reached. Not simply the 'mortal enemy' of history, Serres further argues that the state as stasis can in fact *kill* history—a situation already deemed close to being realized at the time of writing *The Parasite*. Again, it is easy to recognize the realization of just such a state in the instrumentalization of the world known today as the Anthropocene and, more pointedly, the Capitalocene. What from a certain perspective can be seen as a tending toward global equilibrium is instead the running down of metabolic processes on a global scale that is not simply the contrary of *life* but is rather the contrary of *being*:

As soon as the world came into being, its transformation began. . . . My body is an exchanger of time. It is filled with signals, noises, messages, and parasites. And it is not at all exceptional in this vast world. It is true of animals and plants, of air crystals, of cells and atoms, of groups and constructed objects. Transformation, deformation of information (72–73).

In 'All Life Is Artificial Life' (2019), Colebrook makes the important point that it remains insufficient to simply acknowledge that fabrications such as the polity are 'not made by man as some godlike external artist' but are rather 'formed in ongoing adjustment that is never fully in command of itself' (6). While it is clear that particular forms of artifice are fundamental to the constitution of Western politics, she writes, the 'types and proximities' of artifice in question are always rigorously policed and proscribed. As such, the ordering of the 'body politic' ultimately allows for only two possible models, that is to say, as either an organic model which conceives of the body as 'an artwork that emerges according to its inner expressive imperatives, or—after modernism—as a counter-organic and pure constructedness that works against the laziness of bourgeois and everyday functionality' (6–7). Here, the apparent opposition between organicist and modernist frameworks serves to obscure the fact of their common founding upon the same unfounded assumption, namely that *artifice is like art* or, more specifically, '*like the art work*' insofar as artifice is, or at least should be, the result of self-making (7).

Formulated by Socrates in the first instance, this normative conflation of artifice and artwork can be found at work all throughout the histories of philosophy and politics in the West. Contrary to this entrenched tradition, however, Colebrook argues that if we are to think artifice beyond the notion of the artwork, it thereafter becomes possible to 'generate a conception of life (including human life) that did not rely upon ownness' (8). Leaving aside for a moment the desirability or otherwise of generating a further concept of life at all, we have already seen in the first chapter how the metaphysical Socratic two-step safeguards not truth or wisdom, but rather a restricted system of ownness in service and in thrall to ownership, exclusion and the defence of lines and limits of property. Whereas the normative conception of life as an exclusive property and process of self-making or, better, of auto-generation relies upon a paradoxical automaticity that ultimately leaves nothing of life behind, to think of artifice other than as a work of art introduces a very different kind of automaticity, one that, by contrast, lets loose the illimitable inventiveness inherent in the mindless process that is iteration.

Bodies, cells, atoms, algorithms, groupings, technologies and fabrications: everything we can think of, as well as the myriad other things we cannot, *are* only insofar as they are, in Serres's phrase, *exchangers of time* and, as such, have the potential to host a 'child' in an ecstatic fashion that in some way or in some sense makes of itself 'more or less' that child's home. Furthermore, at its black-boxed core is a noisy imbrication of eternity, contingency and automaticity that makes possible the formal articulation of being and orders time's arrow 'with only one direction' (Serres, *The Parasite*, 80). In addition, at and as every moment of being, parasited metastable entities take place in the form of marks, masks and memorials of the unceasing material whirr of profoundly mindless iteration. As Colebrook argues, poiesis in general and autopoiesis in particular are rather normative concepts that conceal at once the artifice of invention and the inventiveness of artifice. In contrast to the sovereign work of art lionized by poiesis according to which entities are 'created to stand alone, be set apart, and to continue through time as though mind were extended by artifice,' writes Colebrook, mindless artifice concerns instead 'the variations of matters that generate all forms and relations of life, and nothing would be more improbable than life in its human or supposedly non- or pre-artificial forms' ('All Life Is Artificial Life,' 8). This point is crucial if we are to have any hope of escaping our present instrumental capture. As things currently stand, continues Colebrook, we are allowing 'the matters that compose bodies and objects to operate without the morality of the living body,' when in truth we cannot even begin to address questions of ethical concern until we recognize the priority "of a general artificiality that does not extend life but continually undermines any possibility of 'a' life" (8).

So just what becomes of life in general, and of our lives in particular, should artifice cease to be 'moralized as having its only proper form in the art object' (10)? From all across the political and religious spectrum today, millenarian polemics of fear decry as but a short step away the terrifying rise of the machines ushering in the total destruction of civil society and, ultimately, the end of all life (as we currently know it, anyway). As previously argued, however, all such apocalyptic visions, irrespective of their underlying political orientation, are constructed on the basis of a fundamental system error insofar as it presumes that the existence of a secure ontological distinction between living beings and technological artefacts is not only possible but is in fact the fundamental condition of all that follows, from culture, politics and law to knowledge, virtue and morality, and from truth and falsehood to life and death and everything in between.

LIVING ON, AND OFF, THE APOCALYPSE

In what in all likelihood will prove its greatest ideological triumph, the power brokers of postwar capitalism in the West set about demonizing the pre-modernist spectre of communism in the hope of being able to exorcize it once and for all. In the process, one spectre comes to be replaced by another, the imminent apocalyptic collapse. The end of capitalism, in other words, becomes synonymous with the end of the world. But what might such an ending of the world entail? Is the end of the world the ending of life itself, or only both the end of the world and the end of life *as we know it*? What possible form or forms might the postcapitalist apocalypse take?

In order to understand the end of capitalism as simultaneous with the end of the world and the end of life, we need only to recognize this *ending* of capitalism in all of its senses, that is, as the termination of the capitalist mode of production but also as its goal and its culmination, its completion and expiration. On this basis, it thereafter becomes possible to ask, as Colebrook does in 'All Life Is Artificial Life,' if we really should

> see the end of life as we know it—the life of the technologically accomplished purveyor of a world of one single, self-forming humanity—as the end of the world? Should we really be panicking that the life that has formed itself as humanity—as a being capable of extending itself and archiving itself through ongoing artifice—might be falling apart? (10).

Instead of seeking the home for humanity in a world of means to be exploited, the world to which all beings comport in complex and partial forms of incomplete and unfinished fabrications is a mesh working of endlessly iterated and reticulated forces, movements and materialities. In clear contrast to the imaginary privilege of perfect monadic closure in which the sovereign human body is deemed both star and sole player, the role of fundamental actant in the ongoing mesh working of worlds is instead taken by—rather than given to—*innovation* as the material force and manifest form of potential nonlinearity at the heart of being and with the spacing of iteration as its percussive beat. The functioning of the relation of *hôte à hôte*, in other words, constitutes the opening of place to the occupation of bodies more or less at home while reiterating an asymptotic limit that *literally makes sense of* being.

In accordance with the normative conception of agency as the exclusive province of the willing and desiring subject, for something to be or become a guest it must have previously been invited. Amid the mindless machinality of artifice, however, agency in this traditional sense is—just like the life it claims to condition—a supplementary effect produced by a series of artifices. Here, it is not the host who decides whether or not to open their property and in so doing bestow guest status upon another, but rather the guest who mindlessly takes upon itself a very different kind of agency that precedes and precludes any possible invitation insofar as its relation to the host is the prior condition of relation 'itself.' As Colebrook writes, whatever it is that 'we' take ourselves to be 'is the effect of matters that have no stability or life without the contingency of relation, without artifice' ('All Life Is Artificial Life,' 9).

That said, of course, it remains difficult indeed to recognize such a world as our own, and even more so to recognize our own part and place within the mesh working of that world. It is helpful in concluding this section to call upon another of reason's principles, namely that of Occam's razor. Also known as the law of parsimony, Occam's razor states that when faced with competing hypotheses about the same prediction, the hypothesis with the least number of assumptions should be selected. This principle remains a cornerstone of the scientific method to this day insofar as theoretical simplicity facilitates testability in accordance with the falsifiability criterion upon which the method is based. So how does this help us? What assumptions are conveyed by a world of property-owning hosts compared to this world populated by abusive guests always already riven by senseless parasitic static?

In the tradition of the former, the existence of the host as both sovereign body and conscious agential subject assumes that the possession of a home and the intentional act of inviting another respectively must precede the existence of the guest, who (and not which) only comes into being as a result of this prior invitation and which, as a consequence of its capacity to receive and to respond to this engendering invitation, is similarly assumed to be both sovereign body and conscious agential subject. It assumes, in other words, a willed opening to relation that is nonetheless ontologically prior to, and thus absolutely distinct from, any and all relation, thus making of the conscious host a sovereign presence in its constitutive withdrawing from existence as the condition of possibility of relation, which is to say, of being itself. Life deemed by us to be conscious and willing—primarily that of human being along with a mobile but tiny fraction of other species largely in service to economic edicts—thus pre-exists the world as its prime mover. In bringing Occam's razor to bear, can we really accept the idea of a universe composed of existing beings that maintains itself by way of its necessarily prior and mute echo in the supernatural shadow realm populated not by gods or archetypal forms, but by an infinite number of inexistent sovereign hosts—infinite because each subsequent relation in the realm of existence demands one more of these windowless monads as its necessary precedent?

HERE AND NOW AND FOR THE FIRST TIME IN HUMAN HISTORY: MALABOU'S GENERATIVE FORCE

In their very different ways, for both Heidegger and Colebrook we come to find ourselves today as occupying a singular nexus of position, disposition and dispossession as and at the end of human history—an articulation without precedent that not only is that which defines the way of being of any and every historical juncture, but which further conspires a locus, and perhaps even the chance of something like a home, with such potential as to impact profoundly the trajectories and the histories of the future in ways and forms that are as potentially world-transforming only inasmuch as they remain unthinkable. Such, then, is the paradoxical promise of posthuman times—a paradox and its promise that can be further clarified by turning now to the recent work of Catherine Malabou.

In *Before Tomorrow: Epigenesis and Rationality* (2014), Malabou argues that—here and now and for the first time in human history—the 'generative force proper to thought' becomes available through the figure and process of *epigenesis* (25). Here, it will be argued that epigenesis, as the reciprocity of interference and transformation that brings about the fusion of times, serves to further clarify the automatism definitive of emergence and articulation by facilitating a reworking of the concept of *machinality*. As we have seen, the intrusion of a parasitical element necessarily precedes every form of auto-mated production—such is the contrary and inhuman force of *machinality* at work. In addition, it follows too that this unbecoming force at work in machinality is the same inhuman force that, here and now and for the first time in history, makes manifest the site and sense of our contemporary his-torical fracture. Above all else, machinality names the *a priori* fallibility of the machine and thus the potential emergence into being of entities without classical causes.

In turning attention now to epigenetic fallibility, it is nonetheless important for us not to overlook or ignore certain concerns identified by Colebrook. First of all, as evidenced most clearly by the oxymoron that is 'artificial life,' our engagement with emergent technologies today remains primarily *phar-macological*, that is, as "a 'pharmakon' or poisoned chalice . . . which poses a risk to us but that might be managed and harnessed for our future" ('All Life Is Artificial Life,' 9). To this, Colebrook suggests that we think instead about 'the forms of artifice that have brought humanity into being, including the forms of imperialism, colonization, slavery, and industrialization that allowed *homo faber* to think of artifice as self-extension' (9). Second, it is imperative that the notion of artifice be liberated from the human and this 'concomitant fetishization of the notion of artifice as a supplement' (10).[3] Only then, she continues, does it thereafter become possible for us

> to entertain forms of artifice that do not fetishize holding onto one's own-ness: perhaps what is often imagined as the end of the world—the loss of the technological maturity that has brought most humans into a global connected-ness—is better thought of as the dispersion of artifice and the opening to other ways of being (12).

Here then, once again we find ourselves returned and reoriented toward that 'something like' an inhuman formal power that 'dislocates humanity from itself [and] opens humans to an infinite or non-living future' (Colebrook, 'Fragility,' 257).

Finally, in 'The Time of Planetary Memory' (2017), Colebrook sounds a timely note of warning that we as philosophers and theorists would do well to heed:

> Like the modern and modernist discourses that preceded the Anthropocene, stratigraphic claims for a new era do not deny that other modes of human existence have existed, but they do claim that for the purposes of the present (and future) those other pasts will be caught up in a single anticipated future from which there is no escape. Those who criticize the 'anthropos' of the Anthropocene, like those who contest the 'man' or 'subject' of modernity, are nevertheless forced to contend with the brute fact of memory and inscription. ... The Anthropocene's timeline is not that of European 'man,' but of the earth, an earth that—despite the differences of the past—will ultimately subsume (and thereby constitute) us all. Just as modernism wrote as if every voice in the present reinscribed and recalled 'all' the past, at once opening 'humanity' and yet closing it in upon the West and its others, so the Anthropocene opens a planetary memory that leads to a single global predicament. In this respect, one might see the Anthropocene as a reclamation of modernist (universal/human) time; *the more it acknowledges other timelines and modes of existence, the more those other modalities can only appear as lost* (1019–1020, italics added).

What, then, remains for us in the future? What or where is the chance, if indeed there is any chance at all, of engineering an escape *from* the future before it will have been already too late? What chance, as Malabou writes with such precision, before tomorrow?

IF NOT NOW, WHEN?

As was touched on briefly in the reading of Heidegger in the previous chapter, in *Before Tomorrow* Malabou embarks upon a close reading of Paragraph 27 of Immanuel Kant's *Critique of Pure Reason* (1781/1787, versions A and B). Here, Kant introduces the concept of biological epigenesis so as to better illustrate the differing paths available for the transcendental deduction of the concepts of understanding. There are, he argues, 'only two ways in which a *necessary* agreement of experience with the concepts of its objects can be thought: either the experience makes these concepts possible or these concepts make the experience possible' (*CPR*, B166–167). Kant immediately dismisses the first way as 'a sort of *generatio aequivoca*' in that it supposes the generation of one sort of thing out of another, essentially different sort of thing. As with the appropriation of the biological notion of epigenesis as definitive of the second way, so too Kant here employs a biological process to best illustrate the folly of this first way—that of 'the supposed generation of flies from rotting meat' (B166). Consequently, he continues, 'only the second way remains (as it were [*gleichsam*] a system of the *epigenesis* of pure reason): namely that the categories contain the grounds of the possibility of all experience in general from the side of the understanding' (B167).

As Malabou establishes at some length, this restriction by Kant to only the two possible ways by which the principle of reason can be thought—either as self-thought first principles or as developing over time consequent with experience, that is, as either innate *a priori* or manufactured *a posteriori*—has given rise to an irresolvable schism among readers of Kant that continues to this day. With Kant himself explicitly refuting the possibility of dialectical sublation or indeed any 'middle way' whatsoever that might ultimately bridge the two positions, for centuries scholars have been unable to resolve definitively the question of the ontological or empirical status of the concepts of the understanding. By contrast, what makes Malabou's critique as timely as it is important is her recognition that 'the challenge of §27 derives from the tension that it incites, rather than soothes, between preformation and transformation' (*Before Tomorrow*, 159). The Kantian figure of epigenesis, in other words, 'constantly sets off the conflict it is supposed to settle' (159).

Rightly maintaining that there can be no escape from this conflict, for Malabou the figure of epigenesis serves instead as a 'flagrant marker of the instability of the transcendental' (113). That said, however, the figure of epigenesis does not simply memorialize the site of a fundamental indecision with respect to the definition of reason. Crucially, as we shall see, the figure of epigenesis is the failure of the principle *of* reason understood in both its genitive and nominative cases. Epigenesis, writes Malabou, "takes place exactly at the articulation, which Kant terms an *opportunity*, between the presence of the categories as they '*lie ready*' in the understanding and their implementation in experience" (38). As the 'trigger point' in the relation between pure concepts and experience, the figure of epigenesis thus initiates the opportunity—and opportunistic leave-taking—of reason even as it sets the time of its return. This is no mere rhetorical extravagance. Rather, the figure of epigenesis describes the reciprocity of interference and transformation that animates both old and new in the 'process of bringing the fusion of times to fruition' (158).

In the remainder of this chapter, I aim to further clarify this opportunistic process of temporal articulation by focusing on the alleged inseparability that Malabou seeks to establish between epigenetic temporality, the biological process to which it refers, and the future of the living being. To this end, I will be guided by three related questions. First, why is it that only life possesses the capacity to manufacture within itself the future revelation of prior meaning? Second, on what basis can epigenesis be distinguished from automatism? And third, what exactly is the 'newly figural' element of life that for Malabou transforms both the principle of reason and the entire system of critique?

TIMES OF OUR LIVES

According to Malabou, the manifest schism between innate *a priori* and *a posteriori* manufacture—and thus between atemporality and contingency—is symptomatic more broadly of our failure thus far to think the figure of epigenesis. Such a figure, she argues, configures a possible line of flight from our claustrophobic confinement within the rigid prior accord of preformation on one hand and the magical inorganicism of *generatio aequivoca* on the other. Moreover, it is a possible escape that ultimately transforms the principle of reason itself insofar as it makes available for the first time the generative force proper to thought.

To engage this generative force is to understand that the adequation of category and object is in fact produced, is a product of an epigenetic relation whereby the understanding 'imposes, of itself, a form on the given and thereby constitutes knowledge as the product of its own activity' (*Before Tomorrow*, 25–26). Epigenesis, in other words, names a dynamic, creative and self-forming relation and, as such, is not to be confused with genesis. There is no epigenetic origin story awaiting its redemption in the recovery of its genetic past, no originary depths to be plumbed for the judgement of its previously hidden truth. Whereas genesis forever drags the new back to the old, writes Malabou, epigenesis by contrast 'marks the current valency of the meeting point between the old and the new . . . the embryo of a specific temporality' (158).

For Malabou, this specific epigenetic temporality cannot be divorced from either the biological process described by the discourse of epigenetics or from the future of life itself. In the first case, 'epigenetics' refers to the subfield of molecular biology that takes as its object the complex interrelation of universal genotype and individual phenotype. As Malabou writes in *Morphing Intelligence: From IQ Measurement to Artificial Brains* (2019), epigenetic modifications 'determine the activation and inhibition of genes in the process of constituting the phenotype, that is, biological individuality' but without bringing about any change in nucleotide sequences and thus without affecting DNA (61). In other words, epigenetic mechanisms are those that modify in dynamic and creative fashion the functions of an ordering sequence in such a way as to produce an agreement or adequation on an elective or opportunistic bias of activation and silencing, but without ever modifying the sequence that gives rise to those mechanisms. This last point is crucial insofar as it makes clear the essential and continuing role that the *a priori* still has to play in the creative and self-forming relation that epigenetics describes.

As befitting its disciplinary foundation, epigenetics discourse focuses almost exclusively upon biological material, that is to say, upon living matter. Malabou takes this further, however, arguing that this exclusive coincidence of epigenetic modification with living being is in fact a *necessary* condition of the epigenetic process itself. This argument for causal necessity is based in the first instance on there being one 'essential aspect' common to all traditional, biological and contemporary forms of epigenesis, and that is the defining of 'ontogenesis, or individual development, as an autonomous, self-formed, and formative growth' (79). This formative process is then further clarified by the discourse of epigenetics which, in mapping the originary co-implication of *a priori* and *a posteriori*, that is, of genotype and phenotype, discloses as fundamental to all existence 'a transmissible memory of changes linked to environment' (82). This notion of 'transmissible memory' as fundamental to enduring being is of profound importance. However, Malabou does not stop here, going on to further identify existential malleability as the 'ability of an organism [*capacité d'un organisme*] to react to an environmental input with a change in form, state, movement, or rate of activity' (82).[4]

Our attention is caught here by Malabou's apparent reservation of the ability to respond to an external milieu for organic entities alone. However, there is nothing in this text that would necessarily exclude inorganic beings from the life of epigenetic development as expressed in accordance with the twofold criteria of self-formed and formative. To better understand this, it is helpful to first of all reconsider the terms. By definition, an organism is an organized entity. As such, it is a thing, quite possibly even a self, but whatever it is it is *also* a metastable open system set adrift in the anarchic ocean of energy and flows. Metastable processes, as Dorian Sagan and Eric Schneider maintain, 'underlie the things we mistake for things. . . . [W]e too are metastable flow systems with billions of years of history as dissipative structures' (*Into the Cool*, 112). Forms of being, in other words, are emergent, energy-driven processual structures, at once self-formed product and formative producer of material cycles and self-reinforcing networks constituted through the transmissible memory of changes linked to a given environment. Considered in this way, all living organisms are metastable epigenetic organizations, but not all metastable epigenetic organizations are organisms.

So what does this mean for Malabou's thesis in *Before Tomorrow* and beyond? Does Malabou's concept of epigenetic plasticity, in contrast to both traditional epigenesis and the epigenetics of molecular biology, in fact offer us something other than servos fabricated for exclusive use in the self-differentiation of living beings? In order to answer these questions, we must first consider the roles Malabou attributes to life, contingency and purposive organization in the opportunistic process that is epigenetic modification.

Epigenesis, Malabou argues, is a figure that has thus far failed to find its place in time. As we have seen, Malabou locates its taking place within the manifest schism dividing the innate *a priori* from *a posteriori* manufacture, whence it articulates and as such animates the old and the new in the same space by way of opportune reciprocal processes of interference and transformation. But what, exactly, is going on here? According to Malabou, the space of epigenesis is at once the meeting place of the archaic and the teleological as well as the 'median point where birth is prepared' (*Before Tomorrow*, 158). Teleology, she further clarifies, "is a prospecting tension towards the future which rectifies after the fact the primitive or 'archaic' dispositions that made it possible" (158). The epigenetic process, in other words, prepares for the space of origin insofar as it brings together the old and the new—the archaic and the teleological—in an animating relation of mutual interference and transformation. The old and the archaic interfere with the new and the futural as the new and the teleological interfere with the old and the ancient, always already transforming and retransforming one another in the process. Epigenesis, in short, is a taking place in the mode of futural causality.

Put more schematically, insofar as it marks and is marked by the confluence of the discrete temporal dimensions of protention and retention, this shared impact space 'is' the movement of time as such. Furthermore, in marking in space the taking place of embryonic temporal contact, the epigenetic process requires its own specific hermeneutic strategy: 'Meaning therefore lies in the way in which a principle becomes its result' (158). The simultaneously prospective and retrospective movement of epigenesis is therefore mapped directly onto the hermeneutic movement, bringing together meaning and valency in one and the same impact space and, in the process, transforming even the principle of reason itself.

The concept of *valency* here is particularly intriguing, not least because Malabou herself does not use the close equivalent term '*valence*' in the original French text.[5] Nonetheless, Carolyn Shread's translation here is both inspired and illuminating insofar as valency, like epigenesis, also posits the concurrence of both molecular and hermeneutic economies. From the Latin *valere*, meaning 'to be well' or 'to be strong,' from which we get *valentia*, meaning power or competence, the term 'valency' in the discourse of chemistry refers to the combining power of a given element, as measured by the number of atoms it can either combine with or otherwise displace. Similarly, in linguistics 'valency' denotes the number of grammatical elements with which a given word, usually a verb, combines in any particular sentence. In Shread's translation, we recall, epigenesis marks the 'current valency [*l'actualité*]' of the shared impact space of old and new, *a priori* and *a posteriori*. The introduction into this context of the concept of valency thus serves to further clarify the formal relation of this temporal encounter insofar as it denotes a quantitative capacity to formally combine with, or displace, that which lies outside through reciprocal processes of interference and productive of a given meaning. We must, however, be very careful not simply to assume the presence somewhere of an intending cognitive subject overseeing the operation of this epigenetic production, and the supplementary valences of chemistry and linguistics thus render explicit the error of just such an assumption. Rather, the combining power of an element concerns the *formal competence* of that element. Strength, of power as competence, is the power of combining and at once of being combined, the power of displacing and at once of being displaced. Valency is what Kant calls opportunity: the opening of a reciprocal deferral to meaning in the convergence of embryonic temporality.

In *Morphing Intelligence*, Malabou describes this epigenetic process as an activity directed toward equilibrium that is 'constantly in process because its temporal horizon is undefined' (69). Hence, she writes, a 'position has been established between a strict adherence to the *a priori* and pure empiricism. The structure is stable, but . . . equilibrium is supple and adjustable. There is no constancy, stability, or permanence other than what is constantly modified' (75–76). Moreover, this ceaseless mobile practice of 'equilibration' takes place over time and along the following 'main axes': 'successive coordinations (combinativity), reversals (reversibility), detours (associativity), and conservations of positions (identity).'[6] Epigenetic equilibration, in other words, accords with the valency of formal competence described above. Once again, however, it would be a serious mistake to assume the shadowy presence of an actively ordering subject hard at work behind the scenes. Forms of being, we recall, are emergent, energy-driven processual structures constituted through the transmissible memory of changes as correlated to formal competence.

ANIMATING TIME: KANT'S OPPORTUNITY OR DEWEY'S EXPERIENCE?

Thus far, we have neither located the precise place of the living organism in Malabou's recent work nor identified its unique animating function. What makes this task particularly difficult, however, is that the very same logic of epigenetic machination that animates the future with the past must also animate life as both an ongoing process and the product of itself. In a very real sense, the concept of life remains in epigenetic flux throughout Malabou's later texts. However, in order to sharpen the critique contained therein, it is important that we understand exactly what can—and, more importantly, what cannot—be attributed solely to biological lifeforms.

In *Morphing Intelligence*, Malabou traces the three main metamorphoses in the formulation of the concept of intelligence: 'genetic fate, epigenesis and synaptic simulation, and the power of automatism' (14). Of particular importance here is the distinction Malabou draws between epigenetic intelligence and automatic intelligence. In discussing the power of automatism, one passage in particular would seem to offer an unequivocal response to our question as to whether the living biological organism should or should not be afforded privileged status:

> Yet the approach that claims that only the living is plastic—never the machine— still dominates today. It seems that for many people the 'intelligence' of reorganization remains the unique domain of organisms. There are two approaches to the plasticity of reorganization: scientific and philosophic. One reserves it for the living; the other extends its power to the machine (117).

Here, it is clear that Malabou is siding with the philosophical approach that extends to the inorganic realm the possibility of 'intelligent' reorganization, thus endowing the machine with the ordering power of plasticity. This occasion of extension and inclusion is, I believe, the single most important event to befall philosophy today. However, and while the reasons underlying this claim will be further developed below, this inclusion of the inorganic is conspicuously absent elsewhere in *Morphing Intelligence*. Earlier in the same chapter, Malabou introduces John Dewey's concept of experience, describing it as at once mediator and midpoint between *a priori* and *a posteriori*. This recourse to Dewey's experience thus plays an identical role in *Morphing Intelligence* that does Kant's concept of 'opportunity' in *Before Tomorrow*, which we recall Malabou defines as the articulation between the innate *a priori* of the categories and their *a posteriori* implementation in experience.

While Dewey's concept of experience and Kant's concept of opportunity occupy the same terrain in the different texts, the differing contexts adhering to these two concepts over time carry along with them some very different inferences. Most importantly, the concept of opportunity has recourse to neither will, desire, intelligence nor consciousness as its condition of being but only the timeliness of potential formal competency that enables the chance emergence into being of a hitherto unheard-of organizational form. By contrast, the capacity for experience is traditionally reserved for only those bodies deemed by us to constitute consciously desiring subjects of a life—a highly selective and elitist club the membership of which has only relatively recently been opened up to include some (but by no means all) nonhuman animals. In Malabou's words, 'Experience is the continuum of life, which moves forward thanks to various specific experiences that extend it every day' (106–107). Malabou then reiterates this point with a direct quote from Dewey's *Art of Experience* (1934): 'Experience occurs continuously because the interaction of live creature and environing conditions is involved in the very process of living' (Dewey, cit. 107). Moreover, we can follow this concept of experience as mediator and midpoint all the way through to Malabou's concluding remarks, wherein she argues that '[o]riginally, becoming is metabolism. This means that the work of intelligence . . . derives just as much from the initiative of the organism in its interactions with its environment as from intellectual dispositions' (141). And again, in the very last sentence of *Morphing Intelligence*: 'There is one life only' (144).

Staying with the work of intelligence, however, Malabou argues tha, as a consequence of becoming being originally metabolism, such work entails the operation in tandem of distinct methodologies, the possibility of which in turn depends upon the presence of preexisting capacities—namely, capacities to disclose connections, to reduce indeterminacy, to make sense and to resolve practical problems. As with the twofold criteria of self-formed and formative, however, here too there is nothing that would necessarily exclude inorganic and nonliving beings from partaking in the work of intelligence.

There is nothing to be gained from pointing out further examples of lively organic privilege in *Morphing Intelligence*, and everything to be gained by turning instead to what Malabou describes as the philosophical approach to the plasticity of reorganization, that is to say, an approach that 'extends its power to the machine' (117). To this end, let us now take *this* Malabou at her word, a word and a work devoid of any organismic or vitalist trapping. To this end, writes Malabou, the 'critical task is to rediscover the pathway for interrupting automaticity so as to better emancipate automatisms' (133). It is to this task of critique that we must all now answer.

AUTOMATIC FALLIBILITY

What does it mean to 'interrupt automaticity'? And how might the rediscovery of its critical path enable us to better emancipate our enslaved automatisms? We get an initial sense of the terrain involved when Malabou asks herself if 'a programmable and programmed plasticity [is] still plasticity? Not that plasticity is the opposite of the concept of program on principle. Epigenetic mechanisms are programmed genetically. Biological plasticity is, if you like, programmed not to be programmed' (*Morphing Intelligence*, 91). This idea of emergent forms being 'programmed not to be programmed' is definitive of the formative and self-forming process of epigenesis in particular, and of plasticity in general. More than this, however, the concept of a programmed breach of its own programming discloses the machinic process at work in the production of its own interruption—discloses, in other words, the machinery at work in the otherwise indeterminable production of an event. Hence, the event marks the failure of programmed necessity or, as Malabou puts it, 'The midpoint between necessity and contingency is the true space of life for automatisms' (121).

If everything does indeed start with metamorphic plasticity that 'trumps all determination,' as Malabou previously claims, then it remains necessary to ask first of all whether plasticity therefore risks dissolving into nothing by becoming everything.[7] Is it even possible, in other words, to make value distinctions in a universe that is already and everywhere both the production and the product of a prior plasticity? As previously noted, organized forms of being are emergent, energy-driven processual structures, at once product and producer of material cycles and self-reinforcing networks. However, as Malabou points out in various places, it is important to understand that, while metastable systems are constitutively open, they are *not* therefore open to infinite flexibility or unfettered polymorphism. Rather, the emergence of novel forms or patterns is dependent upon both the current system *and* its history of prior states. Plasticity, in other words, inscribes the potential for unpredictable and irreversible transformation as a constitutive condition of metastable systems. Formed by iterative feedback loops, however, this discontinuous transformation is nonetheless constrained by historicity, that is, by the memory of prior states of being.

Here, let us recall once again the well-worn definition of insanity as doing the same thing over and over again and expecting a different result. By contrast, therefore, the definition of sanity resides in knowing the effect of every cause in advance. Interesting here is that the logic of insanity specifically concerns the expectation or anticipation of a breakdown of determined causal relationships. Hence, we are dealing here with a strange form of causality, one that is more insane than insane insofar as the effective event constitutes an interruption of determinist causality that is *not*, however, the breakdown of causality but rather the literal breakdown of a perverse but nonetheless pervasive form of machine logic. It is, in other words, to inscribe fallibility as the prior condition of the machine; to be 'programmed not to be programmed.'

While counterintuitive, this point is absolutely fundamental. As Malabou writes, "[T]he imbrication of automatism and plasticity does not 'robotize' plasticity but rather inscribes within the machine a fallibility that alone makes it intelligent. In return, the 'mechanization' of brain plasticity paradoxically signals its undetermined nature, not its routine" (*Morphing Intelligence*, 113–114). In other words, the indeterminacy that is machinic fallibility is a 'power of interruption that is, again, inscribed within automatism and that constitutes its intelligence' (118).

The implications of this, as we shall see, are as varied as they are profound. Before that, however, it is important that we first understand the broader context against which this argument is posed. First of all, the long-held supposition that posits the existence of an internal principle unique to biological organisms that governs the organization of living forms of matter still largely prevails to this day. This principle is neither innate nor aesthetic, but rather serves an ideological function, propping up the value distinction that divides lively occurrences from lifeless mechanisms on the basis that organicity— i.e., the auto-organization of the organic—is deemed to be lacking from inorganic matter. Moreover, this distinction remains fundamental to how we think of ourselves as human beings today, a process of identification that is repeatedly fed back to us in the form of some of our worst collective nightmares. Whether as an internally organized yet entirely inorganic lifeform or as an organic body formed by a will entirely external to itself, these are indeed the stuff of nightmares: on one side are technological dystopias populated by affectless automatons programmed to kill and enslave all organic life, such as Schwarzenegger's Terminator, the Cylons of *Battlestar Galactica* and *Star Trek*'s Borg, and on the other are mind control experiments large and small, ranging from the production of mindless clone armies and the surrendering of control to sentient yet malevolent AIs all the way to reanimated dead matter in the form of zombies entirely in thrall to an alien impulse. We could continue with this list almost indefinitely—viral contagions, bioengineering, cultic control, apocalyptic visions, demonic possessions and so forth—but this suffices to illustrate the *monstrousness* of thinking both organicity and inorganicity with one and the same concept.

FORECLOSING THE MACHINE

In the opening pages of 'Typewriter Ribbon: Limited Ink (2),' Jacques Derrida addresses this monstrosity of concept by first drawing our attention to the polysemy at work in 'what we could call in Greek a *mēhkanē*, at once an ingenious theatrical machine or a war machine, thus a machine and a machination' (71). Key here is that even at its origin, *mēhkanē* bears within itself the contradiction of being something that is at once mechanical and strategic, both automated and intentional at one and the same time. Immediately after this, Derrida employs a striking formulation in stating as his subject 'both the event and its *mēhkanē*' (71)—not both the event and the machine or *mēhkanē*, but rather the event and *its* machine, that is, the mechanics and the machina-tions *of* the event or which belong *to* the event, be that as condition, compo-nent, attribute or property. The machine, in other words, is always already an event-machine. For us, this monstrous concept of an event-machine as both automated and intentional opens up a very different area of inquiry. What would happen, for example, what event would befall that literally vital essence that was for so long imagined definitive of the event *and* of life itself? What becomes, in other words, of the concept of affect once detached from the constraints of subjectivity, that is, of living consciousness? And what event might thereafter befall inorganic desire?

Traditionally, the concept of affect describes the response of an entity to an event that impacts it. However, neither the event nor the response is necessarily sensible, insofar as events need not impact consciousness in order to take place, in the same way that an affective response to an event need not be perceived directly by the senses in order to constitute an affect. The claim that living organisms alone are born with an instinctive—that is, automatic—capacity to 'experience' in some manner or form an *in*sensible affect thus offers a clear contradiction. In other words, both the event and its affects always already refute any exclusive metaphysical attachment to the well-worn concepts of will, desire and intention. So where does this leave us? How can we now draw a secure line of exclusion that would maintain the privileged isolation of pure affect by denying it any possible contact with the oily, machinic underbelly that is instrumental effect? In accordance with such a model, we need only know that nothing has ever happened, and nothing will ever happen, outside of life's umbrella. The undeniable, as Derrida reminds us, is that which in truth can *only* be denied insofar as it allows of no other form of refutation.

Before we can go much further, it is necessary to first break free of the hold of two habitual presumptions that currently stymie our thinking: one, that thinking of the event necessarily presumes living organicity, and two, that thinking of the machine necessarily presumes inorganic repetition. It is, as Derrida argues, just as difficult 'to conceive of a purely machinelike appa-ratus without inorganic matter' as it is difficult 'to conceive of a living being to whom or *through* whom something happens without an affection getting *inscribed* in a sensible, aesthetic manner right on some body or some organic matter' ('Typewriter Ribbon,' 72). It is at this point that Derrida adds the further correlated pairing of spontaneity–automation to those of the event–machine, living–nonliving and organic–inorganic binaries. 'The automatic-ity of the inorganic machine,' he writes, 'is not the spontaneity attributed to organic life' (72). The life of a machine, if we can put it that way, is generally conceived as being one of indifferent, calculable repetition with neither affect nor auto-affection, existing always in a 'state of anesthesia . . . nonliving, sometimes dead but always, in principle, unfeeling and inanimate, without desire, without intention, without spontaneity' (72).

It is here that Derrida's argument dovetails with Malabou's accounting of the automaticity, and thus fallibility, of intelligence: 'Intentionality forecloses the machine. If, then, some machinality (repetition, calculability, *inorganic* matter of the body) intervenes in a performative event, it is always as an accidental, extrinsic, and parasitical element, in truth a pathological, mutilating, or even mortal element' (74). Derrida's strategy here, its textual machination, is readily apparent. We find that now it is the *machine* that is seen to bear the traits of unpredictability, singularity and spontaneity, traits that are only in fact disclosed by way of relative contrast to the 'working' of the event. In other words, we have a strange kind of evental meta-machinality—meta-repetition, meta-calculability, meta-inorganicity—that interferes in every occasion of an event as something both external and, insofar as it is wholly contingent, fundamentally unpredictable. Moreover, this arbitrary and extrinsic machinality—already an apparent contradiction in terms as it stands—intrudes into any given event in the *form of a pathological element* that functions parasitically upon it and which, in the process, mutilates and perhaps even kills its host. Whereas the event traditionally implies an unpredictability, singularity and spontaneity deemed exclusive to organic life, machinality here breaks loose from its quarantined confinement as something predictable, calculable and replicable. Instead, machinality—if not the machine itself—is ultimately disclosed as a pathological parasite that preys upon the singularity of the event even as it ordains its demise. The real perfection of machines, as Malabou writes, 'is not really dependent on increased technological performance but rather on a wider margin of indeterminacy' (*Morphing Intelligence*, 113).

In a close reading of Derrida's work on animality, it is here that Colebrook makes the crucial point that, for Derrida, 'there is something like a formal power that dislocates humanity from itself, that opens humans to an infinite or non-living future' ('Fragility,' 257). As noted previously, Colebrook elsewhere clarifies this 'something like a formal power' as that which opens 'another counter-logic of artifice that is not quite counter to life, but that is perhaps best thought of as a destructive and inhuman force within figurations of artifice' ('All Life Is Artificial Life,' 1). As 'not quite' counter to life and thus off to one side of the array of exclusive oppositions constitutive of biological life, this inhuman formal power rather describes the destructive fallibility of automation itself. As we have seen, the formative epigenetic process discloses the transmissible memory of changes of relation, both internal and external, correlated to formal competence as a fundamental condition of being. Epigenesis, in other words, describes a ceaseless process of creative 'equilibration' that takes its place along the axes of combinativity, reversibility, associativity and identity in the production of unpredictable yet metastable forms of being. As something like a formal power, it is this opportunistic valency [*valere*] of competence [*valentia*] that, as a quantitative capacity productive of deferred meaning, answers to Colebrook's 'destructive and inhuman force' always already at work within forms of automatism.

In the discussion of artificial intelligence in *Morphing Intelligence*, Malabou cites David Bates's claim that 'digital brains—brains modeled on and simulated by computers and increasingly *formed* by repeated interactions with our digital prostheses—will reveal their genuine plasticity only when they rediscover the power of interrupting their own automaticity.'[8] My argument, however, is that any such revelation that might befall us in the future of intelligence will indeed be a *re*discovery, as Bates states here, and necessarily so, insofar as the thoughtless machinations of formal automatisms already and everywhere disclose a genuine machinic plasticity that cannot fail to interrupt automaticity itself.

THE CRITIQUE OF REASON IS A CRITIQUE OF VITALISM EVERYWHERE

In order to further clarify the stakes of this argument, it is important to understand just how the fallibility—the epigenetic indeterminacy—of machinic instrumentality transforms even the principle of reason. Insofar as enduring in being is composed through the reiteration of metastable forms of organization, the risk of its own abrupt and destructive interruption that arrives with neither warning nor reason is thus an *a priori* condition of being itself. Furthermore, this poses a serious challenge to one aspect in particular of Malabou's argument in *Morphing Intelligence*. As we know, Malabou identifies three distinct stages in the formulation of the concept of intelligence since its inception in the West in the early part of the nineteenth century, namely 'genetic fate, epigenesis and synaptic simulation, and the power of automatism' (14). However, once we finally let go of our habitual presumption that living organisms everywhere possess a unique and distinct ontological privilege that by definition excludes inorganicism and automatism, there is no longer any basis upon which can be constructed epigenesis and the power of automatism as mutually exclusive processes. Rather, *the time of epigenesis is the power of automatism as the force of epigenesis is the iteration of automatism*. This point is absolutely critical.

Turning our attention now from the process of epigenetic indeterminacy to the figure that is its product, we already know that such a figure only ever *achieves* its meaning from the coming into being of its own deferred future.

Moreover, argues Malabou, insofar as it 'is neither a pure product from out-side, nor the revelation of a preformed meaning,' this newly futural figure poses a profound challenge to the principle of reason upon which Western tradition has been built (*Before Tomorrow*, 159). This point is fundamental to Malabou's accounting of the logic of epigenesis, as well as to the concepts of valency and competency introduced herein.

At this point, however, our accounts again diverge. As we have seen, the critical trajectory that is the epigenetic deferral of meaning to the future thus introduces an external *a posteriori* element that is nonetheless internal to the archaic *a priori*. According to Malabou, however, this 'element that the figure of epigenesis already introduced covertly in [Kant's] first Critique and that profoundly transformed the entire system, is life' (160). For Malabou, in other words, the outside element internal to its own transcendental condition is that of life itself. In a rather dizzying manner therefore, this move also defers the meaning of epigenesis itself insofar as life thus becomes the later figure through which the meaning of the old figure of epigenesis is to be ultimately revealed.[9]

So in what way does Malabou's newly figural element of life transform both the principle of reason and the entire system of critique in the process of generating the meaning of its own generative figure, namely epigenesis? In accordance with the epigenetic trajectory it describes, Malabou argues that the meaning of Kant's initial invocation of the analogous figure of epigenesis is deferred until the *Critique of the Power of Judgment* (1790), wherein Kant 'identifies for the first time the specific question that the living [*le vivant*] poses to reason' (*Before Tomorrow*, 160; translation modified). This question, continues Malabou, derives in the first instance from the common condition of living beings as constitutively excluded from reason: lifeforms 'are neither ideas, nor concepts, nor forms. They do not immediately have any transcen-dental status. Indeed, they seem to come from outside [*Ils semblent justement venir du dehors*]' (160, translation modified). Life, in other words, is able to address itself to reason precisely on condition of being excluded from it and, as such, 'seems' upon taking place to have somehow arrived from somewhere outside of the traditional purview of reason. Moreover, this seeming external-ity is defined as a property unique to biological lifeforms on the basis that all such forms of life lack an immediate transcendental status. Forms of life, in other words, are never immediate but rather always already mediated through an epigenetic giving and receiving of form outside of itself that excludes it from categories of the understanding.

Staying with the reading of the first and third *Critiques*, Malabou argues that Kant gradually comes to recognize the existence of certain appear-ances—primarily that of the beautiful and the living being—that do not mani-fest in experience as common objects of experience, and which in fact 'do not present themselves as objects at all' (161). As such, this specific manner in which these apparitions present themselves betrays a fundamental resistance to the categories of the understanding in that they 'expose the transcendental to the factuality of life' (161). Consequently, writes Malabou, the recognition of this unreasoned resistance of the living organism ultimately serves to transform, and be transformed by, the Kantian categories of the understanding in giving rise to a series of three interlinked categorial modifications, namely, 'the specification of causality through the intermediary of purposiveness [*la finalité*]; the constitution of purposiveness as an autonomous concept; and, above all, as a result of all this, the transformation of the category of necessity' (161). The stakes are thus clearly very high. Put simply, as an appearing of contingent lawlessness, the spectre of the living being here makes available a specification of causality that, by way of autonomous purposiveness, transforms the understanding of necessity itself.

Malabou's reasoning here is impeccable, and the stakes of her reading are indeed very high. However, this does nothing to detract from the problematic role attributed to life in her account, an engagement with which in fact promises to extend and intensify exactly what is at stake here and going forward. As previously stated, epigenesis and automatism do not constitute two distinct processes, as Malabou argues, but are rather reciprocal aspects of the same process in accordance with which the time of each aspect is the force of the other. To better understand this as well as further clarify the stakes of this argument, it is important to understand that it is in fact the fallibility—or epigenetic indeterminacy—of machinic instrumentality that ultimately transforms the principle of reason, before then moving on to consider exactly how all of this impacts so dramatically the *a priori* concepts of causality, purposiveness and necessity.

First of all, let us briefly recap the steps taken by Malabou in construing the exclusive role of the biological organism within the formative epigenetic process, which are as follows: (1) the process of epigenetic indeterminacy is the production of such a figure that only achieves its meaning from the coming into being of its own deferred future; (2) this play of epigenesis introduces within an ordered system an element from outside that is nonetheless internal to its own transcendental condition; (3) this formative outside element is necessarily that of life, insofar as only biological lifeforms 'appear' to have arrived from somewhere outside of reason by reason of their particular factuality; and (4) this particular factuality is initially made manifest by an absence of manifest presence, insofar as biological lifeforms do not present themselves to common experience as objects.

Here, the specific problem presented by the living thus centres in the first instance upon phenomenological notions of factuality, presentation and appearance, which Malabou identifies as constituting a prior condition of the epigenetic process. But of what is this prior condition composed? As we know, Malabou argues that it is *because* they fail to present themselves as objects that biological lifeforms must therefore present themselves— i.e., their particular factuality—as having its basis outside of the domain of reason. Tellingly, however, Malabou argues that this manifest failure to make manifest, which subsequently grounds the privileged externality attributed to life, is itself based upon a further prior condition: the living organism, she writes, 'self-forms [*s'autoforme*] and has no need for categories' or, at least, it 'appears to do without' the ideas, concepts and categories constitutive of reason (*Before Tomorrow*, 161). The singular form of life, in other words, resists all categorization insofar as it initially and automatically presents itself as a preconceptual form of being.

But what of all those 'other' forms of being deemed to *lack* the necessary capacity to fail that is definitive of living beings everywhere? What is it about nonliving and inorganic forms of organization that makes them so successful when it comes to presenting themselves as objects? What of war machines, of algorithms, technologies and clouds? What of artificial neuronal networks and emergent synaptic forms? Here, the seemingly opposed concepts of 'nature' and 'artifice' abruptly converge, coming together beneath the rubric of automatism. From hurricanes to the Higgs boson, all such organized forms of being habitually supposed to be devoid of life are thus deemed as such on the grounds that they *lack the lack* that serves to define living beings other- wise. The absence of apparent life, in other words, is the lack of the capac- ity to fail in presenting itself as an object. Put simply, nonliving beings are defined by a lack of *fallibility*.

Of course, the deriving of exceptional status on the back of a common lack has had a long and storied career within the humanist metaphysics of Western philosophy. By contrast, we recall that, on at least one occasion, Malabou argues that the critical task facing philosophy today concerns the exten- sion of the power of plasticity so as to include the machine generally, and in particular to disclose 'the pathway for interrupting automaticity so as to better emancipate automatisms' (*Morphing Intelligence*, 133). We also recall that for Malabou the notion of 'being programmed not to be programmed' is definitive of the formative and self-forming process of epigenesis in particu- lar, and of plasticity in general. However, insofar as an event constitutes an interruption of determinist causality, the epigenetic process is always already constitutive of the breakdown of the imagined infallibility of the automatism. Epigenesis, in short, inscribes automatic fallibility as the condition of the machine in its broadest possible sense.

Indeed, in *Morphing Intelligence* Malabou draws our attention to just this when she writes of the 'imbrication of automatism and plasticity' that 'inscribes within the machine a fallibility that alone makes it intelligent'

(113–114). A few pages later, she further clarifies machinic fallibility as a 'power of interruption' inscribed within automatism and constitutive of its intelligence (118). However, it is important to note that this argument takes place within a broader discussion regarding the likely role of synaptic chips for the future of artificial intelligence in general and of brain modelling in particular, which here Malabou maintains as distinct from the formal power of interruption characteristic of epigenesis. This distinction not only obfuscates the necessary concurrence of epigenesis and automatism in one and the same process, but it is also what makes it still possible to redraw a simple line of demarcation between living organisms and lifeless machines.

Returning to Malabou's claim for biological privilege, we recall that this privilege is a consequence of a particular *factuality* that, unique to living beings, gives the appearance of having been engendered outside of the realm of reason insofar as it resists conceptualization and thus objectification. But can we really say that the manifest factuality common to all forms of life is different in kind to the manifest factuality common to all forms of nonlife? First of all, in attributing a constitutive lack of fallibility to forms of nonlife, Malabou thus reiterates the timeless instrumentality of classical causality, in accordance with which the lifeless realm functions like a kind of perpetual motion machine, insofar as the prior impossibility of interference determines the impossibility of any entity defined as such to be anything other than what it is right now. By contrast, both epigenetic innovation and automatic fallibility concern the strange external and internal causal machinery at work in the production of an *in*determinable event, disclosing in fact the necessary absence of such impossibility. They disclose, in other words, the impossibility of a *general* factuality. The event, in its making manifest of a particular factuality, marks the failure of programmed necessity. Hence, it is factually, not the factuality of life, which makes manifest the appearance of a founding resistance to the concepts of pure reason. Echoing then the claims made by Malabou on behalf of the singular form of life, we find instead that it is the *singularity of form* that resists categorization, insofar as it initially and automatically presents itself as a preconceptual form of being.

FINDING OUR INTERMEDIARY PURPOSE

Before concluding, it remains for us to now consider the impact of this thesis upon the fundamental philosophical concepts of causality, purposiveness and necessity. While there are 'clear and undeniable' similarities in the arguments favouring epigenesis proposed by Kant in the first and third *Critiques*, writes Malabou, there is also a profound difference, one that 'must be called a difference in causality' (162). In the first *Critique*, epigenesis is called upon to validate the determinist mechanism constitutive of what Kant understands as the 'universal lawfulness' of nature (*CPJ*, §81). By the time of the third *Critique*, however, epigenesis instead comes to be "analyzed within the framework of the 'teleological principle,' which assumes 'an intentionally acting cause to whose ends nature is subordinated, even in its mechanical laws.'"[10] It is a shift that proves crucial for Malabou as well as for Kant, both of whom note that mechanism and teleology denote entirely different kinds of causality and thereby lay down the challenge "to arrive at their 'unification'" (162). What are we to make of this 'other' necessity as described by teleological causation, and why does it matter? The answer resides in the mirroring of being. According to the metaphysical tradition of the West, writes Malabou, 'the necessary is that whose opposite is impossible, while the contingent is that whose opposite is possible' (171). Such definitions, however, only work when dealing with mechanical or determinist causality, whereas under the sway of teleological or epigenetic causation, a very different concept of necessity emerges, one in which the *must* is inextricable from the *might*. Thus, writes Malabou, if we are to meet such a challenge, we must first introduce the concept of *purposiveness* [*la finalité*] described in Paragraph 81 as a further, particular kind or space of causality. Purposiveness, she continues, enables the introduction of a space of play hitherto unavailable within the incommensurable relation of two other causalities—the mechanistic and the teleological—and does so in such a way as to effect a dramatic transformation in the categorial order.

Malabou argues that Kant clearly demonstrates in Paragraph 81 of the *Critique of the Power of Judgment* that 'epigenesis is a form of teleological judgment,' thereby supplanting the apparently mechanist explanation initially proposed in the *Critique of Pure Reason* (163). More precisely, in the case of the first *Critique* 'the dual causal pulse of, on the one hand, the archaic or archeological (the fundamental metaphysical principles of nature, as Kant himself said) and, on the other, the teleological is not yet identified' (163). Of particular note here is the introduction of the economy of *nature*. According to Kant, this economy is composed of two parts: first, there is 'nature' understood as referring to both 'the set of laws and the subsuming of all appearances to these laws,' and second, there is the 'order *of* nature' [*Naturordnung*], which 'describes the tendency of these laws to combine together into a system' (163). As *a priori* lawfulness, Malabou writes, 'nature' is on the one hand 'subject entirely to the jurisdiction of the understanding' while, on the other hand, it 'tends towards another order, which is the systematic order incumbent on reason' (163). Shared thus by both the order of reason and the order of nature, it is this latter systematic tendency that Kant calls purposiveness.

In short then, purposiveness describes the tendency of laws to combine into a system. However, between the *Critique of Pure Reason* and the *Critique of the Power of Judgment*, this concept of purposiveness undergoes a pronounced modification with respect to its subject if not its definition, starting with causal determinism and ending with teleological causality. Purposiveness, in other words, now addresses itself toward *ends* and, as such, shifts focus away from the causal efficiency of the physical realm and toward the domain of biology in general and toward epigenesis in particular. Furthermore, as Malabou makes clear, this causal shift discloses an odd contradiction at the heart of the Kantian system. Thus, at the time of the first *Critique*,

> mechanism (necessity) and purposiveness (systematic order) complement one another without any other form of process. The system of pure reason is described as an 'end.' Indeed, its privileged figure is the organism. And yet purposiveness does not describe the natural living [*la finalité ne caractérise pas en proper le vivant naturel*] (164).

Let us pause a moment here. In the *Critique of Pure Reason*, Kant deems the existence of physical entities as being entirely necessary insofar as they are subject to the mechanistic order, that is, subject in their entirety to the purposiveness definitive of simple causal determinism. Moreover, this ordering of the physical world has no need of supplemental forms of process, has no need of extra elements, mechanisms or techniques in order to accomplish its task of bringing material forms to completion. Furthermore, as far as Kant is concerned, the concepts of organized being and living being are one and the same, coming together as one in the privileged figure of the organism. Hence, the set of necessary self-organized existent forms [*s'autoforme*], that is, of purposive material beings, therefore includes within itself at this stage the subset of all self-forming *living* beings [*s'autoforme*]. However, according to Malabou, mechanism and purposiveness, necessity and systematic order, does not and, what is more, cannot at this time account for the 'natural' living beings. Indeed, as we saw in the previous section, such an account must await the recognition by Kant of such entities as do not present themselves in fact as the common objects of experience or, indeed, as objects in any real sense. In the process of this recognition, however, the mechanism of 'self-forming' constitutive of all forms of being in the first *Critique* is thereafter denied to the common objects of our experience and is reserved instead for *un*apparent entities only. In other words, it is only the apparitions that turn out to be real.

In accordance with this move, Kant's focus shifts away from efficient causes and toward the perceived *ends* of systematic order. Of course, the concept of the 'end' already presupposes at least two different senses: namely, both *goal* and *completion*. As such, Kant is careful to define the ends of an organized totality, that is, its *purposiveness*, on the basis of three distinct logical principles of systematic unity—principles that, as Malabou pointedly remarks, remain consistent across all three *Critiques* and which find perhaps their clearest articulation in the appendix to the Transcendental Dialectic in the *Critique of Pure Reason* (A657-8/B685-6, 598). With clear reference to zoological classifications, these principles are as follows: one, a principle of sameness of kind in the manifold under higher genera; two, a principle of variety of what is same in kind under lower species; and three, a principle of the affinity of all concepts offering a continuous transition from every species to every other species. We can, writes Kant, further define these logical principles of sameness, variety and affinity, as 'the principles of the *homogeneity*, *specification* and *continuity* of forms' (*CPR*, 598).

It should be noted, however, that in his further gloss on these principles, Kant has recourse to both mathematical and topological frameworks in addition to that of the zoological. In fact, it is by way of mathematical nomenclature—and of what, following Georg Cantor, we now think of as set theory—that Kant most clearly and at length develops what he defines explicitly as three interlinked *logical*, rather than *biological*, principles. First, writes Kant, let us regard a concept as a single point on a plane from which the 'multiplicity of things' stretching all the way to the horizon can be represented and surveyed (*CPR*, 599). Moreover, within this horizon there must also be given a multiplicity of points (i.e., concepts) stretching to infinity and each of which in turn has 'its narrower field of view'—every set of things, in other words, contains further *sub*sets in accordance with the law of specification and, as such, look out over the logical horizon that 'consists only of smaller horizons' (599). In bringing together the many different sets and subsets of the manifold within a 'collective' or 'common horizon,' it then becomes possible to 'survey collectively from its middle point, which is the higher genus, until finally the highest genus [that] is the universal and true horizon' is attained, namely the set that comprehends all possible sets, subsets, subsets of subsets and so on. (599). Last, this staging of the seemingly endless ascendance and descendance of forms can give neither space nor time to 'points that have no domain,' that is, to the individual as a singular and thus autonomous form of being (599). In other words, the universal field of view presupposes the impossibility of original and primary points or sets in that this latter presupposes a necessary and absolute isolation from all other points, a separation that presumes an empty intervening space of demarcation that the principles of homogeneity and specification already render unavailable.

As such, continues Kant, the 'logical law of the *continuum specicrum* (*formarum logicarum*) . . . must therefore rest on pure transcendental and not empirical grounds. For in the latter case it would come later than the systems; but it really first produced what is systematic in the cognition of nature' (600).

Here, in what is ultimately an elicitation of teleological causality, Kant has no other recourse than to introduce temporality as the very condition of systematic unity. In other words, the transcendental *a priori* status of the law of the continuity of forms is in fact founded upon the empirical production and development of those same forms that it necessarily precedes as their prior condition. This point will prove crucial to what is to follow, for two reasons. First of all, the transcendental deduction of the principle of the continuity of forms thus inscribes a necessary time of purposiveness, that is, an *a priori* time of systematization, of organization. Moreover, in following Malabou we now recognize this fundamental time of purposiveness as the time of epigenesis. Second, and recalling the impossibility of autonomous forms of being, this introduction of teleological causality therefore orders all organized forms of being—that is to say, orders *all forms of being*. Here, it is important to situate this particular argument of Kant's within the broader context of the transcendental deduction. Kant, we recall, introduces the concept of biological epigenesis as illustrative or analogous of the single possible path available for the transcendental deduction to follow. This all changes, however, once epigenesis ceases to be read as biological analogy but rather as an *example* of the epigenetic mechanism constitutive of all forms of being.

So, just how is it that such a tiny shift in grammar from metaphor to example can occasion such dramatic change? Paragraph 27, as we know, has long served to incite arguments over the roles played, or not played, by preformation and transformation in the first *Critique*, arguments which ultimately give way to Malabou's extraordinary reading of epigenesis as an originary co-implication of *a priori* and *a posteriori*. Here, however, instead of defining purposiveness as a process of development analogous to the growth of living organisms as Malabou claims, the development of purposiveness or systematic unity is rather exemplified by the growth of living organisms. Rather than distinguishing living beings as exclusively self-forming entities, in other words, the teleological causality of epigenesis serves instead to constitute any and all metastable systems—including sets, genera, concepts, subsets and forms—of which the living organism is but one example among a seemingly infinite number of forms.

Returning to *Before Tomorrow*, Malabou argues instead that Kant 'completes' the inscription of the fundamental relation between system, purposiveness and organism by thereafter distinguishing between the whole as 'articulated (*articulatio*)' and that which is merely 'heaped together (*coacervatio*)' (*CPR*, 691; cit. Malabou, 164). Here, Kant is making a distinction based on the systematic relation between the parts and the whole they compose, that is, between growth as simple accumulation and growth as purposively arranged. In this way, Kant implicitly distinguishes between two discrete forms of causality—mechanistic or 'technical' aggregation on one side and teleological causality on the other. Hence, writes Kant:

> The systems seem to have been formed, like maggots, by a *generatio æquivoca*, from the mere confluence of aggregated concepts, garbled at first but complete in time, although they all had their schema, as the original germ, in the mere self-development of reason, and on that account are not merely each articulated for themselves in accordance with an idea but are rather all in turn purposively united with each other as members of a whole in a system of human cognition (*CPR*, A835/B863, 692).

Malabou cites the above passage in support of the claim that we 'therefore have proof of the close association between purposiveness and the mode of development of organic life' (165). However, while the close relation between purposiveness and organic development is undeniable, it does not necessarily follow that purposiveness is exclusive to the development of organic life as a result. As we know, the logical economy that closely associates purposiveness with organic lifeforms is not *bio*logical but rather *teleo*logical. Ultimately, it is teleological causality that orders the development of systematic unity in general, teleological causality that articulates the unity of the system as a whole, and it is teleological causality that, in our current historical moment as much as in Kant's, is manifest most clearly through—is exemplified by—the development of organic life. The development of organic systems, in other words, serves a profoundly heuristic purpose in disclosing the movement of teleological causality—i.e., of epigenesis—as fundamental not simply to the constitution of forms of life but to the constitution of form *as such*.

All that said, however, Malabou herself remains very clear on the fact that systematicity in the *Critique of Pure Reason* 'leaves no place for biology' (*Before Tomorrow*, 165). Citing Philippe Huneman, she explicitly states that, throughout the time of the first *Critique*, purposiveness 'is only a language to say what the natural sciences explain, and provide it with a heuristic; this language is immediately coextensive with the territory of physics' (165). From this perspective, continues Malabou, 'the systematic unity of cognition, as the end of reason, matches the necessity of the mechanism perfectly' (165). In attending more closely to these differing heuristic roles attributed to purposiveness, however, we are thus able to clearly locate the point of divergence between Malabou's account of epigenesis and my own. For Malabou, the language of purposiveness in the *Critique of Pure Reason* is the appropriation—or rather *mis*appropriation or metaxis—of a figure parachuted in from a very different discourse to serve as an aid to comprehension. In my account, the direction is in fact reversed insofar as organic purposiveness, rather than serving as a metaphorical figure, is in fact an empirical example of the teleological causal process that Kant discloses as fundamental to the development of all forms of being.

NECESSARY ENDS

As we have seen, the figure of epigenesis—and, by normative inference, that of life itself—constitutes a 'flagrant marker' of transcendental volatility insofar as it both holds and anticipates the place of a future that has yet to return. Following on from this, Malabou makes the crucial point that 'epigenesis is unthinkable without some contingency' (165). In this way, contingency is introduced within causal necessity even as contingency and life are placed in prior relation, insofar as both are excluded from the universal and necessary *a priori*.

In the first *Critique*, writes Malabou, organized beings 'immediately appear stateless in the natural order' (168). As we have seen, the development of systematic unity definitive of organized entities is manifest most clearly through the development of organic life, and so it follows that 'life' too most clearly 'presents' the question of 'the transgressive status of organization' (168). Contrary to Malabou's claim, however, this presentation of a state of statelessness is not exclusive to, and thus constitutive of, organic entities alone. In drawing such a line of segregation, Malabou erases the heuristic value of organic development as it relates to the movement of teleological causality and instead follows Kant in inscribing a simple ontological division between mechanical aggregates on one side and articulated organisms on the other. Here, Malabou redraws the traditional life–matter binary on the grounds of causal and thus temporal distinction: mechanist causality simply 'heaps' matter into non-purposive aggregate forms, whereas teleological causality organizes specific articulations of forms of life in accordance with an intermediary purposiveness ordered by the dynamic and creative process of epigenesis.

At this point, an odd kind of inversion seems to threaten the coherency of Kant's thought. In the first *Critique*, the systematic architectonic of pure reason is defined in opposition to the contingent accumulation characteristic of the aggregate. Similarly, organized forms of life are excluded from the *a priori* forms of reason on the basis of an epigenetic contingency that confounds mechanical necessity. Consequently, writes Malabou, reason is thereby forced 'to identify another nature for nature—purposeful nature—whose articulation it fails to understand' (168). In other words, the contingency that arises from being exposed to constitutive temporality necessarily situates all such beings outside of the limits put in place by the principle of reason. For Malabou, the concept of 'natural ends' proves critical insofar as

the bringing to light of the reflecting aspect of teleological judgment and, consequently, the regulative aspect of the concept of 'natural end' makes it possible to
recognize, without understanding, that is to say, paradoxically without leading
back to their cause, both the singularity and the regularity of the status of the
living being among appearances (*Before Tomorrow*, 168).

Of course, the recognition of this paradoxical status of the living being as
both regular and singular remains insufficient in isolation, and this leads Kant
in Paragraph 81 to attempt to somehow reconcile the irreconcilable regimes
of mechanical regularity and teleological singularity.

The mechanism of nature, writes Kant, is insufficient 'for conceiving of the
possibility of an organized being' and must therefore 'be subordinated to an
intentionally acting cause' (*CPJ*, 290). Moreover, he continues, the teleological ordering of such a being is also and 'equally inadequate for considering
and judging it as a product of nature unless the mechanism of the latter is
associated with the former, as if it were the tool of an intentionally acting
cause to whose ends nature is subordinated, even in its mechanical laws'
(290). This is the puzzle that Kant sets for himself in Paragraph 81: How are
we to comprehend the unification or *necessary* association of two entirely
different kinds of causality—that of nature in its 'universal lawfulness' on the
one hand and, on the other, that of an idea that limits said universal lawfulness 'to a particular form for which nature does not contain any ground at all'
(290)? Kant's answer is simple: we can't. Any possibility of such a union,
he argues, is necessarily unavailable insofar as 'it lies in the supersensible
substrate of nature,' about which we can determine nothing beyond its phenomenal façade (290).

All that said, writes Kant, we are nonetheless able to pose certain necessary principles with respect to the domain of natural beings. First of all, and
irrespective of whatever we might 'assume to belong to this nature and to be
a product of it,' all such beings must nonetheless remain subject to the universal governance of mechanical laws 'since without this kind of [determinist]
causality organized beings, as ends of nature, would not be natural products'
(290). And second, given that we must assume the function of an intimately
associated teleological principle of generation—an assumption, according to
Kant, that simply 'cannot but be the case'—then it necessarily follows that
'the cause of their internally purposive form can be grounded in either occasionalism or prestabilism' (291). Moreover, continues Kant, the system of
epigenesis contrasts with occasionalism and humanism in bringing along with
it 'the least possible appeal to the supernatural' insofar as it 'leaves everything
that follows from the first beginning to nature . . . [but] without, however,
determining anything about this first beginning' (292).

In the third *Critique*, as we know, Kant introduces the distinction between the phenomenal manifestation of common objects of experience and such phenomenal appearances—as exemplified by living organisms—that do not in fact manifest as objects at all. These latter, writes Malabou, 'are appearances which, while also subject to natural determinism, have their own form, a form that is irregular as a consequence of obeying only themselves' (*Before Tomorrow*, 169). But just what, exactly, are we to make of this?

Staying with Kant's privileged examples, we can say that the existent forms of both the beautiful and the living organism exceed the universal lawfulness of nature to which all things are necessarily subject, and do so insofar as their forms of being are also subject to purposive organization under sway of the causality of ends. In the first narrative, however, mechanism (as necessity) and purposiveness (as the tendency toward systemic order) function in perfect accord insofar as the physical world requires neither supplemental processes nor additional elements in order to bring material forms to completion. Moreover, the teleological causality of ends is initially introduced as definitive of the epigenetic system of pure reason. And so, is it even necessary in fact to introduce 'life' as an additional, supersensible element upon which to found a 'special,' exclusive teleology of organic beings? Despite the terminology, the concept of purposiveness has need of neither an intending subject nor an organic or biological substrate. As such, this raises any number of follow-up questions: What then of machine epigenesis? What of material forms and forms of life organized by differential gradients and energetic feedback loops? What of quantum systems and algorithmic engines?

Purposiveness, we recall, is autonomous and intermediary. It places the necessary and the contingent, the mechanistic and the teleological, into a self-forming relation structuring the specification of organized being. Certain forms of being, as Malabou argues, purposively manifest as singular organizations insofar as they obey the universal laws of nature at the same time that they obey only themselves—a spatiotemporal simultaneity of disparate causal regimes that, for Malabou, marks out the supersensible element of life along a fundamental division between organic and inorganic forms and between purposively organized organisms and contingent aggregations of matter. But why must this be so? Would it not be more reasonable to make the argument that, yes, singularly organized forms do indeed obey the universal laws of nature at the same time as obeying only themselves, but that they do so only on the condition that universal law dictates universally. In accordance with this principle, all forms of being must form themselves [*s'autoforme*] in and as the event of their being formed.

In response, Malabou argues that the answer to this lies with the illusory appearance of manifold natural forms. The mechanist productions of nature,

she writes, 'are specific inasmuch as they *in some sense appear* to catego-
rize themselves, *as if* they were self-sufficient, *somehow* their own judges,'
and it is precisely this phenomenal phantasm of a transcendent order that
'enable[s] the faculty of judgment to present as universal' at the same time as
'rendering thought useless through their independence' (169, italics added).
Paradoxically, it is therefore through the illusion of teleological causality
that the reconciliation of nature and freedom becomes possible and does so
primarily "because certain natural objects appear simultaneously naturally
free and necessarily autonomous. Their 'form' derives from their independence" (169). Kant's reasoning proceeds as follows: insofar as they appear
'self-formed [and] self-normed,' both beauty and life are thus forms of nature
that present reason with the 'enigma of factual rationality' (169). Malabou
sums this up beautifully: factual rationality, she writes, 'is the unique rationality in which meaning is given without us, in the chance alliance of nature
and freedom' (169). Life, simply put, demonstrates the profound indifference
of organized beings.

Indifference, continues Malabou, 'is the lining [*la doublure*] of meaning.
. . . That which is indifferent makes meaning all alone. This is just what life
gives to us to think. It makes meaning in order to stand for itself alone' (169,
translation modified).[11] With this, we arrive at perhaps the most important
moment of Malabou's critique. Let us briefly retrace our steps: first, insofar
as forms of life appear *as if* self-organizing as the result of a chance of nature
and freedom, such forms therefore manifest or manufacture a unique factual
rationality all their own. And second, insofar as forms of life *appear* to produce meaning for themselves alone in this way, the meaning or sense of such
forms can thus only be that of indifference. Forms of life, in other words,
can thus present only the sense of a profound withdrawal of sense; that is,
for a meaning to be 'given without us' it necessarily gives of itself only as
an enigmatic absence of meaning that is the indifference of factual rationality
as such.[12]

So the appearance of life 'gives to' or 'prompts' us (in Shread's translation)
to think the indifference of meaning alone, and what is more, it does so in
order to stand only for itself. This claim, however, raises a number of questions centred on the concepts of intentionality, autonomy and automaticity.
While the apparent organization of the living organism may well indeed serve
as the impetus behind the thinking of both purposiveness and indifference as
properties of epigenetic organization, it does not follow that the purpose of
this indifference of purpose is therefore to prompt 'us' to do or to think anything whatsoever. By definition, indifference is indifferent to everything, and
that includes its auto-formative drive toward the appearance of systematicity.
Similarly, as the indifference *of* meaning, an epigenetic organism can never
make meaning in order to *do* anything at all. As such, a given lifeform cannot

therefore make the indifference of its organization meaningful in order to, first of all, deny epigenetic causality, and thus systematicity and purposiveness, to all nonbiological forms of organization; and then in a second, complementary move, recuse itself from the mechanistic indifference of nature on the basis of its exceptional access to this same teleological causality.

AGGREGATION AND ARTICULATION

Purposiveness, writes Malabou, "appears precisely as the 'meaning of the fortuitous existence of meaning'" (*Before Tomorrow*, 170).[13] In concluding Paragraph 81 of the *Critique of the Power of Judgment*, Kant attempts to organize or systematize this introduction of errant contingency at the heart of matter itself. To this end, he calls upon the contemporary work of anatomist Johann Friedrich Blumenbach as offering further proof of a necessary organization–aggregation distinction. However, whereas life was previously seen to emerge from outside of the mechanistic realm of nature in and as the form of a newly figural and transformative element, Kant now follows Blumenbach in declaring that 'natural mechanism' still has a role to play in all of this, albeit a role he describes as 'indeterminable but at the same time also unmistakable,' insofar as it is subject to the 'inscrutable principle of an original organization' (*CPJ*, 292). As with the supersensible element of life, however, this principle of originary order too remains largely without content and, well, inscrutable. Nonetheless, we are able to discern two distinct points. First, mechanist causality (necessity) not only performs a definite and distinctive function within the larger movement of teleological causality (contingency), but this functioning is itself *in*determinable and thus not subject to mechanist causality. And second, this role or function is somehow 'left' to natural mechanism 'on account of which he [Blumenbach] calls the faculty in the matter in an organized body (in distinction from the merely mechanical formative *power* [Bildungs*kraft*] that is present in all matter) a formative *drive* [Bildungs*trieb*] (standing, as it were, under the guidance and direction of that former principle)' (292–293). Mechanist nature, in other words, functions in a contingent manner in response to a formative drive or faculty—be that an ability or a facility—appended to base matter by the very fact of its originary organization and in explicit contrast to the formative power exhibited by mechanical aggregations of matter. At this point, and regardless of whether this undetermined yet determinist natural response to the formative is itself necessary or contingent, it is clear that Kant's argument is at risk of becoming enmeshed within the circularity of its own reasoning.

It is perhaps fitting, therefore, that we should now find ourselves returned once again to a distinction founded upon the systematic relation between the parts and the whole they compose, that is, between an originary formative drive that tends toward a self-forming articulation of the whole and a formative power according to which matter is merely 'heaped together' in the absence of any purposive organization. We recall too that, in making this distinction, Kant is further distinguishing between two discrete forms of causality—situating mechanistic aggregation on one side of the line and teleological articulation on the other—an assumed dichotomy that, according to Malabou, thereafter renders it 'impossible to separate epigenetic temporality from the biological process it refers to, from organic growth, from the future of the living being' (*Before Tomorrow*, 176).

So just what are we to make of this formative impasse, of this face-off between drive and power that would seem to concern nothing less than the meaning of life itself? To answer this, we must first consider the standing and the sway of *germs*. A germ is, above all else, a circulatory of formative matter: germs transfer and transpose, defer and deliquesce, develop and evolve; they invade and exclude, synergize and parasitize; they mutate and lay siege, organizing contact and combat, both inceptions and endings. A germ, by definition, is a process over time. And germs, writes Malabou, 'are the necessary preliminaries for self-organization, not the outlines of preformed living beings' (93). Hence, and in contrast to the genetic relation of transcendent origin, the epigenetic relation is *necessarily* preliminary insofar as its 'preordained' or germinal circularity is formed instead by 'relations of mutuality and reciprocity between the parts' (93). Hence,

> what is at stake in the theory of epigenesis is the idea of a 'force capable of prefiguring the structural and functional organization to be realized, a force that incarnates a sort of immanent plan and that actualizes it by adapting to external and internal circumstances that affect organic development.'[14] Thus there is no hiatus between plan and epigenesis. Here again, the synthesis of the two is organization (94).

In establishing a difference between preformation and preordination, Malabou thus situates and at once sets the boundaries of the epigenetic playing field. Drawing further on the work of François Duchesneau, she argues here that epigenetic force comprises both the structural or teleological formative drive (*Bildungstrieb*) and the functional or mechanistic formative power (*Bildungskraft*), thus enabling the realization over time of an immanent plan subject to all manner of potential contextual contingencies. Thus, the emergent forms of epigenetically organized beings are *necessarily contingent* and thus nonlinear, that is, undetermined, but are at the same time profoundly constrained by the situating context of their emergence, which is to say, they remain *constrained by the very same fact of their contingency*. In conjunction with the preliminary nature of germs, in other words, the machinery and machinations of epigenetic processes are profoundly rooted in the earthy matter of the world and buffered throughout by the empirical vagaries of space and time so as to ultimately give rise to forms of being that are profoundly unpredictable.

It is at this point, however, that Malabou perhaps follows Kant one step too far in thereafter taking this necessary co-incidence of formative power and formative drive to be the marker of life's supersensible element as well as the manifestation of its proper ontological power. Immediately prior to this, however, she makes the crucial point that while the constitutive contingency of the epigenetic mechanism does indeed set a limit on the variety of individual forms available for self-organization at any one moment, this does not therefore 'represent an essential limit to the formative drive; rather it appears as its condition of possibility' (93). We have already addressed the reasons why this must be so in the previous paragraph, and so instead here I want to examine its transitional function within Malabou's argument as a whole. To this end, it is helpful to cite the previous passage in full:

> The limiting of types of individuals capable of self-organizing thus does not represent an essential limit to the formative drive; rather it appears as its condition of possibility. *It is the idea of a living being that would not self-organize that is excluded by the structure of 'generic preformation.'* Any type of vital unity other than the organic unit is inconceivable (*Before Tomorrow*, 93).

Most obvious at first glance is the language employed by Malabou here in referring to teleologically organized forms of being, describing them not as individual forms available for self-organization but rather as 'types of individuals capable of self-organizing.' This suggestion of an active capacity possessed only by certain privileged individuals again recalls to mind traditional machinations of metaphysical and humanist exclusion—a history that demands grave caution whenever it comes to laying exclusive claim to any power or force, as to do otherwise is to risk refashioning this force as yet another self-accredited capacity that serves only to reestablish lines of confinement and containment in the moment of their apparent erasure.

Immediately following this, however, Malabou seems rather to embrace this reactive refashioning. While appearing at first glance to reverse the dynamic of exclusion in recalling to the stage the Kantian structure of 'generic preformation'—a structure that she earlier defines as synonymous with epigenesis in describing it as 'the other name of a structural schema capable of integrating varieties, that is, a system' (93)—closer inspection reveals that

Malabou's adroit use of a double negative in fact serves to facilitate exclusive passage for the living organism. This becomes clear once we resolve the syntactical confusion. It is, writes Malabou, "the idea of a living being that would not self-organize that is excluded by the structure of 'generic preformation.'" While giving the impression that the structure of self-organization is solely a property of living organisms, all that Malabou is actually claiming here is that forms of life are structurally self-organizing and nothing more, thus inferring nothing whatsoever with respect to the structure of *non*living forms of being. Put more simply, Malabou's argument is as follows: epigenetic structure, as the ordering condition of living being, necessarily excludes from possibility the idea of a living being that would not be self-organized. Even now, however, this sentence still remains somewhat difficult to grasp, which is not in spite of its simplification but rather because of it. Once again, the threat of circular reasoning looms large—a threat that will never entirely depart given the nature of epigenetic causality—insofar as it can be reduced to the wholly redundant claim that epigenesis is the structural condition of life *and therefore* forms of life are constitutively structured by epigenesis. Moreover, if we focus on what Malabou refers to as the idea of a living being, things become even more confusing: Why must the epigenetic structuring of lifeforms necessarily exclude from possibility the idea of nonpurposive forms of life? This would seem especially problematic insofar as it was the idea of nonpurposive aggregate forms of being in the first *Critique* that originally served to make possible the thought of purposively organized forms of being.

There are two reasons for our dwelling on this particular sentence at some length. First of all, Malabou herself accords it significant emphasis insofar as she italicizes the entire sentence, a stylistic gesture of which she only rarely makes use. Second, it strategizes a secret exchange between before and after, *a priori* and *a posteriori*, in its assumption of exclusive passage from the epigenetic forms of being of the first sentence to the epigenetic forms of organic life in the third, which states, 'Any type of vital unity other than the organic unit is inconceivable.' There is, however, nothing here that would support such a conclusion. It simply does not follow from the statement that all organic forms of life without exception are purposively organized that its inverse is therefore also true; that is to say, it does *not* follow that all inorganic forms of nonlife without exception are therefore not purposively organized.

Nevertheless, with its ultimate disclosure of the inseparability of epigenetic temporality, organic growth and the future of the living being, *Before Tomorrow* is a work of profound philosophical significance. After Malabou, formative plasticity is itself reformed and thus transformed, describing anew the originary inextricability of epigenetic processes, purposive forms of organization and the ends of teleological causality. Once again, this argument is of fundamental importance. However, it is equally important not to unwittingly constrain the force and scope of this argument through the reinscription of baseless lines of exclusion. Put simply, there is no possible place from which a simple line of demarcation can be drawn that has not always already been transgressed, and it is the factuality of this *in*difference that ultimately releases the full power of Malabou's critical thesis.

THE SENSE OF PURPOSE

In the *Critique of the Power of Judgment*, Kant defines purposiveness as 'the lawfulness of the contingent' (274), a seemingly paradoxical definition that on its own provides sufficiency of reason. For Malabou, this lawfulness is displayed most clearly by purposive development at the cellular level. How, she asks, are we to explain

> the difference between a neuron and a hepatic cell . . . given that their starting point is one and the same, since all the cells of a single organism share an identical genetic heritage? Differentiated cellular development depends on the selective use of certain genes via activation and silencing. Epigenetic mechanisms structure the self-differentiation of the living being (*Before Tomorrow*, 79).

So insofar as cells are organized forms of both organic matter and biological material, are we therefore to conclude from this that every cell at every stage is an individual form or type of life? Can we say with certainty that, in the process of being discarded and thus without any modification other than its location in time and space, a given skin cell is in fact therefore a living or a nonliving form of being? Or is it that this very process of being discarded *is* the movement across spacetime from life to nonlife, from organized vitality to a mere heap of 'dead' matter, and if so, how do we determine the precise location of the line that divides these mutually exclusive states? We already know the answer: the line of demarcation has always already been transgressed. Being alive is necessarily to die, just as for an entity to be dead it must once have been living, and yet to be no longer living necessarily implies the possibility of passage between opposing states that are in fact founded upon the impossibility of passage between them. Matter, in short, cannot be dead, and as such living things cannot 'pass away' into a lifeless realm of organic matter, cannot transform themselves into mere aggregates of biological material.

That said, however, this is in no way suggestive of some form of animist extension, nor is it a call for less stringent entry criteria when determining future membership within the set of living beings. Rather, the supersensible ghost in the teleological machine is the metaphysical concept of life and the debilitating spectre of residual humanism. In its stead, there are only differing levels and magnitudes of formal systematization. As Malabou puts it so well:

> The epigenetic transformation of necessity and causality, starting from reason itself, reveals that contingency derives less from a possible modification of the laws of physics than from the existence of different levels of necessity or lawfulness in which physical necessity is but one dimension (*Before Tomorrow*, 173).

Recalling here what Kant calls opportunity and Carolyn Shread translates as the 'current valency' of the meeting point between before and tomorrow, we are now in a position to define complex systematic forms—of which the biological organism is but one example—as the making manifest of a quantitative capacity to combine with, or to displace, that which lies contingently outside through reciprocal processes of interference and transformation. Epigenesis 'takes place at the moving contact point between origin and the present state of affairs, until their difference disappears right into their contact—tensed origin, retrospective present, future in the making' (157). Stated as simply as possible, formal systems have neither time for nor need of supernatural donations of vitality in the opening of a reciprocal deferral to meaning that is in fact the very definition of purposiveness.

Chapter 4

Ends of Thought

Mad Times, Hyper-Chaos and Difference More Radical Than Différance

Summarizing our thesis thus far, it has been argued that the metaphysical concept of life is at the heart of the reductive and parasitic tendency that is a principal characteristic of the Anthropocene. Essential to its continued functioning, to be conferred or denied the status of a living being serves the normative function of excluding nonliving entities from the domain of ethical concern on the grounds that inanimate objects are ordered in their entirety by instrumental relations of simple cause and effect. By contrast, however, we have argued that the disorderly potential for unpredictable and irreversible transformation is a constitutive condition of all manifest forms of being. Clearly this raises some very serious questions about the legitimacy and potential risk of predicated futures founded upon the erroneous assumption that all beings that are deemed, by us, to lack the magical virtue of vitality, because of this will always behave in a manner that is wholly predictable, by us, on the basis of present being. Whereas the metaphysical concept of life serves to severely restrict entry to the operative enclosure of ethically accountable bodies, the prior inscription of potential disorder as a condition of being rather marks all manifest forms of being as always already demanding of ethical liability.

In the previous chapter it was further argued with Malabou that, in being constituted through the transmissible memory of changes correlated to formal competence, epigenetic processes thus mark in space the taking place of 'embryonic temporal contact' that is itself and all alone productive of meaning. This imbrication of automatism and plasticity thus discloses the machinery at work in the otherwise black-boxed production of an event. Put another way, the indeterminacy of machinic fallibility is the parasitical power of interruption both inscribed within automatism and constitutive of its particular intelligence. The parasite *in* the machine, in other words, *is* the machine.

Building upon these arguments, we turn now to the always thorny question of time 'itself' (as if such a thing were even possible) in the hope of accounting for the paradoxical temporality of the event as at once anachronous and discontinuous and yet simultaneously determined by context and historicity—as, in other words, both an accident *in* time and an accident *of* time. For Malabou, the grounding question of time necessarily crosses the strange causality of the accident understood as a destructive event of metamorphic power that emerges 'not as absence of form but as the form of its absence' (*The New Wounded*, 18). Such accidents, she argues, create literal forms of destruction through the destruction of form, *instantaneous* events that cut the thread of history while remaining beyond any possibility of hermeneutic recovery.

How might the form of the absence of form—the form of destructive plasticity in Malabou's account—emerge as the new figure of an event-machine at the horizon of our present possibilities? This question will prove crucial in what follows. The metamorphic power of destructive plasticity, writes Malabou, makes possible the creation of a past that never took place *and* that of an entirely new being to assume that past in an instantaneous transformation that takes place but not time. The form of absence must indeed resemble nothing, and not least the monster, insofar as it is a figure *without change* and at once *utterly unprecedented*. But how can such a thing *be* and, indeed, *be thought*? In what way or manner can a form of a being be absolutely without precedent *and yet* absolutely unchanged? What challenges might this bewildering temporality pose to the notion of metamorphosis itself? How might it affect our negotiations with the futural and the virtual? Will time ultimately be the undoing of the future? Or is it that, following Derrida, 'this thinking could belong only to the future—and even that it makes the future possible' ('Typewriter Ribbon,' 73)

?

POTENTIALITY, ACT AND THE ACT OF
POTENTIALITY AS POTENTIALITY

As always, we are not done quite yet with the time of Aristotle's *Physics*. Recalling the analysis of time undertaken in chapter 2, the privileging of the present is, from Parmenides to Husserl and beyond, 'what is self-evident itself, and no thought seems possible outside its element' (Derrida '*Ousia* and *Grammē*,' 34). Nonpresence, in other words, is always conceived as a modalization of presence, and the past and the future are always determined as past presents or as future presents. In seeking to challenge this seemingly self-evident restriction *of* thought and *for* thought, Derrida identifies a further binary pairing as fundamental to the ordering of the metaphysical system as a whole, adding *act–potentiality* to those of event–machine, living–nonliving, organic–inorganic, undeterminable–determined, and spontaneous–automated already logged.

At this point, it is likely helpful, maybe even necessary, to reiterate (as Derrida is called upon to do on countless occasions subsequent to the publication of '*Ousia* and *Grammē*' in 1968) that, abstruse and difficult it may be, but the price and the practice of deconstruction is ultimately that of a *systematic* reality check. As Derrida puts it, if we fail to engage critically and rigorously with the system of metaphysics *as* a system, 'the very necessary attention to differences, disruptions, mutations, leaps, restructurations, etc., becomes ensnarled in slogans, in dogmatic stupidity, in empiricist precipitation—or all of these at once; and in any event lets the very discourse it believes it is putting into question be dictated to itself *a tergo*' (39). Rigorous critical engagement with a conceptual system at the level of a system, in other words, remains always necessary in order to avoid the folly of unwitting reinstallation or replacement of the same at the same or at another level of being.

Returning now to Derrida's analysis of time in Aristotle's *Physics*, we recall from the previous chapter that the now is at once necessary *and* accidental; that is, on the one hand it is both constitutive of time *and* a number foreign to time and, on the other, it is both constitutive of time *and* an accidental part. Starting from this fundamental disjuncture, Derrida argues, it thus follows that the 'enigma of the now is dominated in the difference between act and potentiality, essence and accident, and the entire system of oppositions that follows from them' (61). This is further confirmed, he continues, in Paragraph 222a of the *Physics*, wherein Aristotle "reassembles the entire system of the various points of view one might have about the now . . . according to which 'the same things can be said in terms of potentiality and act'" (61–62). Crucially, however, this reductive and systemic reordering of the many into the one is only possible on the basis of a specific definition of *movement*, the ambiguity of which 'necessarily has a double consequence as concerns time' (62). Produced in the 'decisive' analysis of Book Three of the *Physics*, continues Derrida, this ultimate order and definition of movement that henceforth organizes the plurality and distribution of significations is henceforth that of the 'entelechy of that which, as such, exists potentially' (cit. 62). Hence, we return once more to the 'movedness that form is.'

At first glance, perhaps, this elevation to the status of supreme movement might seem to add little to the concept of *phusis*-being that composes a cornerstone of Aristotle's philosophy and which to this day retains its extraordinary power of organization and correlate exclusion in such fields as biology and bioengineering, for example, and in the definitive skin of autopoiesis. Coupled with *energeia* and in concert with *arkhe* and *kinesis*, as we have seen, the concept of *entelechy* here again describes the ordered movement of the unfolding of being *as* living being, which is to say, entelechy is the process of an *a priori* ordering *such that* it unfolds over time. In Book III of the *Physics*, however, not only does Aristotle claim that the movement definitive of *phusis*-being is in fact wholly reducible to the determining act of potentiality *as* undetermined potentiality—that is, of potentiality *as such*—he then further elevates this movement to supreme status as that which orders and organizes in their entirety the plurality and distribution of being and not being, thus bringing to the argument the particular decisiveness identified by Derrida.

THE STUBBORN OBSCURITY OF BEINGS

To better understand this decisive significance, it is necessary for us to restage the steps of Aristotle's argument in Paragraph 201 of the *Physics*. As we shall see, Aristotle begins by arguing that 'movement or change'—with the conjunctive here serving to mark these terms as interchangeable and thus indistinguishable and not as mutually exclusive alternatives—is the fundamental characteristic of all forms, types and ways of being. From there, he seeks the dissolution of metaphysical systems founded upon binary antonyms—principally the zero-sum game apparently proposed by Socrates—by situating the operation of fundamental movement-or-change as taking place along a continuum ranging asymptotically between polar limits of potentiality and fulfilment. Last, argues Aristotle, it follows from this that it is the way of every being to be plurally and multiply distributed insofar as *to be* is always already to be manifold ways of being *as* at once potential *and* fulfilled. In concluding, Aristotle then offers something vaguely akin to a summary definition of fundamental movement-or-change, or at least a 'suggested mode of definition, namely that it is a sort of actuality, or actuality of the kind described, hard to grasp, but not incapable of existing' (202a). Clearly, or rather *un*clearly, this definition of fundamental 'movement or change' does little to clarify Aristotle's argument, the double negative 'not incapable' serving only to muddy the waters further. That said, however, the resistant obscurity of Aristotle's definition is less an expository failing than it is symptomatic of the resistance and obscurity definitive of beings.

Considering the three steps making up this argument in more detail, Aristotle starts from the claim that there can be 'no such thing as motion over and above the things' (*Physics*, 200b33). There exists, in other words, no movement *as such*, but only ever things that move and things that are moved.

Most important, however, is that which for Aristotle composes the set of 'things,' which he further qualifies by arguing that movement only ever takes place 'with respect to substance or to quantity or to quality or to place that what changes changes' (200b34). Hence, movement does not 'belong' only to substantial forms of being commonly understood as independent, *factual* objects, but also to every possible *predicate* of all such factual beings, meaning that 'there are as many types of motion or change as there are of being' (201a7). In this way, 'substance' no longer takes precedence over quantity, quality and place, but becomes instead just another predicate with the potential to move and to be moved at once and in an infinite number of ways. As such, Aristotle's concept of movement-or-change dissolves in advance what will become in time the traditional philosophical distinction between substance and predicate.

Despite this, reiterates Aristotle, it is nonetheless impossible for us to abstract a transcendental concept of movement-or-change from out of the differing ways and forms of being (201a3). Rather, movement-or-change 'belongs' to all its subjects strictly insofar as they occupy a place 'between what is in fulfilment and what is potentially; thus *the fulfilment of what is potentially, as such, is motion*' (201a9–10, italics added). Hence, movement-or-change 'belongs' to each of its subjects in either of two ways: with substance as a tension between form and its privation; between contrary qualities such as white and black; between quantities as complete and incomplete; and in the case of locomotion between upwards and downwards or lighter and heavier.

Once again, this tension is definitive of all such subjects and, insofar as movement-or-change necessarily takes place in and over time, can thus never be resolved in and over time in favor of either pole—poles that ultimately prove to be indistinguishable: presuming at one end the paradoxical emergence into being of an eternal and thus timeless sovereign subject and, at the other, pure potential and therefore the eternal impossibility of factual being. One pole, in short, describes the impossibility of becoming and the other describes the impossibility of being. As the *a priori* impossibility of movement-or-change, any distinction between eternal presence and eternal absence dissolves in their timeless perfection. Movement-or-change, put simply, is the *time* of beings *as such*, of beings *as* beings.

This then leads us to the next step in Aristotle's argument, wherein he seeks to challenge the construction of philosophical systems founded upon mutually exclusive, mutually supportive binary pairings. Taking place along a continuum tending between the idealized absolutes of fulfilment and potentiality, he argues, the fulfilment of that which is moveable-or-changeable, *as* moveable-or-changeable, *is* movement-or-change. As Aristotle puts it, 'the fulfilment of what is alterable, as alterable, is alteration' (201a11). Similarly, the fulfilment of what is increasable and decreasable, as increasable and decreasable, *is* increase and decrease; the fulfilment of what can come to be and what can pass away, as that which can come to be and pass away, *is* coming to be and passing away; the fulfilment of what can be carried along, as that which can be carried along, *is* locomotion; the fulfilment of what is learnable, as learnable, *is* learning; and so on. While there are at least as many examples of the fulfilment of movement-or-change as there are verbs, the key point here for Aristotle is that all such examples—the limitless plurality and distribution of their significations—are, as noted by Derrida above, organized by the definition of movement-or-change as the entelechy or fulfilment of that which exists potentially as such, that is, of that which *is* potentiality *as* potentiality. In place of transcendental absolutes, there are only such things as tending toward what is in fulfilment and what is potentially, with 'nothing over and above them' (201a3).

From here, we move now to the final stage of Aristotle's thesis, in which he argues that the tending of any given thing toward one or other pole does *not* consequentially exclude that thing from tending simultaneously toward the opposite pole. Interestingly, Aristotle does try to restrict the scope of fundamental movement-or-change at this point, but in truth his argument already renders null and void any such restriction. In this way he writes that the same thing 'can be both potential and fulfilled, *not indeed at the same time or not in the same respect*, but e.g., potentially hot and actually cold' (201a19–20, italics added). However, not only is Aristotle explicitly *not* playing a zero-sum game with binary antonyms—not *either* potentiality *or* fulfilment—in fact, he is not even playing with *graded* antonyms despite his recourse to the exemplary graded antonym of hot–cold. If we take the relation of potentiality–fulfilment as a graded antonym, as Aristotle is suggesting, then their relation is ultimately reducible to one of simple arithmetic in accordance with which whatever is lost or gained on one side of the dash is necessarily balanced by an identical and opposite gain or loss on the other, with movement-or-change being the unchanging total sum shared across the two sides. While such formulas are a commonplace of classical physics—in dynamics, for example, the Hamiltonian expresses the sum total of kinetic and potential energies as a constant unchanged by movement-or-change that modifies only the proportional relation of kinetic to potential energies[1]—the difficulties with such simplification are readily apparent in the case of Aristotle's definition of movement-or-change as the entelechy of what is potentially as such.

First of all, if the relation of potentiality–fulfilment expresses a graded antonym in the same manner as that of the hot–cold relation, then *more*-fulfilment necessarily equates to *less*-potential and vice versa. As such, the relative *degree* of fulfilment contra potentiality is measurable and thus quantifiable, after which it becomes possible to map the movement-or-change over time of every quality, quantity, place or form either toward or away from a state of fulfilment. However, such either–or accounting of fulfilment and of its relative lack can never amount to anything other than baseless judgements of aesthetic value, reiterating once more the system error definitive of metaphysics in general. Never the play of opposites in a zero-sum game, fundamental movement-or-change is rather that of a tending always and at once toward what is in fulfilment *and* what is potentially as such, factual *and* potential—not being *or* not being but rather at once being *and* not being.

For Aristotle, we recall, a given thing *can* be both potential and fulfilled, only 'not indeed at the same time or not in the same respect' (201a19–20). It should be noted, however, that just as with fundamental 'movement *or* change,' here too the conjunctive marks the time of a thing and the 'respect' or 'way' of a thing as interchangeable and thus indistinguishable rather than as mutually exclusive alternates. Put another way, any given thing can be both potential and fulfilled, only not at the same time, *which is to say*, not in the same respect or way. Hence, to take Aristotle's example, a specific thing cannot, in a strict sense, be both *potentially* hot and *actually* hot at the same time, which is to say, it cannot be so in the same respect or way of 'being-hot.' Nonetheless, the same thing *can* be both potentially and actually hot, but only insofar as one and the same thing at one and the same time composes manifold ways or respects of being in its articulating of fundamental movement-or-change.

> It is the fulfilment of what is potential when it is already fulfilled and operates not as itself but as movable, that is movement. What I mean by 'as' is this: bronze is potentially a statue. But it is not the fulfilment of bronze as bronze which is movement. For to be bronze and to be a certain potentiality are not the same. If they were identical without qualification, i.e., in definition, the fulfilment of bronze as bronze would be movement. But they are not the same, as has been said. We can distinguish, then, between the two—just as color and visible are different—and clearly it is the fulfilment of what is potential as potential that is movement. It is evident that this is movement, and that movement occurs just when the fulfilment itself occurs, and neither before nor after. For each thing is capable of being at one time actual, at another not (*Physics*, III, 201a27–201b6; translation modified).

That which is potential is fulfilled when it operates *as* movable in relation to other things. The fulfilment of that which is potential is thus always already fulfilled, inasmuch as it *will have taken place* within the process of fundamental movement-or-change. Having reached this late stage, we are of course very familiar by now with the complexities of the future perfect tense. Being in fulfilment is, in other words, nothing more and nothing less than being in a relation of fundamental movement-or-change that is both constitutive condition and way of being of all of being. Bronze, therefore, is potentially a statue only insofar as it is movable, that is to say, only insofar as bronze *is movement* and thus always already in fulfilment, wherein to be in fulfilment is to have a contextually specific *capacity* 'to cause to move-or-change' and 'to be caused to move-or-change.' It is *as* moveable, that is, *as* being able-to-move, that bronze is indeed potentially a statue, but only insofar as the fulfilment of bronze *as* bronze is movement-or-change. For this reason, argues Aristotle, the fulfilment of bronze is never reducible to a certain potentiality, such as to this or that particular statue. Furthermore, once we recognize this distinction between fulfilment and potentiality, it thereafter becomes clear that it is the fulfilment of what *is* potential *as* potential that is fundamental movement-or-change. And finally, he continues, it follows thus that fundamental movement-or-change will have taken place only at the moment when fulfilment is made manifest as being movable. In fulfilment as a given actuality *and thus* as movable, in other words, each thing *is* already the potentiality to have been otherwise. Hence, in Aristotle's decisive analysis, fundamental movement-or-change is defined as the entelechy and the act of that which exists potentially as potentiality, the ambiguity of which entails conflicting consequences for the concept of time.

THE TIMES OF AMBIGUITY

In '*Ousia* and *Grammē*,' Derrida summarizes this contradiction as follows: *on the one hand*, he writes, 'time, as the number of movement, is on the side of non-Being, matter, potentiality, incompletion. . . . But, *on the other hand*, time is not non-Being, and non-Beings are not in time' (62). Consequent to the operation of fundamental movement-or-change, in other words, time is *both* not-being, insofar as it accords with the potentiality of that which is not yet being, *and* not-not-being, insofar as any given thing must tend toward actuality and, as such, must take place in time. More importantly, argues Derrida, such a contradiction is inevitable insofar as the 'concept of time, in all its aspects, belongs to metaphysics, and it names the domination of presence' (63). From top to bottom, in other words, the concept of time is founded upon an understanding of being as eternal presence in act, and as a consequence of which 'movement and time are neither (present) beings nor (absent) nonbeings' (62).

Crucial here is Derrida's point that the concept of time belongs to metaphysics *in all its aspects*, by which he means that the concept of time *cannot be thought otherwise* than on the grounds of the metaphysics of presence. We can, he writes, "only conclude that the entire system of metaphysical concepts, throughout its history, develops the so-called 'vulgarity' of the concept of time . . . , but also that an *other* concept of time cannot be opposed to it, since time in general belongs to metaphysical conceptuality" (63). This of course raises any number of important questions, not just within the ontological realm, but also as regards accountability, ethical responsibility and both the production of value and the exclusion from it. For Derrida, the impossibility of thinking time other than in its 'vulgar,' metaphysical form serves in the first instance as an explicit critique of Heidegger's destruction of ontology, insofar as the latter is 'ordered around one fundamental axis; that which separates the authentic from the inauthentic and, in the very last analysis, primordial from fallen temporality' (63).

Of course, it is not simply by chance that Derrida begins his critique of metaphysics with a deconstruction of Heidegger's existential analytic that in turn returns us once more to the crucible that is Aristotle's *Physics*. Rather, as the most radical formulation of temporality and, as such, both the most radical critique of metaphysics *and* its most sophisticated reformulation hitherto, Derrida's aim in taking Heidegger's *Destruktion* as his *first* target is ultimately to topple the entire historical structure of metaphysics in the West by demonstrating, over and over again going all the way back to ancient Greece, the absence of any such foundation to support what, in and at the end, is shown to be a brittle yet catastrophic conjuring trick. Even more important, however, is that in one and the same moment Derrida shuts down any possible recourse to an alternative conception of time, insofar as time can never be thought otherwise than in terms of the present. There can be, in other words, no authentic or primal order of time awaiting only the proper articulation, but only and always the 'vulgar' form of time that ultimately determines the history of metaphysics as a series of—occasionally innovative, often dogmatic but always already futile—attempts to escape the inescapable and deny the undeniable.

Following Derrida following Heidegger, the situation may perhaps seem hopeless, but this is not the lesson with which Derrida, like Nietzsche before him, leaves us. Rather, as Derrida never ceases to argue, to be *truly* hopeless, to be *truly* nihilistic, is to claim to have escaped the inescapable and to have refuted the undeniable. It is *this*, not any supposed vulgarity of time, which is the signature of metaphysics, and its reiteration marks at once the folly and the futility of idealist escape, no matter the banner—humanism, vitalism, etc.—under which it claims to fly. So what, if anything, might still be left to happen? Just what, that is to say, becomes only 'after' time? The answer is to be found in the very ambiguity of time that, as the operation of fundamental movement-or-change, is at once present and absent, at once not-being and not not-being. Hence, writes Derrida, the *other* gesture, 'the more difficult, more unheard-of, more questioning gesture, the one for which we are the least prepared, only permits itself to be sketched, announcing itself in certain calculated fissures of the metaphysical text' ('*Ousia* and *Grammē*,' 65). What follows here is an attempt to articulate this other gesture and, in so doing, to prepare, in some strange sense, for that which we always will have been the least prepared for.

Even here at the very beginning of his oeuvre, however, Derrida offers a number of complex yet nonetheless key provisos that continue to compel any such articulation, and which thus bear citing at length:

> [T]hat which gives us to think beyond the closure cannot be simply absent. Absent, either it would give us nothing to think or it still would be a negative mode of presence. *Therefore the sign of this excess must be absolutely excessive as concerns all possible presence-absence, all possible production or disappearance of beings in general, and yet, in some manner, it must still signify, in a manner unthinkable by metaphysics as such.* In order to exceed metaphysics it is necessary that a trace be inscribed within the text of metaphysics, a trace that continues to signal not in the direction of another presence, or another form of presence, but in the direction of an entirely other text. Such a trace cannot be thought *more metaphysico*. No philosopheme is prepared to master it. And it (is) that which must elude mastery. Only presence is mastered. The mode of inscription of such a trace in the text of metaphysics is so unthinkable that it must be described as an erasure of the trace itself. The trace is produced as its own erasure. And it belongs to the trace to erase itself, to elude that which might maintain it in presence. The trace is neither perceptible nor imperceptible (65, italics added).

If nothing else, this passage makes very clear the extraordinary—indeed, impassable—difficulties that face any attempt to locate and to describe precisely that which, as the production of its own erasure, can neither be located nor described as such. It is with this explicitly in mind, however, that in the remainder of this chapter I stage a comparative analysis of two seemingly very different texts published a decade apart, namely Derrida's 'Typewriter Ribbon: Limited Ink (2)' (1998) and Meillassoux's 'Time without Becoming' (2008).[2] As we shall see, both of these texts take as their subject the radical contingency of causality and its implications for the principle of reason, thus making it possible to situate what Derrida describes as the *nonfigural figure* within what Quentin Meillassoux provocatively identifies as *mad time*. Contrary to familiar claims about the hostile disparity of the two positions, by reading each text in the light of the other we find both Derrida and Meillassoux making the argument that any genuinely postmetaphysical philosophy can have recourse only to the structure of possibility itself. More importantly, in disclosing that thinking of the future is necessarily impossible *at* present and *in* the present, insofar as the machinery and machinations of reason fully obscure the machinery and machinations of the event, their articulation in common heralds the emergence of a new logicity as yet impossible.

THE TIMES AND LOGICS OF MADNESS REVISITED

Given the obvious complexity of the task still before us, however, it is necessary first of all to recap—admittedly in somewhat schematic fashion—the three major steps taken up to this point, in the hope of drawing together, as neatly and as clearly as possible, the various threads of this thesis thus far.

We begin, of course, with the singularly rapacious governance of the calculable, the rationale of which demands a deterministic and thus entirely predictable universe in order to function. In accordance with this seemingly all-powerful schema, perfection becomes synonymous with the absolute calculability of objects, and insofar as modern technology is perceived as coming closest to this engineered perfection, the calculation of reason thus comes to determine the essence of our technological age. On and to the side of this global accounting, however, there emerges a strange and paradoxical form of causality whose effective event marks the breakdown of precisely this perverse yet pervasive form of machine logic. In this way, the insanity of causality thus takes place in one of two distinct contemporary forms, either as a reactive thinking anchored in the past or as a transformative thinking of the future in the present. It is the latter, however, that constitutes the fundamental operation and motor of change and inscribes fallibility, that of being 'programmed not to be programmed,' as the prior condition of the machine itself. This point is crucial. As Malabou writes in *Morphing Intelligence*, "the imbrication of automatism and plasticity does not 'robotize' plasticity but rather inscribes within the machine a fallibility that alone makes it intelligent" (113–114). Machinic fallibility, in other words, describes a 'power of interruption that is, again, inscribed within automatism and that constitutes its intelligence' (118).

Second, the *a priori* nature of fallibility necessitates a complete overhaul of the traditional concept of nature as *phusis*. As we shall see, this transformation is at the centre of Derrida's deconstruction of the traditional event-machine binary in the opening pages of 'Typewriter Ribbon,' wherein he attempts to bring to light a profound homonymic disparity between old and new concepts of 'thought' that are at once identical *and* exclusive, always the same *and* radically otherwise. Here, it will be argued that we find this same fundamental movement of homonymic play at work in Heidegger's argument that nature names both that which can no longer be thought *and* that which remains impossible to think, both that which validates antecedence as it invalidates novelty *and* that which validates the future as it invalidates the past. Similarly, we find the same fundamental movement underpinning the process of *epigenesis* in Malabou's account as that which prepares for the space of origin, insofar as it brings together the old and the new—the archaic and the teleological—in an animating relation of mutual interference and transformation.

Epigenesis, in other words, describes a taking place in the mode of futural causality in accordance with which the old and the archaic interfere with the new and the futural as the new and the teleological interfere with the old and the ancient, the one always already transforming and being-transformed by the other in the process. Moreover, this protentive and retentive marking in space of the taking place of temporal contact is mapped directly onto the hermeneutic movement insofar as meaning, in Malabou's words, 'therefore lies in the way in which a principle becomes its result' (*Before Tomorrow*, 158). In moving from process to the figure that is its product, in other words, a figure only ever *achieves* its meaning from the coming into being of its own deferred future. Hence, insofar as it is neither a pure product from outside nor the revelation of a preformed meaning, this 'nonfigural' figure thus poses a profound challenge to the principle of reason as traditionally understood.

Last, all of this follows on from a single and seemingly simple question: namely, *just what, and how, is form as movedness*? The movedness of metaphysics in the West, as we know, arrives in the form of its own freedom *from* nature as conceptual containment and *into* nature as being *as such*. However, as we know from our discussion of Serres and Colebrook in the previous chapter, it is rather the case that *every* organized form of being, as a system of relations, is always already parasited and as such develops its own laws of survival, insofar as it develops *new* laws of enduring stations and paths by way of relations that take place both on, and to the side of, its host. Moreover, as will be addressed in more detail in the discussions of general cybernetic systems and thermodynamic dissipation in the next chapter, a given system produces its own laws in this manner always through the ceaseless expropriation and consumption of energies not its own and, in the process, produces a new and essentially unpredictable relation of guest to host. Finally, the process of production is necessarily black boxed, obscured by static that is both the noise of the system and the system itself. In this way, as we shall see here, parasitic production names the figural paradox that Meillassoux in 'Time without Becoming' identifies as the dense and real *peut-être*.

EVENT-MACHINES

On the subject of causal disorientation, Meillassoux defines metaphysics as an erroneous belief in the determinability of the future and the predictability of future events. A metaphysician, he writes, is a philosopher who 'believes it is possible to explain why things must be what they are, or why things must necessarily change, and perish, or why things must change as they do change' ('Time without Becoming,' 29). In explicit contrast to metaphysics, therefore, Meillassoux defines *facticity* as 'the absence of reason for any reality; in other words, the impossibility of providing an ultimate ground for the existence of any being' (21). As such, there can be no definite causes and physical laws that give rise to fully determined effects, insofar as 'we shall never find a ground for these laws and causes, except eventually other ungrounded causes and laws: there is no ultimate cause, nor ultimate law, that is to say, a cause or a law including the ground of its own existence' (21). We should pay particular attention to the last claim here, as it will later prove key to Meillassoux's argument more broadly construed. As we shall see, Meillassoux argues that it is reason itself that ultimately demonstrates its own absence, and as such 'the very idea of reason is subjected to a profound transformation, if it becomes a reason liberated from the principle of reason, or, more exactly, if it is a reason which liberates us from the principle of reason' (29). Moreover, he continues, the absence of reason consequently 'becomes the attribute of an absolute time capable of destroying or creating any determinate entity without any reason for its creation or destruction' (23).

Before addressing in detail the insanity of what Meillassoux calls both 'mad time' and 'hyper-chaos,' we turn now to Derrida's thinking on the same topic. In 'Typewriter Ribbon,' he argues that if we are to think together the hitherto incompatible concepts of the event and the machine within one and the same concept, then '*not only* (and I insist on *not only*) will one have produced a new logic, an unheard-of conceptual form,' but one will also "have changed the very essence and the very name of what we today call 'thought,' the 'concept,' and what we would like to mean by 'thinking thought,' 'thinking the thinkable,' or 'thinking the concept.' Perhaps another thinking is heralded here" (73–74). Here, Derrida too is suggesting that the very idea of reason be subject to a profound transformation. Moreover, he writes, such aporetic thinking of the event-machine 'would not block or paralyze, but on the contrary would condition any event of thought' (74). And again as with Meillassoux, Derrida likewise explicitly links the transformation of reason to the question of time, claiming that such thinking 'could belong only to the future—and even that it makes the future possible' (73). Finally, with respect to Meillassoux's concept of radical facticity, Derrida argues something very similar in a number of places throughout his oeuvre, most notably perhaps in 'This Strange Institution Called Literature' (1992), wherein he states that while there are indeed 'contextual elements of great stability,' these elements are nonetheless 'not natural, universal and immutable but fairly stable, and thus also destabilizable' (64).[3]

Thus far we have introduced three intersecting claims, which can be summarized as follows: first, there can be no immutable cause or law; second, that reason itself demonstrates its own absence and as such must subject itself to a profound transformation; and third, unreason is the attribute of absolute time, and the thinking of unreason makes the future possible.

For Derrida, as we have seen, the future is at once made possible *and* heralded by the deconstruction of the event–machine antinomy. Never event *or* machine, he argues, but rather always an event and *its* machine or *mēhkanē*: at once mechanical *and* strategic, theatrical *and* warring, automated *and* intentional. Inseparable, the event and its machine are always already an *event-machine*. That said, however, Derrida is quick to put in place a coda designed to arrest any reckless charge toward a naïve or overly simplistic conclusion. As yet, he writes, we do not even know if it will be possible for us to join in a single gesture 'the thinking of the event to the thinking of the machine. Will we be able to think, what is called thinking, at one and the same time, both what is happening (we call that an event) and the calculable programming of an automatic repetition (we call that a machine)?' (72). This is the task that Derrida puts before us, and he does so explicitly for reasons of the future: '[I]t would be necessary in the future (but there will be no future except on this condition) to think both the event and the machine as two compatible or even indissociable concepts' (72). As alluded to briefly in the introduction, it is thus *in* the future and *on behalf of* the future that the event-machine still remains to be thought. At present, however, *in* the present, thinking of the future is necessarily impossible, the machinery and machinations of the event forever prohibited from contact by the machinery and machinations of reason. Speaking of reason, we are of course referring to reason as defined by the Western metaphysical tradition, the very weight of which prevents any chance of our simply letting it go, in the same way that simply letting go of our faith in the laws of physics is impossible. In both scenarios all things would likely be lost to the void, perhaps even to hyper-chaos, the moment we did so.

The functioning of the event–machine antinomy depends upon the belief that when, where and however something happens, it does so as an event that can be neither calculated in advance nor reduced to repetition, but is rather the manifestation of an incalculable singularity. Moreover, it further presumes that in order to actually *be* an event, it must necessarily happen *to* some*one* and not to some*thing*. For an event to actually happen, in other words, it 'ought above all to happen to someone, to some living being who is thus is affected by it, consciously or unconsciously' (72). With this, we glimpse the empty foundation of metaphysical exclusivity insofar as the event–machine antinomy is shown here to depend for its legitimacy upon a second antinomy—in this case, living–nonliving—even as the living–nonliving antinomy in turn depends upon the event–machine antinomy for its legitimacy. In other words, and as Meillassoux reminds us above, there are no grounds for causes and laws except for other ungrounded causes and laws. It is also important to stress Derrida's final point here, which he subsequently glosses thus: "No event without experience (and this is basically what 'experience' means), without experience, conscious or unconscious, human or not, of what happens to the living" (72). For an event to happen, in other words, it must be experienced *as* an event and *as* it happens. What this means is that for something to happen *in fact*, it must in fact happen *to* someone *and for* someone, thus rendering both the event and the experience of that event as one and the same thing at one and the same time. The spectre of Bishop Berkeley's subjective idealism clearly looms large here, but the solipsism implied by such an account goes further than even Berkeley would likely admit. Indeed, we experience something very strange happening—and apparently we do so even if actually we do *not*, as we shall see—insofar as the event as an experience that must be lived can, however, also be experienced *un*consciously. It is not, in other words, required for the happening of an event that living beings be in any way cognizant or aware of its having taken place.

But what would it mean exactly to experience an event unconsciously? How might we describe or define an unconscious experience? Is this not a clear contradiction in terms? One could perhaps argue that one indeed 'experiences' an unconscious event insofar as one experiences its manifest affects. However, as we have seen, if we are to retain the purity of the event–machine distinction, then it must *also* be possible for a living entity to be unconsciously affected by an event while at the same time it is impossible for a nonliving—that is, nonsentient or nonconscious—entity to be similarly (unconsciously or nonconsciously) affected. Given that the concept of affect describes the response of a being to an event that impacts sensibly upon it, how are we then to distinguish an insensible *a*ffect from an insensible *e*ffect? All the while remembering that, insofar as an event and its affects can be unconscious, this immediately rules out any recourse to the shopworn notions of sovereignty, will, desire and intention.

Clearly the idea that living bodies, and only living bodies, are somehow able to instinctively—i.e., unconsciously—experience an insensible affect is manifestly without sense. Furthermore, it is the very possibility of sensibility, of *making* sense, which ultimately serves to ground the event–machine antinomy: an event must be perceived to happen, and as such a being must be sensibly affected—this is precisely why life is deemed an *a priori* condition of the event in the first place. In other words, the event–machine antinomy is founded upon an absolute yet absolutely untenable causal and temporal distinction between living events that produce novel affects and mechanical causes that reproduce determined effects—a schema according to which nothing has ever happened or will ever happen outside of life's purview. For us, however, the concept of an event-machine opens up a very different critical orientation. Stripped of their vital essence, what thus becomes of the concepts of intention and will once liberated from the constraints of living consciousness and willing subjectivity? What *happens*, in short? What event or events, for example, might thereafter befall inanimate desire or machinic will?

THE ABSOLUTIZATION AND ABSOLUTION OF FACTICITY

In order to better understand what Derrida describes as the 'nonfigural figure' of the event-machine, let us now turn our attention to Meillassoux's critique of correlationism under the governance of mad time. Correlationism, as defined by Meillassoux in *After Finitude: An Essay on the Necessity of Contingency* (2008), names a current of thought based upon 'the idea according to which we only ever have access to the correlation between thinking and being, and never to either term considered apart from the other. We will henceforth call *correlationism* any current of thought which maintains the unsurpassable character of the correlation so defined' (19).[4] Correlationism, in other words, assumes the primacy of the relation over the related terms. Meillassoux further clarifies this argument in 'Time without Becoming,' wherein he describes correlationism as 'the contemporary model of anti-realism' (10). Despite their many and diverse forms, he argues, all correlationisms nonetheless partake of the same 'more or less explicit decision: that there are no objects, no events, no laws, no beings which are not always already correlated with a point of view, with a subjective access' (9). Moreover, continues Meillassoux, correlationist thinking has proven dominant in post-Kantian philosophy, insofar as it presumes a vicious circle that ultimately renders self-defeating any and all claims to a competing realist position. As Meillassoux puts it:

> If you speak about something, the correlationist will say, you speak about something that is given to you, and posited by you. . . . The circle means that there is a vicious circle in any naive realism, a performative contradiction through which you refute what you say or think by your very act of saying it or thinking it (10).

It is perhaps curious to note here the introduction by Meillassoux of the notion of *performative contradiction* as that which can legitimately, or at least sufficiently, serve to disqualify the foundations of realism—after all, the radicalness of Meillassoux's position is centred upon his maintaining that 'an absolute, i.e., a reality absolutely separate from the subject, can be thought by the subject' (albeit under 'very special conditions') (12). As we shall see, however, the power invested here in performative contradiction will quickly be repurposed and turned against correlationist thinking in support of a realist position.

We recall that, for Meillassoux, facticity names the profound absence of reason for existence such that it allows for 'no ultimate cause, nor ultimate law, that is to say, a cause or a law including the ground of its own existence' (21). Here, Meillassoux is setting the limits of what can, and more importantly what cannot, be defined as necessary. For a cause or a law to constitute a necessary condition, he argues, it must therefore include its own ground within itself, that is, include the ground or condition of its own existence. This becomes clear once transposed into the language of set theory, with Meillassoux arguing that formal necessity requires a given set to include itself as a member of that set. For a cause to be necessary, in other words, the set of all possible effects must also include the cause itself, thus rendering the cause an effect of itself—a logical impossibility. It is important to understand this, as Meillassoux maintains that the absolutization of facticity constitutes 'the fundamental answer to any absolutization of the correlation' (22), going so far as to claim only absolute facticity is capable of 'defeating' the argument for the ontological priority of the correlation.

The logic at work here is reasonably straightforward: everything can be conceived of as contingent *except contingency itself*. 'Contingency, and only contingency,' writes Meillassoux, 'is absolutely necessary: facticity, and only facticity, is not factual, but eternal' (24). Here, then, the absolutization of facticity is synonymous with the absolutization of contingency understood as the *a priori* impossibility of causal determinism. Moreover, only absolute facticity is exempt from the trappings of time, because only absolute facticity is absolutely *necessary*; that is to say, only facticity includes its own ground within itself: facticity 'is not one more fact in the world' but is nonetheless itself absolutely without reason (24). The necessity of facticity, continues Meillassoux, 'is not facticity but rather the non-facticity of the facticity . . . the essence of facticity,' which he names the *'fatualite'* or, in English translation, the 'factiality' of facticity, and from which comes the principle that 'enounces the factiality' that he calls 'the principle of factiality' (24).

So how exactly does this absolutization of facticity defeat the binds of correlationism? The weight of Meillassoux's critique rests upon an assumed opposition of the *in-itself* and the *for-us*. This antinomy, he writes, constitutes 'the fundamental opposition in correlationism, even when this opposition is not stated or is denied' (23). Correlationism, that is to say, is founded upon the unfounded assumption that the for-us and the in-itself are ontologically distinct.[5] The argument offered by Meillassoux in support of his claim is as simple as it is powerful: if the thing in-itself and the thing for-us are one and the same thing, then the correlationist logic of *a priori* 'givenness' is indistinguishable from a realist, determinist or positivist position. In other words, if the thing in-itself *is* the thing for-us, then the correlation is always already redundant. Hence, the correlationist thesis necessarily *assumes* or *presumes* that the thing in-itself and the thing for-us are ontologically discrete. As Meillassoux puts it, '[T]his reasoning assumes that we enjoy positive access to an absolute possibility: the possibility that the in itself could be different from the for-us' (24). This brings us neatly to his second point, that in order for us to even *conceive* of an antithetical relation between the in-itself and the for-us in the first place, we have already committed to a further assumption that we can in fact *access* this absolute possibility. Once again, this second assumption is necessary if correlationism is to save itself from redundancy.

Indeed, it is undeniable that the correlationist position assumes Meillassoux's absolute possibility (and thus, as Derrida points out, can *only* be denied). Moreover, this presupposes that the in-itself and the for-us compose a binary antonymic relation insofar as the former must necessarily withdraw in the givenness of the latter. It is this, as Meillassoux rightly argues, which situates correlationism firmly within the metaphysical tradition. Building on this point, Meillassoux then turns his attention to the *condition* for the thinkability of this fundamental metaphysical opposition. On what basis, in other words, are we able to conceive of this antinomic relation in the first place? What *is*—rather than what is *assumed* to be—the prior condition that makes this antithesis, this absolute possibility, available to be thought? Meillassoux's answer is unequivocal:

> [T]his absolute possibility is grounded in turn upon the absolute facticity of the correlation. It is because I can conceive of the non-being of the correlation, that I can conceive the possibility of the in it-self being essentially different from the world correlated with human subjectivity (24).

So just what is the point being made here? Put simply, the thinkability of absolute possibility depends upon the thinkability of absolute facticity. In other words, it is only because we can conceive of everything being otherwise—everything, that is, except for facticity itself—that it becomes possible to conceive of the in-itself as other than that of the for-us. More exactly, writes Meillassoux, it is 'because I can conceive of the absolute facticity of everything, that I can be skeptical towards every other kind of absolute. . . . [and]

this is based upon a precise argument: I can't be skeptical towards the opera-tor for every skepticism' (24). As such, both the correlation and correlation-ist thinking are necessarily contingent, mere facts that, like everything else, exist with neither ground nor reason for being. For Meillassoux, everything can indeed be conceived as merely factual insofar as it depends on 'human tropism,' as humanist proponents of strong correlationism claim—everything, that is, except contingency itself, as we have seen. Absolute facticity, in other words, discloses the correlation itself as *un*necessary. That said, however, the question still remains of whether, simply by accepting what Meillassoux calls 'surcontingence' or 'super-contingency,' we thereafter find ourselves free of all correlational constraints, or if instead this is mere rhetorical tomfoolery, a formal loophole devoid of material content.

According to Meillassoux, it is the very factuality of the assumption of absolute possibility that ensnares correlationist reasoning within a performa-tive contradiction of its own. On this point, however, we should pay par-ticularly close attention to exactly what claim or claims are actually being made here: 'Consequently,' writes Meillassoux, 'it is possible to refute the correlationist refutation of realism—which is based upon the accusation of performative contradiction—as I discover a performative contradiction in the correlationist's reasoning' (24). It is important to note that these mirrored indictments in fact put to work *two* distinct claims—claims that bear directly upon our question about the potential or otherwise of Meillassoux's core concept. These conflated claims run as follows: *either* Meillassoux refutes the correlationist refutation of realism (thus breathing new life—so to speak—into a realist position long left for dead by the philosophical tradition), *or* he discloses a contradiction at the heart of the correlationist position, with which he aims to discredit correlationism on the very same basis as the refutation of realism before it (which not only leaves the refutation of realism intact but actually serves to further bolster the legitimacy of its argument).

The correlationist, we recall, dismisses realism on the basis of a performa-tive contradiction, insofar as whatever is said or thought has already been refuted in the very act of saying or thinking. In his turn, however, Meillassoux claims to successfully refute this refutation through the discovery of a second performative contradiction: namely, that the radical scepticism of modern philosophy is only made possible off the back of the becoming-thinkable of absolute facticity. This leaves us with three fundamental questions. First, how does this argument stand with respect to each of the conflated claims? Second, just what are the consequences both for correlationism and for realism? And third, what becomes of mad time and of becoming itself in all of this? The answers to all these questions concern the concept of thinkability—of the priority of thinkability refuting what is thought and of the priority of think-ability refuting what is assumed as ontologically prior. In this, Meillassoux does not simply reiterate the refutation of naïve realism only this time turned back against correlationism, but instead seeks to lay siege to the latter over the concepts of antecedence and time.

The principle of factiality, he writes, makes it possible to clearly refute correlationism, insofar as 'I can think an X independent of any thinking: and I know this, thanks to the correlationist himself and his fight against the absolute' (24). This latter phrase is particularly telling—the principle of factiality enounces the essence and necessity of facticity and, in so doing, refutes correlationism *on behalf of* or *at the behest of* correlationism. As such, the challenge posed by Meillassoux to the dominant orthodoxy of correlationism on the basis of its continuance of metaphysics echoes the earlier secularization of humanist philosophy, according to which reason itself ultimately demands the death of (the) God it was initially constructed to slavishly serve. As Meillassoux puts it, the 'principle of factiality unveils the ontological truth hidden beneath the radical skepticism of modern philosophy, to be is not to be a correlate, but to be a fact, to be is to be factual, and this is not a fact' (24). Factial speculation, he continues, 'is still a form of rationalism, but a paradoxical one: it is a rationalism which explains why things must be without reason, and how precisely they can be without reason' (29).

So where does this leave post-correlationist realism? As the absolute absence of causal reason, facticity is 'the effective ability for every determined entity, whether it is an event, a thing, or a law, to appear and disappear with no reason for its being or non-being' (23). And just what, asks Meillassoux, 'can we say about this absolute which is identified with facticity? What is facticity once it is considered as an absolute rather than as a limit? *The answer is time*' (25, italics added). First of all, facticity is the effective ability *for* every determined entity rather than *of* every determined entity; that is, it is not a property or possession of every entity but is instead that which *enables* each and every being to appear and disappear without reason. Hence, writes Meillassoux, 'facticity, and only facticity, is not factual, but eternal' (24). Second, entities are necessarily determined *by* facticity and, as such, are necessarily *in*determinable. Consequently, unreason 'becomes the attribute of an absolute time capable of destroying or creating any determinate entity without any reason for its creation or destruction' (24).

MAD TIMES, PETITIONING THE
DENSE AND REAL *PEUT-ÊTRE*

As an absolute, writes Meillassoux, facticity must be considered as time. However, he continues, this time is "a very special time, that I called in *After Finitude* 'hyper-chaos'" (25). Put simply, the time of facticity is the time of all times and none—a hyper-chaotic *meta*-time. The prefixes are important here: whereas chaos generally signifies disorder, randomness and confusion, *hyper*-chaos by contrast names a contingency that 'is so radical that even becoming, disorder, or randomness can be destroyed by it, and replaced by order, determinism, and fixity. Things are so contingent in Hyper-chaos, that time is able to destroy even the becoming of things' (25). The time of facticity, in other words, is such time as renders time itself contingent. The 'supercontingency' that defines absolute facticity is therefore not simply the inevitability of temporal disorder or the necessary increase of thermodynamic entropy but is rather a radical meta-contingency that is 'the equal contingency of order and disorder, of becoming and sempiternity' (25).

For Meillassoux, the radical contingency of 'mad time' constitutes the fundamental operator of being. There can be absolutely no reason why any entity should endure or persist in its being even for a moment—be that entity an occurrence, a thing, a law (whether physical, natural, sociopolitical or juridical), a manifestation, representation, perception, conception or apperception. All such entities, he continues, 'are just facts: you can't demonstrate their necessity' (26). Moreover, in order for us to accept the argument that entities are just facts and that facts are necessarily contingent, we 'should just believe reason' (26); that is to say, we need only keep faith with the principle of reason. While this will likely seem counterintuitive at first, Meillassoux's own reasoning on this point is impeccable. First of all, he clarifies the relation of temporal antecedence: 'Time is not governed by physical laws because it is the laws themselves which are governed by a mad time' (26). He then argues that this absolutization of facticity constitutes a 'rupture' with regard to what he describes as "both principal modalities of metaphysics: 'the metaphysics of substance' and 'the metaphysics of becoming'" (26). With this, we reach the central thrust of Meillassoux's attack on philosophical discourse more generally.

Like Derrida, we recall that Meillassoux too demands that the principle of reason be subjected to profound transformation. It is incumbent on reason, he writes, to explain just why it is that all things—and this includes becoming itself—can always become what they are not. It is up to reason, in other words, to 'reason about the absence of reason' and thus become 'a reason which liberates us from principle of reason' (29). Ultimately, the walls of reason that we have hitherto constructed around ourselves are in fact built upon yet one more groundless binary opposition between *being* (as substrate) and *becoming*, which Meillassoux diagnoses as 'the operator of every metaphysics' (26). As such, it is largely irrelevant on just which side of the dividing line any given thinker may or may not reside. For Meillassoux, metaphysics is defined solely on the basis of its belief in a 'determinate necessity,' and so it makes little difference if that necessity is ultimately attributed to either entities or processes. According to the metaphysical tradition, in other words, 'things must be what they are, or must become what they become because there is a reason for this' (26). That said, however, the metaphysics of becoming offers a further point of clarification when contrasted with Meillassoux's hyper-chaotic meta-time. Not only does metaphysical becoming believe in the necessity of becoming rather than of fixity, but it *also* believes in 'the necessity of such and such a becoming, rather than of others that are equally thinkable' (26). On the contrary, however,

> the notion of Hyper-Chaos is the idea of a time so completely liberated from metaphysical necessity that nothing constrains it: neither becoming, nor the substratum. This hyper-chaotic time is able to create and destroy even becoming, producing without reason fixity or movement, repetition or creation. That's why I think that ultimately the matter of philosophy is not being or becoming, representation or reality, but a very special possibility, which is not a formal possible, but a real and dense possible, which I call the '*peut-être,*' the 'may-be' (26–27).

This last point is crucial and brings us back to the question of whether the concept of absolute facticity enables an escape in fact from our correlational ties or simply makes use of a rhetorical blind. For Meillassoux, it is the very matter of philosophy—in all of its various senses—that is ultimately at stake. Rather than the staging of a formal possible in the manner of metaphysics, the absolutization of facticity precludes any possibility of taking refuge in the formal realm and turns instead to that which can or may be *in fact*.

Before picking up again with Derrida's 'non-figural figure' of the event-machine, it is important to note that Meillassoux too has recourse—and *necessary* recourse at that—to certain conditions of facticity that he calls 'figures.' If reason does indeed destroy reason and leave only facts, asks Meillassoux, how can we ever 'hope to ground the sciences with such a result?' (27). While only absolute facticity is necessary, he argues, this does not mean that being factual implies being just anything at all. Rather, to be factual 'is not given just to any sort of thing. Some things, if they existed, wouldn't obey the strict and necessary conditions for being a factual entity' (27). Once again, after all the talk of super-contingency and hyper-chaos, the sudden appeal here to certain 'strict and necessary' conditions for being will likely baffle some readers in the first instance. Nonetheless, the 'logicity' of Meillassoux's unreason remains sound. All determinate entities, he argues, only exist because they *can* exist—*peut-être*—and no more than that, and entities that do not strictly obey this condition are such things as can*not* exist, 'because if they existed, they would be necessary, and to be necessary, according to the principle of factiality, is impossible' (27). This becomes clear once we consider Meillassoux's exemplary first figure of a necessary modality deduced from the principle of factiality—that of noncontradiction. A figure, as Meillassoux understands it, refers to a necessary condition of absolute facticity, and noncontradiction names one such figure insofar as a contradictory reality 'would already be what it is not' and therefore unavailable for change (28). A contradictory entity, in other words, is 'perfectly necessary' and as such impossible in accordance with the principle of factiality. With this we reach a critical juncture in Meillassoux's analysis: 'If you want to think something necessary,' he writes, 'you have to think it as contradictory, without any alterity, with nothing outside the absolute that the absolute could become' (28).

With this 'first' figure of non-contradiction, Meillassoux thus rejoins the discourse of philosophical reason in the West: 'I maintain that contradiction is impossible—that's why I'm a rationalist' (29). In the same moment, however, reason itself is profoundly transformed: non-contradiction is impossible because it 'is the condition of a radical Chaos, that is, a Hyper-Chaos' (29). Here, Meillassoux is quick to reiterate the logical grounds for his claim, noting that the impossibility of a contradictory being does not mean that a contradictory being is therefore meaningless. On the contrary, he writes, we can in fact *rationally* demonstrate the impossibility of a contradictory entity on the basis of its condition as a necessary being, at which point he concludes with a brief but powerful summation of his argument:

> [I]t is because the metaphysical principle of reason is absolutely false, that the logical principle of non-contradiction is absolutely true. The perfect 'logicity' of everything is a strict condition of the absolute absence of reason for anything (29).

While we can now better understand the foundation upon which Meillassoux's speculative realism is built, this understanding also provides fertile new ground from which to address the 'super monster' that for Derrida constitutes a necessary condition of the future.

MONSTROSITIES OF ORGANICITY

So super-contingency and now a super monster are the braided figures of conditional facticity and nonfigural figures of event-machines that here produce the real and dense *peut-être*. Like Meillassoux, Derrida too is quick to insist on there being a 'new logic' at work in his thinking of the figure and, again like Meillassoux, that this logicity is at once the impossibility of causal determinism. As we have seen, the event–machine antinomy presumes a raft of further metaphysical pairings, most notably living–nonliving, organic–inorganic and spontaneity–automation. Taking the organic–inorganic opposition, for example, Derrida argues that these 'two commonly used words carry an obvious reference, either positive or negative, to the possibility of an internal principle that is proper and totalizing, to a total form of, precisely, organization' ('Typewriter Ribbon,' 73). This issue of totalizing *form* is key, with Derrida here referring to the traditional concept of form as proposed initially by Aristotle in order to make explicit the overt link between organicism and organization—terms which Derrida brings together in the general concept of *organicity*.

The internal principle governing the organization of form is not an aesthetic principle, but rather supports the value distinction dividing lively occurrences from lifeless mechanisms insofar as organicity—the auto-organization of the organic—is deemed to be lacking from so-called inorganic matter. Hence, to think with one and the same concept both the organicity of the inorganic and the inorganicity of the organic is to think of a new logical and conceptual form of being. Not by chance, the mirrored tropes of an internally organized yet entirely inorganic lifeform and an organic body formed by a will entirely external to itself populate our worst collective nightmares in any number of terrifying forms ranging from programmed automatons seeking to kill or enslave organic life to mind control experiments orchestrated by malevolent AIs, from clone armies and zombie hordes to saintly visions and demonic possessions. Such, then, is the *monstrousness* that comes with thinking both organicity and inorganicity in one and the same concept.

These are, however, simple everyday monstrosities, merely symptoms of a very different kind of monster, namely the monstrosity that is the radically new. As touched on previously, Derrida argues that any radically new figure emerging 'at the horizon of our present possibilities' can never 'resemble a monster' because 'resemblance and monstrosity are mutually exclusive' (73). Indeed, the truly monstrous—such as the new figure of an event-machine—would in fact 'no longer be even a figure. It would not resemble, it would resemble nothing' (73). Such a figure is, however, *of* the future insofar as its very novelty—that is, its essential *non*figurality—marks it as an event and, moreover, as 'the only and the first possible event, because impossible' (73). Here, it is clear that some careful unpacking is required if we are to better understand what sounds at first to be a contradictory claim.

First of all, the definitive condition of an event is its very impossibility, insofar as an event is the *emergence and convergence of the radically new set against the backdrop of our present possibilities*. This last point is crucial: an event names an unheard-of emergence into being of something that prior to its becoming-manifest is literally unthinkable. In other words, and no matter how fertile or febrile the imagination at work, anything whatsoever that can be conceived of as in any way possible is thus precluded from achieving the status of an event. Put simply, an event is impossible insofar as it is, by definition, that which cannot be possible and thus predictable in a given state of affairs. Second, insofar as an event is impossible, it cannot therefore resemble something already possible and as such can only resemble nothing. It cannot, in other words, be recognized as something previously recognized as possible, meaning it can only be conceived of as that which cannot be conceived—as, in other words, *a nonfigural figure and form of contemporary absence*. Hence, as a profoundly unpredictable irruption into being that lacks temporal and causal precedence, an event is a singularity insofar as it refers only to itself *as such*, thus resisting any and all attempts to make sense of it: 'An event does not come about unless its irruption interrupts the course of the possible and, as the impossible itself, surprises any foreseeability' (73).

For this reason, Derrida describes the impossible event that would be the unheard-of thinking of the post-metaphysical event-machine as both that which 'could belong only to the future' *and* that which 'makes the future possible' (73). And what is more, he writes, 'such a super-monster of eventness would be, this time, for the first time, also produced by the machine' (73). Here, Derrida raises the stakes significantly. He refers to a new thinking of the event-machine—thinking which is *a fortiori* impossible given our present possibilities—as a 'super-monster' insofar as, through a profoundly new conceptualization of the event-machine, the machinery *of* the event will for the first time be explicitly produced *by* the machine in what is, when considered against the backdrop of our present possibilities, a strangely paradoxical form of machinic reflexivity.

OF DIFFERENCE MORE RADICAL THAN *DIFFÉRANCE*

In contrast to a novel logical argument, this profoundly new logicity entails all too obvious—and ultimately self-defeating—difficulties of articulation and presentation. Following Derrida, and like Meillassoux after him, we have recourse only to the structure of possibility itself, that is, of the *peut-être*, of the real and dense *perhaps*. Perhaps, writes Derrida, 'another thinking is heralded here. Perhaps it is heralded without announcing itself, without horizon of expectation' (73). Just as is the case with Meillassoux, here too there is a great deal at play in Derrida's petitioning of the *peut-être*: the *perhaps* is the herald of another thinking not yet thought and the *perhaps* is the herald that can never be announced within the horizon of our present possibilities. Further compounding the unheard-of conceptual form that would—*peut-être*—come to think at once the impossibility of the event-machine and of machinic reflexivity, Derrida goes on to suggest that such thinking "will have changed the very essence and the very name of what we today call 'thought,' the 'concept'" (73). While somewhat laboured, Derrida's formulation here of the future perfect tense ('will have changed') is nonetheless crucial insofar as the future perfect offers the only possible tense when dealing with the fundamentally impossible *peut-être*. The future perfect, in other words, composes not only the *tense* of the event but also the *time* of the event. Perhaps, says Derrida, just perhaps, another thinking will have been heralded

> by means of this old word 'thought,' this homonym or paleonym that has sheltered for such a long time the name still to come of a thinking that has not yet thought what it must think, namely thought, namely, what is given to be thought with the name 'thought,' beyond knowledge, theory, philosophy, literature, the fine arts—and even technics (73–74).

As might be expected given the difficulties of articulation and presentation indicated previously, this sentence once again requires careful unpacking. First, in this invocation of a new thinking, Derrida in fact interweaves three distinct components: that of the not yet thought 'itself,' the *herald* of that which is to be thought, and the *name* of a new thinking that is still to come. Second, such new thinking will be (or rather will have been) heralded or announced *by means of* the old word 'thought'; that is to say, that which is not yet thought will only become possible by way of, or on the basis of, the *old* 'thought.' Third, the old word 'thought' is not only the condition and the means by which a new thinking will be (or will have been) heralded but, as a homonym or a paleonym, it has also long served to shelter the *name* still to come of a thinking not yet thought. In this, the notion of *shelter* further alludes to the pharmacological role played by the word 'thought,' with the latter not only hiding, obscuring and obstructing the new thinking that it ultimately will have heralded or announced but at the same time keeping thinking *safe*, sheltering it from external threat. As we have seen, this argument is already heralded in '*Ousia* and *Grammē*,' wherein Derrida writes that all of the names given to the trace 'belong as such to the text of metaphysics that *shelters* the trace' (66, italics added).

Staying with this sentence, the *form* of the shelter of 'thought,' according to Derrida, is as a homonym or a paleonym. This latter appears fairly straightforward—Derrida has already said of the word 'thought' that it is 'old,' and *paleonym* is defined by rhetoric as an old proper name no longer in common use. Things get more complicated, however, given its yoking into a partnership with the *homonym*. In rhetorical terms, a homonym signifies each of two or more words that share the same spelling but nonetheless have entirely different meanings and origins. Similarly in biology, a homonym refers to each of two or more entirely different organisms that share the same name. Before we consider these terms in relation, however, we must first consider the relation itself: homonym *or* paleonym. Here, this use of the conjunction *or* offers up two contradictory readings: first, as a relation of mutual exclusion according to which the old word 'thought' is deemed to be *either* a homonym *or* a paleonym, but never both, and second, as a relation of *synonymy* in which the conjunction links together alternative terms considered more or less equivalent. In order to follow Derrida here, it is important that we hold *both* of these modes of relation as functioning simultaneously in an aporetic—rather than antinomic—relation.

With the phrase 'homonym or paleonym,' Derrida in fact stages various facets or components of a thinking not yet thought, setting them swirling vertiginously back and forth between the two terms. First, 'thought' is described as an old word or name whose use and usefulness has disappeared. However, both despite and because of this redundancy, 'thought' is nonetheless the *means* by which a radically new thought will have been heralded. Indeed, as we know, the disused word 'thought' in fact provides shelter for the name still to come of what is not yet thought, thus keeping it safe for the future. Second, the word 'thought' names two or more fundamentally different things with entirely different meanings that have evolved by way of entirely discrete etymologies and genealogies. In summation, therefore, 'thought' and 'thought' in fact constitute two essentially discrete terms that share absolutely nothing in common other than the fact that *one* of the terms has long sheltered the other and despite this other having not yet come into being.

Unfortunately—perhaps—for the mental health of all concerned, the contortions of both grammar and logic do not end here. As a homonym in the biological sense, the word 'thought' is also a name attributed to two fundamentally different beasts. Of particular interest to us here, however, are questions concerning notions of validation, value and antecedence to which the biological conception of the homonym gives rise. Should an identical duplication of nomenclature occur within the biological realm, it is always the newer iteration that is deemed to be without validity and thus value. And this is an entirely reasonable move—without antecedence taking precedence, language ultimately ceases to function. Here, however, we have a *dis*used homonym ('thought') paired with a *non*existent homonym ('thought'). Despite lacking any utility, in this context the old 'thought' invalidates all other 'thought' still to come. In other words, our current conception of thought, despite its being both disused and without use, nonetheless produces as unfounded, illegal and without value that which it shelters and keeps safe for the future.

Derrida thus invokes profoundly disparate versions of 'thought' and of thought that are at once identical *and* exclusive, both new *and* old, always the same *and* radically otherwise. 'Thought,' in other words, names that which can no longer be thought *and* that which remains impossible to think, that which validates antecedence as it invalidates novelty *and* that which validates the future as it invalidates the past. Put as schematically as possible, everything that we now think of as 'thought' is necessarily excluded from radically new thinking and from any radical new 'thought,' and yet what we now think of as 'thought' is also that which obstructs, and in so doing shelters and protects, the possible impossibility of what it *must* think as what will have been. Finally, such thought takes us not only beyond the traditional disciplinary borderlines associated with the homonym 'thought,' but also beyond any borderlines separating life from technics and event from machine.

Moreover, if we take Derrida's oeuvre as a whole, it now becomes possible to identify a philosophical trajectory that, beginning three decades previously with homo*phones* and ending here with the thought of homo*nyms*, marks a significant shift in Derrida's thinking. Hence, in the seminal early text 'Différance' (1968), we find Derrida utilizing differences perceptible only in the *written* form in order to distinguish between the indistinguishable homophones '*différence*' and '*différance*.' As we have seen, however, by the time of 'Typewriter Ribbon,' the difference of *différance* has given ground to a far more radical distinction between '*thought*' and '*thought*' understood as the impossible condition of possibility itself, that is, of the *perhaps*, of the dense and real *peut-être*. It is with this homonymic flight from thought to thought that we begin to gain a sense of just how formal impossibility might emerge as a new, 'nonfigural' figure of an event-machine.

CONCLUSION: FROM METAPHYSICS TO THE MAD MACHINALITY OF HOMONYMIC FLIGHT

So what does this reading in common of lectures by Derrida and Meillassoux enable us to think, and why is this important? First and foremost, insofar as we are denied refuge in determinate necessity, we can no longer lay claim to a readily determinable future at any level of being. For both Derrida and Meillassoux, the principle of reason ultimately demonstrates its own necessary absence and in so doing liberates philosophy from the groundless ideologies constitutive of metaphysical thought. In its place, postmetaphysical speculation instead necessitates a paradoxical rationalism that, in being tasked with explaining *why* things *must* be without reason and *how* things *can* be without reason, is inextricably linked to the question of time. The implications of this causal insanity for ethical accounting and decision-making are as obvious as they are profound, insofar as to acknowledge as necessary the absence of reason for any given reality is at the same time to acknowledge as necessary the mutability of all causes, concepts and laws without exception.

Put simply, every determinable entity—which must necessarily include both time and becoming—carries with it an *a priori* effective capacity to appear and to disappear without reason. Radical contingency thus describes an arbitrary and extrinsic machinality constitutive of structural unpredictability and as such liberates the densely real from the ordered orderly timelessness that defines its deterministic quarantine.

Emerging at the horizon of present possibilities and lacking temporal, causal and formal precedence, by definition the matter of post-metaphysical philosophy cannot therefore resemble something already possible. Hence, it can therefore refer only to itself and its impossibility *as such*, which is to say to the structure of possibility itself. Here, Meillassoux and Derrida thus come together in arguing that philosophy, no longer able to avail itself of metaphysical and determinist deception, has recourse only to the structure of possibility itself and to the matter of the real and dense *peut-être*. Arguably, however, in addressing the homonymic flight from thought to thought, it is Derrida, rather than Meillassoux, who ultimately takes the matter of the real and dense *peut-être* the furthest. As the structuring work of being, the machinale of homonymic flight thus composes a difference more radical than *différance*, insofar as it is ontologically *prior to* the political machinations of performative queering that take place through the positive reappropriation of negatively charged concepts. Here, 'thought' and 'thought' constitute two essentially discrete terms that have nothing in common other than the fact that one of the terms has long sheltered the other, and this despite the other having not yet come into being.

To read Meillassoux with Derrida is to read the *peut-être* as both the fundamental operator of being and the condition of thinkability that itself both discloses and heralds—discloses as it heralds—another thinking as yet impossible against the horizon of present possibles. As the validation-invalidation of both the past and the future, the machinery and machinations of reason facilitate—perhaps—the barest glimpse of reality absolutely distinct from the organizing, interning and correlational subject. Such is the matter of philosophy after metaphysics.

Chapter 5

End Times

Physics and Ignorance

Having arrived so abruptly in end times, it is crucial to understand that, on its own, probability is insufficient to account for the inherent unpredictability of causal relations. Similarly, the introduction of concepts such as feedback and fluctuation into theoretical discourse is insufficient on its own to guarantee an escape from the timeless reversibility characteristic of the classical Newtonian universe. Indeed, as we shall see, the truth of this insufficiency can be seen most clearly in precisely those discourses one would likely imagine to be the least hospitable to such claims, namely quantum theory and thermodynamics. For this reason, I begin this chapter by considering differing ways in which the concepts of probability and feedback are being put to work in contemporary discourse, before then addressing in detail irreversibility, contingency and nonlinearity in the fields of cybernetics, thermodynamics and quantum theory by way of their respective fundamental concepts of system, dissipation and entanglement.

THE INVISIBLE REVOLT

Originally published in the second issue of *Tiqqun* in 2001, the anonymous author(s) of *The Cybernetic Hypothesis* set out to further facilitate what they describe as an *invisible revolt*, such revolt being necessarily invisible for the simple reason that 'it is unforeseeable in the eyes of the imperial system' (130).[1] With this provocation, Tiqqun brings together the various threads that will occupy us throughout this final chapter. Such revolt, it is argued, is unforeseeable to the imperial system because the apparatuses that compose the system can never *aggregate*, whereas fluctuations by contrast disrupt the smooth functioning of the system in favor of amplification, reverberation and superposition theoretically without limit.

On this point, Tiqqun defers to the notion of *fertile chaos* as proposed by Ilya Prigogine and Isabelle Stengers in reference to 'that moment when a system in equilibrium can totter' (128). In *Order Out of Chaos: Man's New Dialogue with Nature* (1984), Prigogine and Stengers locate this moment within a given system in the imminent possibility of bifurcation. Whereas deterministic relations dominate the functioning of a given system in the spaces *between* bifurcations, they write, upon reaching a bifurcation point any recourse to determinism inevitably breaks down insofar as the crossing of such a point is necessarily a stochastic process. Fluctuations describe the introduction of random elements within a given system, and it is in fact the type of fluctuation present in a system that will ultimately govern the choice of the branch the system will follow when faced with potential bifurcation.

Put simply, fluctuations are chance events that, occurring far from equilibrium and concurrently with a potential bifurcation point, make it impossible to predict with absolute certainty any individual trajectory into the future, with chemical chaos for Prigogine and Stengers offering a particularly good case in point. We cannot, in short, 'predict the details of temporal evolution' (*Order Out of Chaos*, 178). Moreover, and in contrast to the deterministic relations that hold sway otherwise than in proximity to bifurcation, the stochastic process determining which of the possible branches a system will follow is necessarily irreversible. These twin conditions—*a priori* unpredictability and ontic irreversibility—will prove fundamental in all that follows. Upon returning anew to our understanding of life and evolution, as Prigogine and Stengers put it, 'we are now in a better position to avoid the risks implied by any denunciation of reductionism' (176).

This brings us to the third fundamental condition definitive of fertile chaos. Irrespective of the particular bifurcating branch selected in this way, the decision is thereafter followed by the system as a whole. The stochastic process of selection, in other words, orders and organizes the entire system, while not itself a selection made by the system as a whole but only by a vanishingly small minority of elements from within that system. As Prigogine and Stengers write:

> A system far from equilibrium may be described as organized not because it realizes a plan alien to elementary activities, or transcending them, but, on the contrary, because the amplification of a microscopic fluctuation occurring at the 'right moment' resulted in favoring one reaction path over a number of other equally possible paths. (176)

In far from equilibrium conditions, in other words, the role played by individual elements takes precedence over that of the system as a whole and ultimately comes to dictate the behavior of the system as a whole. As such, self-organization processes at far-from-equilibrium conditions 'correspond to a delicate interplay between chance and necessity, between fluctuations and deterministic laws' (176).

As is characteristic of nonequilibrium situations in general, such contingent ordering processes raise a number of important questions in related fields of enquiry. In proximity to points of bifurcation, note Prigogine and Stengers, the incidence of fluctuations becomes "abnormally high and the law of large numbers is violated. This is to be expected, since the system may then 'choose' among various regimes" (180). More importantly, they continue, fluctuations 'can even reach the same order of magnitude as the mean macroscopic values' (180). At this point, it ceases to be possible to maintain a distinction between fluctuations at the microscopic level and mean values at the macroscopic level of the system. Furthermore, as will be addressed in detail by way of the Brusselator model below, the feedback processes required to bring about a chaotic—i.e., *non*linear—chemical reaction also entail the emergence of 'spooky' long-range correlations in that particles 'separated by macroscopic distances become linked. Local events have repercussions throughout the whole system' (180). The use of the adjective 'spooky' here serves explicitly to recall what for Einstein was the wholly unacceptable notion of *nonlocal entanglement* as proposed so elegantly by Bell's theorem. While this too must await the section on quantum theory to be addressed in detail, we can nonetheless recognize that the entanglement of noncontiguous particles presumes the sharing of a relational property and state that by definition exceeds the determinable properties and states of an individual system. The entangled sum, in short, is always greater than its localized parts. Insofar as it is individual, in other words, an individual system is necessarily without relation and thus entirely constrained by the principle of contiguity definitive of locality just as, conversely, the given state of an entangled system is therefore indeterminate and thus indeterminable.

Regarding such 'spooky' nonlocal correlations, Prigogine and Stengers rightly stress the fact that they only 'appear at the precise point of transition from equilibrium to nonequilibrium. From this point of view the transition *resembles* a phase transition' (*Order Out of Chaos*, 180; italics added). While we shall consider the allied concept of *phase space* in its relation to technicity and ethics in the conclusion, it is important here that we do not mistake this precise moment of irreversible transition from equilibrium to nonequilibrium for the reversible phase transitions of matter between solid, liquid or gaseous states, as the mobilizing behaviour of particles is very different in each case. In contrast to the global character of phase transitions, the transition from equilibrium to nonequilibrium follows from the increased *amplitudes* of nonlocal correlations. While initially small, the aggregation of such amplitudes rapidly increases with distance from equilibrium to the point of becoming potentially infinite at the bifurcation points. Hence, write Prigogine and Stengers, even before 'the macroscopic bifurcation, the system is organized through these long-range correlations' (180). It is, however, not only that nonequilibrium is therefore a source of order, as stressed by Prigogine and Stengers. More specifically, nonlocal relations constitute the *a priori* condition of novel emergence in being and do so because, in contrast to the apparatuses that compose the imperial system, they alone retain the potential for aggregation, amplification, reverberation and superposition that exceeds the determinable properties and states of an individual system. 'Spooky' action at a distance, as expressed initially by Bell's theorem, is not therefore just some typically atypical quirk of the quantum universe lacking any purchase in the macroscopic world. Rather, it is at once the condition of the new and the refutation of reversibility.

To help further clarify this situation, Prigogine and Stengers introduce the concept of *coherence*. At equilibrium, they write, 'molecules behave as essentially independent entities; they ignore one another' like sleepwalkers oblivious to their surroundings (180). The transition to nonequilibrium causes these monadic entities to 'awaken' and come together in a form of coherence entirely alien to equilibrium. Moreover, feedback processes are critical to coherence at nonequilibrium insofar as the activity of matter

> is related to the nonequilibrium conditions that it itself may generate. Just as in macroscopic behavior, the laws of fluctuations and correlations are universal at equilibrium (when we find the Poisson type of distribution); they become highly specific depending on the type of nonlinearity involved when we cross the boundary between equilibrium and nonequilibrium. (181)

Put more simply, in equilibrium processes instabilities are the result of initial localized fluctuations that spread throughout the system and are possessed of the potential to bring about a change of macroscopic state. If heat is applied to water, for example, a localized temperature gradient is initially produced that is rebalanced by the sharing out of heat energy across the total volume of water, resulting in a mean temperature increase. If sufficient heat is applied over time, this mean temperature will eventually reach 100°C, triggering a phase transition from liquid to gas visible at the macroscopic level. By contrast, in nonequilibrium processes instabilities give rise to an opposite situation. Instead of being 'corrections in the average values, fluctuations now modify those averages. This is a new situation' (178). Rather than being resolved through dissolution within the system as a whole, in other words, at nonequilibrium it is instead the fluctuation that comes to determine the global outcome.

In *From Being to Becoming: Time and Complexity in the Physical Sciences* (1980), Prigogine describes this phenomenon as 'order through fluctuation' such as is characteristic of symmetry breaking—i.e., irreversible—dissipative structures (100–101). As we saw with nonlocal entanglement above, the concept of order through fluctuation has important parallels with probabilistic aspects of quantum theory that have yet to be fully explored. Most notably, while deposing at the quantum level the classical presumption that position and momentum must be simultaneously determinable, Heisenberg's uncertainty relations were nonetheless 'believed to be of no importance for the description of macroscopic objects such as living systems. But the role of fluctuations in nonequilibrium systems shows that this is not the case. Randomness remains essential on the macroscopic level as well' (Prigogine and Stengers, *Order Out of Chaos*, 178–179). Moreover, as will be addressed in more detail below, Prigogine and Stengers identify further parallels between nonequilibrium processes and the wave-particle duality definitive of Bohr's quantum postulate, most notably in relation to the coherent wave behaviour of far from equilibrium chemical systems, which display on the macroscopic level certain properties that were initially thought to exist only at the microscopic level of the quantum.

PROBABILITY: ORDER FROM DISORDER

With these correlations in mind, we are now better placed to ask what becomes of probability in the shift from one discourse to another and in so doing locate the key points of distinction and contention across the fields of cybernetics, thermodynamics and quantum theory. In accordance with classical mechanics, as we noted with Smolin in the introduction, the laws of physics are entirely deterministic and as such preclude the possibility of novel emergence in favour of simple 'rearrangements of elementary particles with unchanging properties by unchanging laws' (Unger and Smolin, *The Singular Universe*, 466). This, however, amounts to a serious and severe over-interpretation of the evidence based upon an erroneous assumption that *reliability* is somehow synonymous with *certainty*. Far from proving the existence of universal physical laws, the reliability of prediction demonstrates only that the *probability* of correctly predicting the future outcome of a given process increases in proportion to the number of successful iterations of a particular process all yielding the same outcome. If we are ever to escape from tyrannical illusions of certainty, then causality itself must be thought anew on the basis that, first, prior iterations of a given system or state offer only a statistical distribution of possible future outcomes in the and, second, insofar as entangled systems necessarily exceed the determinable properties and states of an individual system, any knowledge of past forms of entangled individuals is insufficient to determine their future forms with absolute certainty.

The central question to which the cyberneticians sought an answer, according to the authors of the *Tiqqun* article, was 'the metaphysical problem of establishing order starting from disorder' (*The Cybernetic Hypothesis*, 38). With this statement of temporal and causal origin—whether justified or otherwise—the concerns of cybernetics can clearly be seen to dovetail with our own. The force behind the new science of cybernetics, continues Tiqqun, was the crumbling of Newton's mechanistic physics in the face of 'the probability revolution' in the early part of the twentieth century that gave rise to a 'groping toward a historic compromise whereby laws could be redefined on the basis of chaos, and certainty on the basis of probability' (38). In the wake of the Macy Conferences on Cybernetics held annually between 1943 and 1954, Norbert Wiener, John von Neumann and Claude Shannon emerged as leading figures in the quest for a new theoretical paradigm that would apply just as well to machines as it does to human and nonhuman animals. The result of this 'breathtaking enterprise,' as N. Katherine Hayles writes in her seminal *How We Became Posthuman: Virtual Bodies in Cybernetics, Literature, and Informatics* (1999), 'was nothing less than a new way of looking at human beings. Henceforth, humans were to be seen primarily as information-processing entities who are essentially similar to intelligent machines' (7). Tiqqun describes this same enterprise as an attempt to construct a 'Second Empire of Reason' that in its turn is capable of mastering the 'new' uncertainty disclosed by the probability revolution. At its most fundamental, they write, 'is the desire for an order to be restored and, further, that it have the stability to endure' (*The Cybernetic Hypothesis*, 38). In this, the cybernetic phantasy recalls to being the First Empires of Descartes and Leibniz and, further, the dream of perpetual power as articulated in the first instance in the blueprint that is Plato's *Republic*.[2]

In light of this reactive drive for mastery over uncertainty, it thus comes as no surprise to find that cybernetic theory places the greatest stress on the role and concept of probability. In *The Human Use of Human Beings: Cybernetics and Society* (1950), Norbert Wiener defines our new probabilistic world as one in which statements concerning 'a specific, real universe as a whole' no longer hold, giving way to questions the answers to which instead depend upon multiples of similar universes. Thus, writes Wiener, 'chance has been admitted, not merely as a mathematical tool for physics, but as part of its warp and weft. This recognition of an element of incomplete determinism, almost an irrationality in the world, is in a certain way parallel to Freud's admission of a deep irrational component in human conduct and thought' (11). While this reference to the terrifying formless chaos of Freud's primeval id strikes an odd note given the broader discursive context, its inclusion is particularly telling as to the intense anxiety that drives the cybernetic project. Similarly, the difficulty Wiener has in accepting this new state of affairs is evident throughout: contingency is recognized not as fundamental and constitutive of relation as such, but only as an 'almost' irrational element symptomatic of the fact that, at least for the moment, determinism remains incomplete while at the same time begging the question of just what kind of being it is which Wiener deems 'almost an irrationality in the world.'

Describing the postwar period as one of political as well as intellectual confusion, Wiener then proposes a second, equally surprising analogy. Bringing physicist Josiah Gibbs together with Freud and contemporaneous proponents of probability theory, Wiener declares that by virtue of their shared recognition of 'a fundamental element of chance in the texture of the universe itself, these men [*sic*] are close to one another and close to the tradition of St. Augustine' (11). In the previous sentence, the suggestion of virtue in common is not itself by chance: 'For this random element,' writes Wiener, 'this organic incompleteness, is one which without too violent a figure of speech we may consider evil; the negative evil which St. Augustine characterizes as incompleteness, rather than the positive malicious evil of the Manichaeans' (11). While the characterization of contingency as an element of evil in the world has a long and storied theological history in the West, the distinction Wiener draws here between proper, positively malicious evil and that of a lesser, negative evil that he attributes, via an assumed kinship with St. Augustine, to the random element will prove decisive to the discourse of cybernetics going forward in tying together the desire for mastery over uncertainty, the claim to disinterested objectivity definitive of properly scientific discourse and a Christian moral crusade dedicated to mastering the evil disclosed to be hiding in the very fabric of the physical universe.

We will return to this distinction between the 'good' evil of St. Augustine and the 'bad' evil of the Manichaeans within the broader context of noise, cascades and the law of large numbers in the next part, but for now it is helpful to stay a little longer with the role and function of probability more generally. As mentioned above, central to the cybernetic project was an understanding of how it was possible for order to come from disorder and thus, of all the various kin to St. Augustine listed by Wiener, it is unsurprising that it is the theory of probability as proposed by Josiah Gibbs that he credits as being at the core of 'the new science of Cybernetics' (12). Gibbs's central innovation, he writes, was to consider 'the extent to which answers that we may give to questions about one set of worlds are probable among a larger set of worlds,' and further, that 'this probability tended naturally to increase as the universe grows older' (12). The measure of this probability, he continues, is called entropy. Here, Wiener is clearly basing his claim, along with its scientific legitimacy, on a version of the second law of thermodynamics. Insofar as the measure of entropy within a given system characteristically tends to increase, he writes, the system as a whole inevitably deteriorates and loses distinctiveness, moving 'from the least to the most probable state, from a state of organization and differentiation in which distinctions and forms exist, to a state of chaos and sameness' (12). There is nothing controversial about this interpretation and, given that the strange behaviour of systems transitioning to nonequilibrium had yet to be sufficiently articulated, no attempt is being made here to gloss over the complexity of entropic processes. Nonetheless, it is clear that the behaviour Wiener describes can occur only within a *closed* system at equilibrium, a problem that Wiener initially sidesteps by way of the assumption that the universe as a whole composes just such a closed system. While superficially sensible, however, there can be no possible grounds upon which such a claim could be based. Indeed, Wiener himself is doubtless aware of the problematic nature of this claim, as he further qualifies it almost immediately, stating that 'the universe as a whole, *if indeed there is a whole universe*, tends to run down' (12, italics added). This coda, it should be noted, pulls the ground out from beneath the entire cybernetic project. So why would Wiener single out Gibbs over the Augustinian Freud, for example, to provide the conceptual armature for cybernetics? Why choose entropy to provide the project with much-needed scientific legitimacy when, ultimately, it proves the opposite?

In order to better understand the reasons behind this decision, we need to consider a further direct lineage that Wiener claims for cybernetics in the name of reason itself—that is, in the name of Gottfried Wilhelm Leibniz, a third patrimony that clearly recalls Tiqqun's characterization of cybernetics as an attempt to construct a 'Second Empire of Reason' capable of subjugating the latest and greatest challenge posed to certainty thus far in the form of the twentieth-century 'probability revolution.' Dominated by ideas of communication and keenly interested in machine computation and automata, writes Wiener, Leibniz 'is, in more than one way, the intellectual ancestor' of the cybernetic project (19). Despite this claim for reasoned patronage, however, Wiener is nonetheless quick to distance cybernetics from the monadology proposed by Leibniz. Of particular interest here are the reasons that Wiener gives for this explicit distancing. The living organism, he writes, 'is not like the clockwork monad of Leibnitz with its pre-established harmony with the universe, but actually seeks a new equilibrium with the universe and its future contingencies' (48). Again, the influence of thermodynamics and quantum physics is clear in the terms used by Wiener, who ascribes both irreversibility and unpredictability to living organisms as systems whose 'present is unlike its past and its future unlike its present. In the living organism as in the universe itself, exact repetition is absolutely impossible. . . . Learning, like more primitive forms of feedback, is a process which reads differently forward and backward in time' (48). Key to Wiener's argument here are the related concepts of *repetition* and *feedback*. First of all, reiteration can never be truly repetition because reiteration by definition requires temporal dislocation and thus a contextual difference in the act of its positing: a second iteration presumes temporal succession and, as such, takes place in a new context that contains the history of any and all of its prior iterations. Simply put, a subsequent iteration cannot be its own originary iteration. Second, feedback—and this includes even its 'more primitive' forms—describes the process by which the movement of time's arrow is rendered unidirectional and thus irreversible. Simply put once more, a subsequent iteration cannot be its own originary iteration.

These two claims are not in dispute here, so why should their inclusion be of particular interest for us? The answer concerns the gradual depletion of their critical power over the course of Wiener's account, leading to an enfeeblement that ultimately places Wiener's cybernetics in far greater proximity to Leibniz's monadology than he would obviously like to admit. Things start out simply enough, with Wiener defining feedback as the function by which mechanisms 'control the mechanical tendency toward disorganization, in other words, to produce a temporary and local reversal of the normal direction of entropy' (24–25). Moreover, he notes, such negentropic reversals depend in reciprocal manner upon relations of negentropic feedback composing the cybernetic system as a whole: 'If the feedback system is itself controlled—if, in other words, its own entropic tendencies are checked by still other controlling mechanisms—and kept within limits sufficiently stringent, this will not occur, and the existence of the feedback will increase the stability of performance' (25). For Wiener, as we shall see, this introduction of checks and balances by mechanisms of control at the level of the system as a whole serves both as a definition of technological progress and as the distinction that renders the *apparent* unpredictability characteristic of 'special machines' merely analogous to the actual potentiality that is the exclusive property of living organisms.

As the reader will likely recognize, much of the heavy lifting of Wiener's analogic machinery falls to what, following Humberto Maturana and Francisco Varela in particular, will become known as *autopoiesis*.[3] Writing in the late 1940s, Wiener begins by suggesting the existence of certain, 'special' machines that can be of great service in bettering our understanding of neuropathology. What makes these particular machines special, he writes, is not their enduring correction or perfection of function in contrast to faulty neural assemblages, but rather the similarity of certain 'defects in performance' to those that tend to befall the specifically human mechanism (*The Human Use of Human Beings*, 26). Looking beyond the apparent conflation of the neural with the mechanical for a moment, the notion of the defect is introduced here to describe both a *lack* of perfection and an *incompleteness* of form—a description which, as we have seen, is also for Wiener that of 'good' Augustinian evil. What makes 'some of the newer communication machines' into special, Augustinian machines, writes Wiener, is that they operate in a manner that is 'precisely parallel in their analogous attempts to control entropy through feedback' with that of 'the physical functioning of the living individual' (26). With this, the apparent identity of neural function and the functioning of a small number of privileged new machines is abruptly recast as an *analogical* relation, a distinction that Wiener then further stresses by describing their analogous processes as being *precisely* parallel, which by definition means there can be neither overlap nor continuum, no possible points of contact, breech or symbiosis but only tracks in parallel that define and delineate the abyss between them.

From here, Wiener then establishes a further distinction between living mechanisms and dead machines: in both cases, he writes, the capacity to control entropy is solely a consequence of 'the internal transforming powers of the apparatus, whether it be alive or dead' (26). With this, the defects of function deemed definitive of 'special' nonliving mechanisms now become mere simulacra, analogous to living systems but denied any possibility of life. Furthermore, this vitalist distinction makes it possible for Wiener to thereafter *appear* to be still including the universe of physical systems within his remit, while in the very same moment returning the unprivileged entirety of the evil Augustinian universe to the darkness of determinism. Constitutive of the life of cybernetic systems, in other words, is an autonomous organization through which identity is maintained at the origin of variation by way of relations of reiterative feedback coupled with an *a priori* openness to potentially trans-formative relations with systems external to its self. While this does indeed conform to Maturana and Varela's definition of autopoiesis, it also falls prey to their general critique of such theories that ultimately 'encompass present ideas under comprehensive theories governed by organizing notions, like cybernetic principles, that require from the biologists the very understanding that they want to provide' (*Autopoiesis and Cognition: The Realization of the Living*, 74). Once again, when it comes to *phusis*, lifeforce, *élan vitale* and even that special machinery of cybernetic lifeforms, we need only presuppose its existence in order to be able thereafter to see it. Once again, reason suc-ceeds in finding only what it has itself hidden.

Having returned to life its special privilege, Wiener thereafter reiterates this privilege many times in the guise of its refutation. There is no reason, he writes, why machines may not '*resemble*' human beings, but when 'I compare the living organism with such a machine, *I do not for a moment mean* that the specific physical, chemical, and spiritual processes of *life as we ordinarily know it are the same as those of life-imitating machines'* (*The Human Use of Human Beings*, 32; italics added). As we shall see in a later section, Wiener does not stop there, however, but in fact goes on to deny even to living systems the potential emergence of nonlinear forms by putting in the place of fundamental contingency the ability of lifeforms to make purposive decisions 'on the basis of decisions they have made in the past' (33). Hence, while nonliving machines—be they special, dead or just, well, *machines*—may indeed *appear* on occasion to imitate properly *living* mechanisms, it is only that: mere appearance. That said, however, for Wiener such imitations of living autonomy, while misleading perhaps, are not therefore *nothing*. Rather, he writes, it is the existence of these local and temporary islands that 'enables some of us to assert the existence of progress' (36). In the realms of the technical and the mechanical, in other words, significant transformations make themselves known to us through their seeming imitation of 'proper' living systems.

In the end, the answer comes back to the possibility or otherwise of regaining order from out of disorder—comes back, in other words, to anxiety in the face of the indeterminable and of the irreversible and undeniable loss of mastery. For Wiener, in short, cybernetics answers to a reluctance to cede the position of dominance in the face of indomitable uncertainty:

> In Gibbs' universe order is least probable, chaos most probable. But while the universe as a whole, if indeed there is a whole universe, tends to run down, there are local enclaves whose direction seems opposed to that of the universe at large and in which there is a limited and temporary tendency for organization to increase. Life finds its home in some of these enclaves. It is with this point of view at its core that the new science of Cybernetics began its development. (12)

The original impetus and subsequent driving force behind the 'new science' of cybernetics is here revealed as an attempt *not* to create a new theoretical paradigm with equal applicability to humans, other animals and technical systems, but rather to somehow regain control and thus mastery over probability itself—the undeniable, to paraphrase Derrida, being such that it can only ever be denied. Within cybernetics, the role of probability is therefore recast, by way of the physical sciences in the form of entropy, as further proof of life's *difference* from any and all technical systems rather than their sameness. In the process, *non*living systems are once again reduced to closed, monadic forms of being incapable of external relations and thus, as closed systems entirely at the mercy of entropy's disorderly tendency, returned to the realm of wholly determined and determinable beings. Forms of life, meanwhile, have their superlative status restored on the basis that such forms alone have the capacity to resist entropic disorder, that they alone have the capacity to reverse the determinism to which the rest of the clockwork universe is subject insofar as life alone refuses to simply 'run down.' Returned to life as its defining condition, probability thus disappears as a fundamental problem insofar as it is instead recast as the *a priori* potential of life to resist universal chaos. At its core, the 'new science of Cybernetics' is neither new nor a science: life alone has potential, life alone is unpredictable and life alone composes local enclaves of indeterminable order. Everything else is just clockwork running down—a process that can end only with the end of the universe in the last act of heat death.

Wiener's admittance of contingency as part of the 'warp and weft' of the universe thus results in a conception of probability that in fact *dis*allows that same contingency to all but the tiniest fraction of beings, while at the same time divesting probability of its inherent irrationality by recasting it as merely a symptom of incomplete determinism that remains to be resolved. Despite appearances to the contrary, the threat posed by probability to the problems of mastery and control over the implications of a stochastic universe for predicting the future are abruptly nullified. From the jaws of chaos, from the formless horror of a universe in disarray, order is ultimately restored, and God once again does not get to play dice. With the heavy irony so often provided by hindsight, probability is thus forced to serve the cybernetic project in the guise of a newly restored vitalism, reinscribing yet again the absolute metaphysical distinction between living and nonliving beings, with life alone deemed to possess an *a priori* capacity for external interaction and thus the potential for unpredictability. Moreover, with the introduction of entropy as a scientific *evil*, as we shall see below, Wiener pushes this distinction much further than traditionally has been the case. Contradictions regarding the universality of contingency aside, evil for Wiener would seem to inhabit the warp and weft of everything from the quantum to the cosmological, albeit with a special form of 'malicious' evil that, in strict accord with traditional edicts of Christian morality, exists only at the level of individual, reasoning subjects. As previously suggested, and in an uncanny echo of Einstein's response to the problem of constitutive probability decades before, Wiener's cybernetic program proposes a Hidden Values Theory of universal determinism that ultimately discloses God's hand at work, instigating on the one hand a new Christian mission in the name of St. Augustine and, on the other, a new objective science in the name of Josiah Gibbs.

OF EVIL INCOMPLETE AND OTHER
ERRORS OF PROBABILITY

Given the clear echo of Einstein's steadfast refusal to countenance the possibility of a God with a gambling problem in the 'good' Augustinian evil of universal incompleteness, it is helpful at this point to briefly address this same erroneous conflation of constitutive probability and incompleteness that has dogged quantum theory since its inception. In *The Physical Basis of the Direction of Time* ([1984] 2007), H. Dieter Zeh offers a concise and precise summary of what can best be described as a fundamental system error insofar as it marks a failure to understand one of the most basic premises of quantum theory, and as such warrants citing in full:

> The quantum theory is kinematically nonlocal. For example, the generic many-particle wave function $\psi(r1, r2, \ldots, rN)$, which represents a 'pure' quantum state, describes quantum correlations that are not due to incomplete information (even though they may lead to statistical correlations in measurements). Similarly, a state of quantum field theory is given by a wave functional of fields which are defined all over space. This 'entanglement' is a direct consequence of the superposition principle. In quantum theory, the state of the whole does not define states of its parts. This is in fundamental contrast to the completely determined many-particle state of classical mechanics: a point in phase space (that is, a definite state) remains a point when projected onto a subsystem. The kinematical indeterminacy of the parts in quantum theory describes a non-trivial 'wholeness' of Nature, which cannot, as in classical physics, be interpreted as a mere dynamical interconnectedness (that may lead to statistical correlations in an incomplete description). Quantum nonlocality is not just a 'spooky action at a distance' that would affect hidden local states (86).

We will of course return to this in more detail in the final section dealing with the implications of Heisenberg's uncertainty relations for our concepts of contingency and entanglement, but for the moment I wish only to draw attention to the parallel misconceptions of probability that have from the start marked both quantum theory and cybernetics in order to draw a further parallel here with Ludwig Boltzmann's order principle in the field of thermodynamics.

In accordance with Boltzmann's order principle, to each distribution of the velocities of the molecules that compose a given state there necessarily correspond a number of different ways, termed *complexions*, in which that velocity distribution can be realized via the attribution of variable velocity to each molecule. Entropy (S) is then related to the probability of a state as measured by the number of complexions (P), with the increase of entropy corresponding to the evolution toward the most probable state. As the basis of the Second Law of Thermodynamics, Boltzmann's order principle is of particular importance for us here in that, as Prigogine points out, it was through this 'molecular interpretation of irreversibility that the concept of probability first entered theoretical physics' (*From Being to Becoming*, 11). Prior to this, however, the Second Law as formulated initially in the mid-nineteenth century by mathematicians William Thomson (Lord Kelvin) and Rudolf Clausius was 'more a program than a well-defined statement, because no recipe was formulated by either Thomson or Clausius to express the entropy change in terms of observable quantities' (78). This initial lack of clarity, suggests Prigogine, is likely one of the main reasons 'why the application of thermodynamics became rapidly restricted to equilibrium, the end state of thermodynamic evolution' (78). Notably, Prigogine singles out Josiah Gibbs as particularly influential in this regard insofar as his work 'carefully avoids every incursion into the field of nonequilibrium processes' (78).

On its own, the measurement of entropy in terms of probability expressed by the number of available complexions offers no challenge whatsoever to classical notions regarding the determinism and consequent reversibility of being. Given sufficiently fine measuring apparatus, the probability of states of being remains entirely determinable both forwards and backwards in time on the basis of any present state of being. Nonetheless, Boltzmann's order principle makes possible a number of surprising yet compelling findings regarding the role of contingency in relation to emergent coherence at nonequilibrium. In disordered states generally, the number of complexions is necessarily very large insofar as any given state of disorder presumes a wide dispersion of possible velocities. Coherent motion, by contrast, is defined by a large group of molecules all moving at roughly the same velocity and as such composes a state of being with a narrow dispersion of possible velocities and thus a small number of complexions. Indeed, it is such a low number that any chance of self-organization would seem to be so vanishingly small as to be discounted in practical terms. And yet, all the more remarkably, self-organization does indeed occur. From this chance miracle, write Prigogine and Stengers, we see therefore 'that calculating the number of complexions, which entails the hypothesis of an equal *a priori* probability for each molecular state, is misleading. Its irrelevance is particularly obvious as far as the genesis of the new behavior is concerned' (*Order Out of Chaos*, 142–143). Furthermore, they continue, 'the age-old problem of the origin of life [now] appears in a different perspective. It is certainly true that life is incompatible with Boltzmann's order principle but not with the kind of behavior that can occur in far-from-equilibrium conditions' (143). That said, of course, while life is indeed marked by the remarkable emergence of metastable states of coherent motion, metastable states of coherent motion in turn always already refute every possible attempt to make over such states into a property exclusive to life alone.

Similarly, the application of Boltzmann's order principle and the subsequent focus on equilibrium conditions served for many years to obscure the fundamental role played by fluctuation in the transition to nonequilibrium states of matter, insofar as accordance with Boltzmann's principle denies fluctuation of any impact by ultimately 'dooming it to regression,' to paraphrase Prigogine and Stengers's particularly apt description. Employing the Bénard instability as their privileged example, Prigogine and Stengers demonstrate instead how the fluctuation of a microscopic convection current is rather 'amplified until it invades the whole system' (143). Crucially, this process proves definitive for the emergence into being of a *new* molecular order: 'Beyond the critical value of the imposed gradient,' they write, 'a new molecular order has thus been produced spontaneously [which] corresponds to a giant fluctuation stabilized through energy exchanges with the outside world' (143). We have already seen how Wiener is ultimately able to withdraw potential indeterminism from all nonliving states of being simply by denying them the chance of relations of exchange with the external world. On the contrary, however, living systems are disclosed as but infinitely diverse subsets of the infinitely diverse material history of gradients; they nonetheless are no less remarkable for that fact.

What fluctuation, bifurcation and coherence give us to think is not a *reduction* of life to a mechanistic universe of determinable and reversible physical processes but rather, given a coexistence of reversible and irreversible processes, an opening up of universal potential that, from the most basic to the most complex of exchanges, can be neither controlled nor predicted once and for all, and it is this which is remarkable indeed. Moreover, we are now in a position to draw a preliminary conclusion: *viz*, the potential nonlinearity of metastable systems necessarily *exceeds* the *control* of the broader system within which and from which it emerges, and does so in ways that, as literally and constitutively unthinkable, can be neither foreshadowed nor formulated in advance of its always monstrous emergence. As has been argued throughout, it is through the power of the instrumental and on the basis of the determinable that humanity dreams its dreams of systematic world domination that ultimately achieves its ends in the reductive form of a general polluting and parasitic power that, in triumphant destruction of its own fundamental tendency, seeks to systematically and mechanically overcode all other relations.

Defining and defined by the Anthropocene, this is at once the end of the capitalist mode of production and ultimate validation. As a single—and, as we shall see, singularly cancerous—inclination that now orders the system as a whole, capitalism has indeed proved itself victorious in rendering impossible any other systemic forms or order. The very undeniability of its total victory, however, is also an expression of its weakness insofar as it makes clear that potential change must be such that it emerges *within* its overarching system and, in one and the same process, *accelerates* its auto-destruction. Colebrook, we recall, terms such thinking *inhuman* 'precisely because the creation of the single system or axiom . . . would need to be annihilated to give way to differentials along a different axis' ('Posthuman Humanities,' 182). Here and now, we occupy a place *before* tomorrow that is—perhaps—the inhuman chance of a future other than that which the hubristic presumption of determinism imposes upon being.

Following on initially from the classical theory of linear dynamics, the attempted generalization of thermodynamic processes on the basis of the theory of minimum entropy production inevitably collapses in the face of fluctuations that are irreducible to simple linear functions of forces. This is itself a fundamental point of bifurcation within the physical sciences insofar as the precise moment of irreversible transition from equilibrium to nonequilibrium marks the precise moment after which stability ceases to be the consequence of the general laws of physics. In this brave new world, a stationary state always retains the potential to react differently to different types of fluctuations produced by either the system or its external environment and which, in some cases, 'may be amplified and invade the entire system, compelling it to evolve toward a new regime that may be qualitatively quite different from the stationary states' (Prigogine and Stengers, *Order Out of Chaos*, 141). Given the lack of any universally valid law capable of delineating the overall behaviour of a system into the future, every system of relations must henceforth be considered as a specific case with the potential for unpredictable and thus qualitatively distinct behaviour. That said, however, an important general result is indeed obtained in the transition to nonequilibrium, identified by Prigogine and Stengers as

> a necessary condition for chemical instability: in a chain of chemical reactions occurring in the system, *the only reaction stages* that, under certain conditions and circumstances, may jeopardize the stability of the stationary state are precisely the 'catalytic loops'—stages in which the product of a chemical reaction is involved in its own synthesis (145).

The necessary involvement of the product of a relation in its own synthesis: this definition of catalytic feedback looping further specifies the point of bifurcation leading to the emergent coherence of qualitatively distinct behaviour. Rather than simple mechanisms employed to control the mechanical tendency toward disorganization, as Wiener contends, this catalytic condition of feedback relations in systems at far from equilibrium is the first of two conditions that still remain to be addressed when considering the turbulence and instability of dissipative structures. The second is that, just as with the concept of reversibility that precedes it, irreversibility too is not a universal property. We must, write Prigogine and Stengers, 'accept a pluralistic world in which reversible and irreversible processes coexist. Yet such a pluralistic world is not easy to accept' (257).

THE CYBERNETIC SYSTEM: ENTROPY AND EVIL

Having summarized some of the ways in which probability and feedback have developed in tandem in the fields of cybernetics, thermodynamics and quantum theory, we are now in a position to consider how the concepts of irreversibility, contingency and nonlinearity inform their respective fundamental concepts of system, dissipation and entanglement.

As we know, in his hugely influential account of the cybernetic project in the years immediately following the Second World War, Norbert Wiener makes the claim that mechanisms of control, operating at the level of the system as a whole, impose checks and balances at every level of its various partial and subsystems that account not only for technological progress, but also for the seemingly unpredictable character of this progress that is ultimately dismissed as merely analogous to the 'proper' unpredictability that is the property of living organisms alone. We recall too that Wiener sets up a distinction between the 'good' evil of incompleteness as personified for him by St. Augustine and for us by Einstein, and the properly 'bad' evil that drives the world of material darkness in its constant struggle to destroy the spiritual world of light such as espoused by the Manichaeans dating all the way back to the third century CE. Of particular interest here are the roles played by these negative and positive forms of evil in the constitution of the cybernetic system by way of a strange imbrication of universal contingency with *scientific* evil. As we shall see, such scientific evil describes—and ultimately proscribes—the cascades of noise and parasitic contagion that befall the perfect system in abjuration of its general laws of both order and number. Last, this recalls too Claire Colebrook's urgent call for a futural concept of humanity capable of interrogating the single, generalized inclination that, as definitive of our late-capitalist era, 'now precludes the dynamisms, systems and disturbances of anything outside its own terrain' ('Posthuman Humanities,' 183).

Returning to Wiener's *The Human Use of Human Beings*, the invocation of the Manichaean and Augustinian devils takes place within a broader context concerning the appearance of 'universal systemic purposefulness' that Wiener locates in the residual patterning displayed by way of W. Ross Ashby's concept of machines that learn as well as by the Darwinian concept of nature, and which he argues possesses significant potential as regards 'highly useful technical developments in the task of automatization' (38). Always in search of order and organization, writes Wiener, science is thus engaged in a perpetual game against its arch-nemesis that is the form of disorder and disorganization. But, he continues, what is the precise *nature* of this devil that is opposed to godly science in this manner? Is it, in other words, 'a contrary force opposed to order or is it the very absence of order itself' (34)? Is it Manichaean or Augustinian? This is a crucial distinction for Wiener, as it is only through knowledge of the difference in their respective powers that the correct game to be played against them becomes apparent, along with the correct tactics to be used in each case.

First and foremost, argues Wiener, the Manichaean devil is 'an opponent, like any other opponent, who is determined on victory and will use any trick of craftiness or dissimulation to obtain this victory' (34–35). The specific evil that defines Manichaean devilry, in other words, is that of a willingness to win at all costs. Without compunction he will lie, mislead, distract, cheat and confuse his opponent while all the while making sure the opposing player is kept entirely in the dark regarding his Manichaean 'policy,' with the latter aspect proving crucial to the ultimate success of the strategy overall. More specifically, writes Wiener, the Manichaean devil is 'playing a game of poker against us and will resort readily to bluffing' (35). Drawing on John von Neumann and Oskar Morgenstern's *Theory of Games and Economic Behavior* (1944), Wiener makes the important point that a willingness to bluff 'is intended not merely to enable us to win on a bluff, but to prevent the other side from winning on the basis of a certainty that we will not bluff' (35). The 'refined' maliciousness of Manichaean evil, in other words, rests in the fact that it eliminates from games of chance even the tiniest chance of *certainty*. When playing a game against the Manichaean devil, the winning hand can always still lose.

By contrast, Augustinian evil concerns the mobilization of stupidity. The Augustinian devil, writes Wiener, 'is not a power in itself, but the measure of our own weakness' (35). To further clarify this notion of 'power in itself,' it is helpful to consider the distinction found in the French language between the terms *puissance* and *pouvoir*. While both terms translate into English as *power*, only *puissance* describes power *in itself*, that is, power as *positive force*, like gravity, which may be harnessed and put to work. The power of *pouvoir*, by contrast, is that of *being able to*, that is to say, it refers to a capacity or capability, an *ability* to do this or that thing. Hence, as the measure of our own weakness, of our own *impouvoir*, Augustinian evil is the name of our *being* un*able to*, our *in*capacity or *in*ability to do this or that thing. In contrast to the positive force of Manichaean evil then, Augustinian evil is a negative force, a nonpower or a forced *lack*. Crucially, therefore, *Augustinian evil only ever expresses the relation of human intelligence to the universe outside of it*, and nothing other than that. Here, it is important to recall from our earlier discussion that, for Wiener, Augustinian evil is a universal constraint operating at every level of being, whereas the inherent uncertainty defining the maliciousness of Manichaean evil instead only ever plays out at the level of living, i.e., autopoietic, organisms.

Hence, against the uncertainty derivative of deceptive practices definitive of Manichean evil—evil, it should be noted, which overlaps precisely with the devilish rhetorical practices that Socrates ascribes to his Sophist opponents—the reliability arising from the literality and truthfulness of the 'stupid' Augustinian devil is such that it retains for us, as players, the tiniest chance of certainty whilst remaining within the limits of the game being played. Once again, Wiener is seeking, by any means possible, to return certainty to a probabilistic world that is nonetheless orchestrated by contingency. He further clarifies the nature of Augustinian evil as that which 'may require our full resources to uncover, but when we have uncovered it, we have in a certain sense exorcised it, and it will not alter its policy on a matter already decided with the mere intention of confounding us further' (35). The Augustinian devil, he continues, 'plays a difficult game, but he may be defeated by our intelligence as thoroughly as by a sprinkle of holy water' (35). Here, the references to exorcism and holy water further render explicit the specifically Christian theology that underwrites the differing roles being played by each of Wiener's cybernetic devils.

While it may be arduous and intellectually taxing to do so, the Augustinian devil *can* be beaten in the end and, having been conquered, can further be relied upon to thereafter withdraw completely from the game and from the world, never to return. As the measure of our own weakness, in other words, the *lack* that constitutes Augustinian evil can and will be erased by human intelligence, given sufficient time. That which is currently lacking and thus incomplete will eventually be conquered, erasing every mark and measure of that lack in the moment of victorious completion. In short, the Augustinian devil is a fair player and, in the end, a good loser once faced with the certainty of its imminent defeat. In contrast, the Manichaean devil is a liar and a cheat who changes the rules so as never to lose a game, ensuring in turn that the game never ends and the play is never complete. While the universe will, in the end, be forced to surrender itself completely to the will of human intelligence, the Christian struggle between good and evil in the battle for control over each and every human soul remains a ceaseless and uniquely human game that cannot *not* be played.

It is not simply by chance, therefore, that Wiener turns to Einstein for a suitable aphorism that best describes the 'nature' of the Augustinian devil, one which 'is more than an aphorism, and is really a statement concerning the foundations of scientific method': namely, "'The Lord is subtle, but he isn't simply mean'" (35). The word 'Lord' here, Wiener explains, 'is used to describe those forces in nature which include what we have attributed to his very humble servant, the Devil, and Einstein means to say that these forces do not bluff' (35). Nature, in other words, does not dissemble just as God does not play dice—the one aphorism following on from the other. As the site of Augustinian evil, he concludes, nature inevitably 'offers resistance to decoding, but it does not show ingenuity in finding new and undecipherable methods for jamming our communication with the outer world' (35–36). The forces of nature, in other words, are neither malicious nor ingenious but only stupidly resistant to knowledge and thus, once defeated by human intelligence, can thereafter be relied upon to behave in a predictable, that is, *determinable*, manner.

Having established the differing nature of the twin devils that face us, argues Wiener, we are now able to discern the correct game to play and the correct tactics to be used against them: 'This distinction between the passive resistance of nature and the active resistance of an opponent suggests a distinction between the research scientist and the warrior or the game player' (36). As we have seen, the measure of Augustinian evil is only ever the measure of the material universe that still remains to be conquered and thus exorcised by human intelligence; that is, it denotes nothing else but the measure of our stupidity at any given time. Augustinian evil, in short, is the measure both of the incompleteness of the current state of human knowledge and of the progress made by science to date in its struggle to master the universe that contains it. Hence, science needs but a single tactic in order to ensure ultimate victory over the Augustinian devil, that of *patience*: 'The research physicist has all the time in the world to carry out his experiments,' writes Wiener, 'and he need not fear that nature will in time discover his tricks and method and change her policy' (36). For this reason, the Augustinian devil is an honourable opponent, and so the scientist need not fear that, should she make a single mistake, the Augustinian devil will not take advantage of it to defeat her.

The same cannot be said, however, of the chess-playing Manichean devil, who will keenly take every advantage of the very worst moves of his adversary and thus cannot be considered to be playing the game in an 'honourable' fashion. The value of such 'honour' is dubious indeed, however, insofar as for Wiener it seems that what makes the universe an honourable opponent is that it never tries to actually *defeat* its human adversary but rather accepts its own defeat before even the first play is made. Wiener's cybernetic universe—overseen by Einstein's Lord and God—simply does not play, and never will, but only meekly awaits the inevitable arrival of its colonizing masters.

THE PURPOSELESS PURPOSE OF
WIENER'S SPECIAL MACHINES

So how do these twin devils fit into our brave new probabilistic world under the heel of the Second Law of Thermodynamics? In order for us to become masters of our sympathetic and ultimately subservient universe, suggests Wiener, human intelligence needs only an almost infinite patience. He immediately follows this claim, however, by stating, 'Of course, in the long run, the great trivial purpose of maximum entropy will appear to be the most enduring of all' (38). The universe, it would seem, will have the last laugh in the end, having merely being playing possum to human hubris while all the while orchestrating a final, devastating descent into absolute and universal disorder that prohibits any and all possible chance of order. This returns us to what Wiener describes as the appearance of universal and systemic purposefulness, as exemplified in the patterning of Darwinian nature and Ashby's learning machines, and the use of this apparent purposefulness in further developing the task of automatization.

Crucially, insofar as it takes place in a realm that is necessarily discrete from the realm of human will which alone harbours the possibility of malicious evil, such universal and systemic purposefulness is simple verisimilitude, an illusory consequence of the tendency of human cognition to seek out patterns in the patternless, order in disorder. In addition to the two 'special' machines listed above, Wiener here offers a third example, that of the autonomic mammalian nervous system. All three machines, he argues, are 'fundamentally alike' insofar as they share a common trait that sets them apart and makes them special, namely that they are all 'devices which make decisions on the basis of decisions they have made in the past' (33). Knowing what we know of Augustinian evil, however, it is clear that Wiener's use of the term 'decision' is idiosyncratic at best, given that it cannot signify a *willed* decision but only an automatic calculation, that is to say, a decision*less* decision. Special machines—and this of course includes the *cybernetic* machine as well—are automatons whose function is such that they *appear* to produce more or less meaningful patterns that would seem, wrongly, to signify a sovereign will at work making reasoned decisions behind the scenes, but which are simply projections of human cognizance. Augustinian evil, and the universe along with it, dissolves: first as a measure of human intelligence and then again as a figment of human imagination.

More interesting for us, however, is the potential for significant developments in technical automatization that Wiener contends is to be found in what he tellingly describes as '*unpurposeful*' machines. In seeming to us to display meaningful purpose, in other words, certain 'special' machines, while remaining purposeless in themselves, nonetheless serve a higher, that is, *human*, purpose, insofar as such 'seeming to' offers itself to thought in such a way as to stimulate technological progress and, ultimately, its own Augustinian erasure under the all-conquering steerage of humankind. It is not by chance that Wiener, feeling the need to invent a single term that would 'embrace the whole field' to be hashed out at the annual Macy conferences, went with cybernetics as derived from the Greek term *kubernetes*, which is generally translated as 'steersman' and from which comes the word 'governor.' Demonstrated above all by 'Ashby's brilliant idea of the unpurposeful, random mechanism which seeks for its own purpose through a process of learning'—an idea described as 'one of the great philosophical contributions of the present day'—Wiener argues that henceforth not only 'can we build purpose into machines, but in an overwhelming majority of cases a machine designed to avoid certain pitfalls of breakdown will look for purposes which it can fulfill' (38). It is difficult indeed to understand what Wiener intends by this statement, and in particular how this impacts contemporary developments in automatization. It seems that by including some share of *human* purpose within such machines of the future that otherwise definitively lack any and all *actual* purpose, we can produce special machines that, without requiring any further input from their human creators and masters, will function thereafter and all alone in a fashion that mimics the functioning of human cognition. Such a machine, in other words, is designed to independently search for possible purposes that are within its own capacity to fulfil.

But how does this serve to further develop machinic automatization? No matter how 'human' such machines appear in the production of seemingly purposeful patterns and meanings, they remain fundamentally Augustinian and thus always already divorced from the uniquely living realms of will and purpose. The special machines of our future, in other words, are such that they all alone *appear* to mimic purposeful action in what can only ever be closer and more complex simulations of human behaviour produced by machines which, without the animation bestowed upon them by human intelligence alone, are themselves entirely purposeless and incapable of independent decision. Just as with the brooms brought to life by the Sorcerer's Apprentice, the machines beholden to cybernetic steerage remain determined and determinable, made special only by virtue of independently displaying an ersatz similarity to human intelligence.

The privileged position that cybernetics in general accords to automatization or automatism is closely tied to the image of the cybernetician as 'steersman' to the Augustinian universe that is the measure of their incomplete mastery. Hence, it comes as no surprise that progress in the field of automatization is for cybernetics synonymous with the capture and captivation of universal contingency that is temporarily resistant to human control. That said, however, the conception of total automatism is in fact always already invalidated, serving instead as a blind that obscures the nonlinear evolution of form through processes of concretization. Automatism, as philosopher Jean Baudrillard argues in *The System of Objects* (1968), rather 'amounts to a closing-off, to a sort of functional self-sufficiency which exiles man to the irresponsibility of a mere spectator. Contained within it is the dream of a dominated world, of a formally perfected technicity that serves an inert and dreamy humanity' (147–148). Current technological thinking, continues Baudrillard, "rejects this tendency in principle, and holds that true perfection in machines—one genuinely founded on an increasing level of technicity, and hence expressing true 'functionality'—depends not on more automatism but on a certain margin of indeterminacy which lets the machine respond to information from outside" (148). As we have seen, it is precisely this indeterminacy arising from an actual (rather than simulated) responsive relation to that which comes from outside that Wiener denies to the entire universe of Augustinian evil, and which transforms that same universe into what Heidegger terms the 'standing reserve,' that is, into a passive and purposeless receptacle unwittingly awaiting the intercession of human ingenuity to ultimately provide it with its meaning.

Despite its rejection in principle, however, the projection of automatism continues to this day to be celebrated as the pinnacle of technical abstraction, possessing a peculiar fascination that, as Baudrillard suggests, is 'so powerful precisely because it is not that of a technical rationality' (148). While too often overlooked in contemporary accounts of technology, Baudrillard here offers a bravura analysis of this paradoxical fascination, arguing that we in fact 'come under its spell because we experience it as a *basic desire*, as *the imaginary truth of the object,* in comparison with which the object's structure and concrete function leave us cold' (148, italics added). Later, he further qualifies this by adding that the 'perfect and perfectly autonomous monad which is the governing dream of subjectivity is thus also very clearly the dream that haunts objects' (150). Again, knowing what we know about the genesis of cybernetics, this reference to the 'governing dream of subjectivity' thus betrays its particular importance.

Automatism, continues Baudrillard, is both a simple technical deviation and at the same time 'the true inaugurating moment of the modern age' (152). As part of the consolidation of instrumentality in the form of the standing reserve, in other words, objects lose their very objectivity in the imaginary projection of consciousness otherwise embodied in the valorization of automatism. This, Baudrillard writes, amounts to a *cancer* of the object insofar as the resulting proliferation of alien astructural elements actually functions in opposition to the evolution of technical form, immobilizing the potential for transformation beneath the triumphalism of 'redundant forms and tricked-up materials, and . . . demiurgic formalism' (152). Such changes in form and style, writes Baudrillard, are a sign not of progress but rather of immature and transitional states, and the 'error of capitalism as a creed lies in the attempt to make this period of transition a permanent one' (168). Interestingly, Baudrillard configures this 'fundamental antagonism between the verticality of technology and the horizontality of profit' as an antagonism between open and closed thermodynamic systems, with the metastable openness allowing for the continuing self-transcendence of technical invention being systematically and mechanically overcoded by 'the closedness of a system of recurrent objects and forms beholden to the goals of production' (168). As an attempt to master the contingency of our probabilistic universe in general and the disorderly tendencies of entropic processes in particular, it is with considerable irony therefore that the mastery envisioned by Wiener's cybernetic project ultimately 'becomes an even greater obstacle than the space over which mastery was sought in the first place' (171).

THE KILLERS OF TIME

Identified by Baudrillard as marking the shift from industrial capitalism into its postindustrial variant, it is something of a paradox therefore that the permanence of the transitory that takes its definitive form in what we know today as the Anthropocene is itself the permanence, that is, the *in*transience, of the capitalist mode of production. Recalling capitalism's triumphant autodestruction of its own tendency through the imposition of a single reductive inclination, we can now better understand Tiqqun's claim in *The Cybernetic Hypothesis* that the acceleration of circulation serves as the dark side of the maintenance of accumulation by 'maximizing the volume of commodity flows while minimizing the events, obstacles, accidents that would slow them down' (65). To this end, they write, it is postwar cybernetics that 'supplied capitalism with a new infrastructure of machines—computers—and more importantly with an intellectual technology that made it possible to regulate the circulation of flows in society, making them exclusively commodity flows' (68). In order to facilitate this reductive inclination, two concepts take on particular importance: *insecurity* and *predictability*.

Inseparable and correlated, insecurity and predictability work in tandem 'to maximize fluid circulation to its limit point, the speed of light,' disclosing in the process the tendency of cybernetic capitalism to 'abolish time itself' (65). As such, time—as well as the noise it brings with it—is both an ally and a technology insofar as it is inscribes radical innovation and machinic repetition as an *a priori* condition of being. As we know, the Second Law of Thermodynamics promotes entropy to the status of natural law, and it is on this basis of an apparent sharing of scientific terrain that cybernetics initially attempts to explain, legitimize and—at least upon attaining the end times of humanity—resolve all such forms of disorder, disequilibrium and dissolution that currently impact the sociopolitical and socioeconomic realms. Here, then, the implementation of the cybernetic project is clearly aligned with the generalized reduction to a single tendency definitive of the postindustrial era of the Anthropocene. In the very same moment, however, it also announces its refusal to adhere to the established conventions that currently govern the legitimacy or otherwise of scientific endeavour and, in so doing, its incommensurability with those same physical sciences that cybernetics simultaneously calls upon to validate itself as a legitimate field of study. It is this contradiction that the figure of Augustinian evil both articulates and at once obscures.

There are a number of reasons for this refusal, but the most important is also the most simple: entropic resolution, by definition, cannot be resolved. As markers of temporal ordering, in other words, entropic processes of dissolution and decomposition dissolve without being dissolved, decompose without being decomposed. Against this, cybernetics instead produces its *own* veridictions to such an extent that, as Tiqqun put it so well, it is now '*the most substantial anti-humanism*, one that is determined to maintain the general order of things while priding itself on having gone beyond the human' (27, italics in original). What we are seeing in process, they continue,

> is the most advanced form of contemporary individualism, onto which is grafted the Hayekian philosophy for which every uncertainty, every possibility of an event is only a temporary lack of knowledge. *Converted into an ideology*, liberalism serves as a cover for a new collection of technical and scientific practices, a diffuse 'second-order cybernetics,' which deliberately blanks out its Christian name (57, italics added).

This Christian name obscured in second-order cybernetics, it should be clear, is that of Saint Augustine, joined in the first-order pantheon by Albert Einstein as the patron saint of divine predictability.

Tiqqun locates the catalysis at the heart of the cybernetic project in the pair of incompleteness theorems introduced by mathematician Kurt Gödel in 'On Formally Undecidable Propositions of *Principia Mathematica* and Related Systems' ['*Uber formal unentscheidbare Sätze der* Principia Mathematica *und verwandter Systeme*'], published in 1931. Ostensibly, these theorems concern the logical limits of provability in relation to formal axiomatic systems, but the impact of Gödel's extraordinary theorems—quickly followed in 1933 by Alfred Tarski's undefinability theorem—far exceeds not only the narrow specialism of deductive logic but also the field of mathematics as a whole. Put in simplest terms, Gödel's incompleteness theorems demonstrate that any consistent axiomatic system is necessarily incomplete insofar as there will always be statements of the language of that system that can neither be proved nor disproved from within that system, and from which it follows that any consistent axiomatic system cannot therefore demonstrate its own consistency. Tarski then takes these theorems a logical step further by demonstrating that arithmetical truth cannot be defined within the formal system of arithmetic, from which it is deduced that the truth of any seemingly consistent formal system cannot be defined within that formal system.

While a detailed analysis of these proofs and their importance for the development of Set Theory is clearly outside of the scope of this book, we can nonetheless take note of their specific challenges to the established scientific thinking of the day.[4] Having held true for more than two millennia, it was long accepted as a truism that it is indeed possible to establish the truth of axioms from which 'both the truth and the mutual consistency of all the theorems are automatically guaranteed' (Nagel, *Gödel's Proof*, 5). Key here is the mapping of truth to mutual consistency, with consistency being such that it is impossible to deduce mutually contradictory theorems from the axiomatic postulates that found a given system, insofar as to do so would be to fall foul of the exclusionary strictures imposed by the principle of reason, namely the now shopworn laws of noncontradiction and of the excluded middle. It is this systemic founding by way of an automatic production of proof, truth and consistency—as demonstrated par excellence by the axiomatic system of Euclidian geometry—that Gödel's and Tarski's theorems' refutation of the axiomatic method disallows thereafter. As Ernest Nagel writes,

> A climate of opinion was thus generated in which it was tacitly assumed that each sector of mathematical thought can be supplied with a set of axioms sufficient for developing systematically the endless totality of true propositions about the given area of inquiry. Gödel's paper showed that this assumption is untenable. (6)

Above all, what Gödel's and Tarski's theorems demonstrate is that certain cognitive abilities previously imagined to be inalienable markers of human exceptionalism—namely, provability, perfectability, definability and predictability—are instead disclosed as *a priori in*abilities. Moreover, these supposed abilities—to be able to render certain proof, to render the imperfect perfect, to render definitions that lack nothing and are therefore absolute and to render predictions with absolute surety—are *a priori* conditions for the rendering of completeness and consistency. For a given system to be consistent, in other words, it must be perfect and, as such, formally definable and absolutely determinable. Having already addressed the play of imperfection and incompleteness in Wiener's account of cybernetics, we now turn briefly to the roles of perfection and predictability in the broader context of security and the general production of threat.

SURPLUS INFORMATION AND
MEANINGLESS EXCHANGE

In attempting to somehow sidestep the constitutive uncertainty of systemic enclosure, Wiener first resituates the problem by converting the problem of uncertainty into a problem of information in a bravura move that in large part defines first-order cybernetics. Just as *a priori* imperfectability is restaged as simple incompleteness, so too is *a priori* uncertainty recast as incomplete information—that is, as part of a "temporal series where certain data are already known, others not yet known . . . and in *considering the object and the subject of the knowledge as a whole*, a 'system'" (Tiqqun *The Cybernetic Hypothesis*, 39; italics in original). Translated into a problem of information, in other words, constitutive uncertainty instead becomes an ordinary lack of complete knowledge awaiting its eventual dissolution beneath the steamrolling *telos* that is the promise of human intelligence. As to what this utopia of total information envisioned by the cyberneticians might consist of, Tiqqun cites 'its most zealous French ideologue' Abraham Moles, who argues that it is "'conceivable that a society taken as a whole, a State, could be regulated in such a way that it is protected from all future accidents: such that in itself only eternity changes it'" (cit. 31). As noted in the introduction to this chapter, this phantasy of a cybernetic utopia mirrors the same dream of perpetual power first articulated by Plato in the *Republic* and, indeed, does so to such a degree that it can be considered as its updated blueprint.[5]

As demonstrated by the failure of various—and not infrequently ingenious—attempts aimed at circumventing Gödel's theorems in the years immediately following publication, however, it quickly becomes clear that the translation of a problem from one domain to another or from one model to another does not serve to resolve the original problem, only to displace it. Of the many attempts made to guarantee consistency in this manner, most notable for us here is mathematician David Hilbert's translation of the axioms of Euclidian geometry into algebraic truths. On this basis, Hilbert was able to demonstrate the consistency of Euclidian geometry by showing that its postulates are indeed satisfied by an algebraic model. Despite the elegance of Hilbert's algebraic translation, however, what it states in fact is only that if the truths of the algebraic model are mutually consistent, then so too are the postulates of Euclidian geometry—the consistency of one, in other words, is dependent upon the relative consistency of the other, while the original problem of determining absolute consistency remains unaffected.

This is not to say, however, that the cybernetic displacement from the physical realm of metastable entropic processes to the realm of information is without significant consequences. In fact, the failure of these initial attempts at guaranteeing consistency through the conversion from one domain into another likely helped to obscure these consequences behind what appeared to be just another translation always already lost to the circularity of the relative and as such of little actual consequence. Of course, this *does* indeed describe the cybernetic shift to the realm of pure information, but at the same time the peculiar efficacy of its functioning is such that it remains unperturbed by the fundamental inconsistency of its claims for consistency. There are two reasons for this, one that is general to translation and another that is specific to information: first, the concepts of translation and conversion describe formal processes of *exchange*, and second, the realm of information constitutes as its mirror an infinite realm of data. In accordance with the first, it is the *exchange value* of information that comes to govern the entire world of beings and relegating consistency, or at least the *appearance* of consistency, to just one more commodity like any other in the process. As regards the second point, information and data are mutually constitutive concepts, meaning that each term is the condition of the other. Data, in other words, describes only that which is not yet information, and information describes only that which is no longer data. Key here is the moment of transition: at the very moment wherein the *ability* to convert data into information becomes possible, the infinite and infinitely diverse forms of being are thus retroactively constituted as a repository of pure data awaiting its teleological transformation into information. Finally, in an all too familiar move, the ability to turn data into information is uniquely reserved for human animals as a transformation enacted through the *a posteriori* application of *human* meaning to the hitherto formless mass of data that this same transformation constitutes as necessarily without meaning. Newly alone amid the universe of data, the power and privilege of human reason is once again restored.

Hence, far from being just another futile and largely inconsequential attempt to outwit a universe abruptly turned uncertain and inconsistent by Gödel and other mathematicians, the response of the cybernetic project as initially hashed out by Wiener and von Neumann over the course of the postwar Macy conferences is that of a universe of beings that is *a priori* without meaning aside from the meaning, and thus value, that humans ascribe to it *a posteriori*—value that is itself readily exchangeable within the realm of information. With this simple gesture, the cybernetic project dissolves the universe into a newly *digital* form of Heidegger's standing reserve that is far better suited to the vastly increased speed of exchange definitive of digital capitalism in the Anthropocene.

GLOBAL THREAT AS SINGLE INCLINATION

Before moving on to consider in conclusion the precise definition of catalytic feedback along with its role in the reproduction of dissipative structures, it still remains for us to examine the role played by feedback in the construction of cybernetic systems within the broader context of the Anthropocene and its facilitation of the globalizing tendency of postindustrial modes of production.

As movement in one direction only, the conversion of data into information is entirely insufficient for purpose. Rather, writes Tiqqun, information must thereafter 'return to the world of beings, binding them to each other, in the same way that the circulation of commodities guarantees their placing into equivalence. Feedback, the key to the regulation of the system, now demands a communication in the strict sense' (*The Cybernetic Hypothesis*, 41). Here, Tiqqun identifies two distinct stages in the transition from data to information. In the first, the world of beings is displaced into the realm of potential information and is retroactively constituted as an undifferentiated mass of data in the process. In the second stage, information then returns to the world of beings as a *binding* function in the form of regulative feedback that determines their equivalence as potential subjects of value. As the imposition of meaning and thus value upon an otherwise senseless universe that knows nothing of value or its absence, information is thereafter detached from concerns regarding truth and falsity and from the testable provability of all such claims and becomes instead a marketable commodity and thus a wealth to be extracted and accumulated.

In tandem with this dissolution of the universe into a standing reserve available for expropriation, *predictability*, as a source of confidence, increasingly becomes a source of profit to be mined. As Tiqqun notes, "*Insecurity, much more so than scarcity, is the kink in present-day capitalism.* As Wittgenstein realized on the basis of the crisis of 1929, and Keynes in his wake—there is a very strong connection between the 'state of confidence' and the curve of marginal efficiency of Capital" (67–68, italics in original). Initially at least, it seems that coupling of cybernetics to the operation of postwar capitalism is the result of a shared anxiety and a common enemy that transcends the incommensurability of their differing starting positions. Of course, this should come as no surprise given the superlative capacity of the capitalist mode of production since its inception to adapt and evolve in concert with changes to its external environment, eventually *becoming* the environment, as signalled by the introduction of the Anthropocene and the Capitalocene as ordering concepts at the epochal level.

As we know, the driving force behind the cybernetic project is anxiety over the founding role of contingency in the constitution of being and the fundamental uncertainty that follows as its result. Hence, the primary aim of cybernetics is to find a way to restore consistency and thus return certainty to a world otherwise chaotic and unpredictable. By contrast, the cyberneticians' concerns are not at all those of postindustrial capitalism, preoccupied only with the extraction of surplus value. The value of cybernetics to the operation of capitalism is threefold: first, as we have seen, by translating the world of beings into the realm of commodifiable data and information systems; second, by ensuring the increased efficiency of commodity transactions in accordance primarily with developments in technology; and third, by facilitating further effective control through mechanisms of systemic regulation. Hence, writes Tiqqun, the 'entry of cybernetics into the operation of capitalism aims at minimizing the uncertainties, the incommensurabilities, the expectation problems that might interfere with any commodity transaction' (69). At the same time, and here Tiqqun cites a passage from Jean-François Lyotard's *Libidinal Economy* [*Économie libidinale*] (1993/1974):

> There is in every cybernetic system a unit of reference which allows the disparity produced by the introduction of an event into the system to be measured; then, thanks to this measure, this event can be translated into information for the system. Finally, if it is a matter of a homeostatically regulated whole, this disparity can be annulled and the system led back to the same quantity of energy or information that it previously had (*Libidinal Economy*, 212, cit. Tiqqun, *The Cybernetic Hypothesis*, 72).

Here, it is worth staying with *Libidinal Economy* a little further. Immediately following the passage above, Lyotard clarifies this functioning of homeostatic regulation by way of Piero Sraffa's 'commodity standard':[6]

> Sraffa's commodity standard fulfils this function. If a system's growth were regulated, it would alter nothing of the loop-functioning (*feedback*) model: it is simply that the scale of reference is then no longer u, but Δu. The model is the same as that which Freud had in mind when he described the working of the psychical apparatus. . . . This Eros is centred on a zero: the obvious zero of homeostatic regulation, but more generally annihilation by the *feedback* (that is to say by the repetition of the binding function), of the system's every insignificant disparity, of every threatening event (212).

In its simplest terms, cybernetic feedback serves to bind a given system to its past in order to close itself off from any chance of contingent emergence.

As such, it in fact serves the *opposite* function to the feedback constitutive of dissipative systems insofar as it persists in the regulation of the same by returning a system to an ordered state prior to the contingent emergence of instability, looping back around with the aim of annulling the potential threat of that which cannot have been predicted on the basis of that prior state. Regulative feedback, in other words, is always subsequent to the *a priori* potential for fluctuation and mutation definitive of constitutive feedback—a futile and belated attempt to control uncertainty by reestablishing an order that never was.

In the case of postindustrial capitalism in the Anthropocene, the fact that *a posteriori* regulative feedback is a self-defeating concept matters not at all. Quite the opposite; its regulative *power* rests with its necessary failure insofar as this failure ensures that a final resolution is impossible, ensures that order can never be obtained and maintained once and for all and as such begets conservative regulation as a continuous and all-pervasive process that needs to be applied at every level of being in order to keep the world of commodity exchange safe from the continuous and all-pervasive threat posed to it by the uncontrolled and unpredictable. All forms of repression, writes Tiqqun, 'are given new life in a system entirely turned toward *the fear of threat*' (*The Cybernetic Hypothesis*, 71; italics in original).

Put simply, cybernetics and capitalism come together in the attempt, or at least the appearance of such an attempt, to order and organize feedback processes so as to effectively annul any chance of evental emergence. In accordance with this model of regulative feedback, writes Tiqqun,

> disruptions in a zone will be stifled all the more effectively as they will be absorbed by the closest sub-zones of the system. If repression has the role, in cybernetic capitalism, of forestalling the event, prediction is its corollary, insofar as it is for the purpose of eliminating the uncertainty that's associated with any future. It is the major concern of the statistical technologies (74).

Hence, while cybernetics initially 'borrows' from the language of thermodynamics in order to gain legitimacy as a strictly *scientific* endeavour, it is clear that the same terms play very different and often contradictory roles within their respective fields of enquiry. At the heart of this disjunct is the concept of feedback, as can be seen most clearly when comparing the diagrams of regulative feedback with that of catalytic feedback in the form of the Brusselator model.[7] Whereas the former seeks to stifle disruptions and profit from confidence in an imaginary future deemed certain and safe in its quiet predictability, the latter renders such confidence an idiot's phantasy, an illusion of control that always already disappears when faced with the unruly noise of the universe.

NOISE AND THE STEERSMAN: A FABLE

Wiener's cybernetics, as we have seen, seeks to impose regulatory feedback mechanisms upon the scientific evil of Augustinian incompleteness in the hope of proscribing the cascades of noise and parasitic contagion that nonetheless continue to befall the perfect system in abjuration of its general laws. In this way, the cybernetician as steersman [*kubernetes*] claims to have once more restored human cognition to its proper place at the helm of our postindustrial ark, posed heroically, telescope and microscope in hand, ready to introduce meaning to the data of the past so as to unerringly inform the future in service to a strictly human *telos*. Suited more to fables of the modernist and positivist eras, this figure of the heroic steersman is already long out of date, and deliberately so, insofar as it serves to recall the perceived *security* of the positivist period deemed to be lost in the transition to a probabilistic universe. Repackaged for the so-called information age, the figure of the cybernetic steersman promises to navigate a sure and certain course through the contingency and disorder of the contemporary world and beyond, through all of time and space, sloughing away angst and anxiety at every step along the way to the destined end, both teleological and temporal, of human intelligence. Faced once more with this familiar hubris, it is helpful to recall the absurdity of Nietzsche's gnat who, in common with the cybernetician, similarly imagines herself as being the ordering centre of the universe.[8]

Such common delusions of gnat, human and cybernetician fade away into nothing behind the unremitting *roar* of noise that orchestrates every silence, articulates every system and shatters every waking dream. Noise, as Tiqqun suggests, is indeed our ally:

> In the framework of the cybernetic hypothesis, panic is understood as a change of state of the self-regulated system. For a cybernetician, every disorder can only start with variations between measured behaviors and effective behaviors of elements of the system. So-called 'noise' is a behavior that would escape control while remaining refractory to the system, that is, one that cannot be processed by a binary machine, reduced to a 0 or a 1. Such noises are the lines of escape, the divagations of desires that are not yet entered into the circuit of valorization—the non-inscribed (*The Cybernetic Hypothesis*, 125).

Here, panic is indexed to the potential threat of an unforeseeable systemic change emerging from out of the very system it changes and doing so in a manner that is fundamentally unpredictable. At the same time, it is this same system that is tasked with eradicating this ineradicable threat by feeding back upon itself a previously determined form of itself in a regulative process that can only be implemented *subsequent to* that system having been systematically transformed into a wholly new and thus discontinuous order of being. It is clear from this that the mechanism of regulative feedback cannot be maintained insofar as it presumes a temporal and sequential order of process that does not meet the logical conditions of precedence and antecedence. Any accrual of commodifiable confidence founded upon calculations of risk turns out to be yet another confidence trick in service to the accumulation of more and more wealth. More specifically, noise here serves to index the 'non-inscribed' and, as such, immeasurable differences between the predetermined behaviour of elements that conform to a prescribed system and the actual behaviour of the elements that form a system at any given moment. Importantly, as non-inscribed, noise describes the part of every system that necessarily escapes systemic control but nonetheless remains an obstinate part of that same system.

As we know, the noise of a system is a necessary and parasitical process of that system and at once that which the system is not. As such, it cannot be accounted for by the system of which it is a part, nor can it be expropriated for exchange. Instead, noise is that which marks the potential for mutation and transformation definitive of every form of being. It is, put simply, that which at once *is* and *is not* part of every articulated form. Noise marks the imbrication of being *and* nonbeing as the *a priori* potential for any form of being to become radically other than itself. In this way, the constitutive and parasitic character of noise discloses its obvious parallels with that of temporality as addressed previously, revealing too its role as the soundless sound of the irreversibility of time's arrow.

In relation to the regulative work of the cybernetic steersman, noise marks instead the *over*-steering of a given system that always already takes place prior to the attempt to direct it. As a collective noun, 'noise' discloses here a further key characteristic that is presupposed by the parasitical relation but is not immediately obvious. Noise, in other words, describes that which has the capacity to increase dramatically in series, that is to say, an unlimited capacity for iterated aggregation over time. Noise on top of noise is still noise, and this potential for aggregation and amplification constitutes the potential for an automated 'over-steering' or overproduction of a given system through processes of catalytic feedback giving rise to unforeseeable bifurcation points. The parasite, recalling Serres, is being and nonbeing, relation and nonrelation, whereas noise is can make the parasite immediately disappear insofar as a noise of the system 'can only be supplanted by noise . . . thus noise is the fall into disorder and the beginning of an order' (Serres, *The Parasite*, 79). This, continues Serres, 'is why the relation of exchange is always dangerous, why the gift is always a forfeit, and why the relation can attain catastrophic levels' (80). Catastrophic potential is catalytic feedback at work in far from equilibrium conditions and at once the noise that silences the cybernetic steersman by stripping every probate of its validity and every prediction of its confidence.

THE MEANING OF SPACE AND TIME

In *From Being to Becoming*, Prigogine argues that, at far from equilibrium, 'an unexpected relation exists between chemical kinetics and the space-time structure of reacting systems' (103). This relation, he continues, is *in addition* to those of typical short-range interactions, such as valency forces and hydrogen bonds, insofar as at far from equilibrium conditions the dependence upon global characteristics plays a decisive role that at or near equilibrium is negligible. This supplementary dependency is fundamental to the nonlinear evolution of metastable structures insofar as it composes the crucial further condition that sets irreversible processes apart from reversible ones. This last point is central to an understanding of that which reason, in the form of Voltaire's *Dictionnaire Philosophique*, dismisses as ludicrous: namely, that there do indeed exist certain events that are necessary and others which are not, or in other words, that 'a part of what happens had to happen and another part did not' (cit. Prigogine and Stengers, *Order Out of Chaos*, 257). As such, it will serve as the focus of this final part.

The most obvious example of this supplementary dependence at far from equilibrium conditions concerns the size and complexity of a given system, in that 'the occurrence of dissipative structures generally requires that the system's size exceed some critical value—a complex function of the parameters describing the reaction-diffusion processes' (*From Being to Becoming*, 104). Hence, writes Prigogine, we can therefore state that instabilities at far from equilibrium 'involve long-range order through which the system acts as a whole' (104). Furthermore, he continues, this 'global behavior *greatly modifies the very meaning of space and time*' (104, italics added). As we shall see, this claim that the behaviour of far from equilibrium systems somehow alters, and not in a trivial way, the meaning of space and time, is both astonishing and at once utterly banal. Critically, this claim can be read in two different ways: first, that the newly disclosed behaviour of systems in far from equilibrium conditions requires the current understanding of space and time to be reworked in order to take this 'new' behaviour into account; and, second, that the specific behaviour of a given system correlated to its singular far from equilibrium conditions significantly modifies the meaning or sense of space and time at the precise locus of that system's becoming dependent upon a supplementary external relation that radically impacts its global behaviour. These different interpretations can be seen to address the same problem at the level of the general and the singular respectively and, as we shall see, both are empirically valid.

Reading Prigogine's initial description of the supplementary relation more closely, we find two distinct processes at work: (1) an emergent and unexpected relation takes place between the activity of chemical kinetics and the *structure* in space and time of the system that is reacting to that activity, and (2) a correlate behaviour in turn modifies the *meaning* of space and time. As we saw with the analysis of regulative feedback mechanisms in the previous section, here too it is important to consider the validity or otherwise of these respective processes in terms of precedence and antecedence—a question that proves far more complex than before. For this reason, it is worth stressing again that this is *not* a relation that takes place unexpectedly between kinetic activity and the reaction of a system to that activity, but is rather a supplementary relation that takes place unexpectedly between kinetic activity and the *structure in spacetime* of its given system. How are we to account for this unpredictable dependency at far from equilibrium conditions? Indeed, given that these processes involve unpredictable relations with specific structures in spacetime coupled with a synchronous modification of the meaning of space and time, is it even possible to pose questions of discontinuous temporal and spatial ordering that are not already either presumptive or belated?

To begin thinking through precedence and antecedence in dissipative systems, that is, in systems operating at far from equilibrium conditions, we must first consider the functioning of temporal and spatial ordering at its most basic level. Simply put, ordering in space or time describes the displacement of a given being from one point in space and time and its replacement in a subsequent point in space and/or time. While this is of course a gross over-simplification, it nonetheless provides us with a useful starting point going forward, insofar as it presumes that displacement–replacement in spacetime follows along a single smooth trajectory moving from the past and toward the future, a presumption which is in turn premised upon Euclidean and Newtonian concepts of space and time, the articulation of which precludes any possibility of irreversible processes. As Prigogine writes:

> Much of geometry and physics is based on a simple concept of space and time, generally associated with Euclid and Galileo. In this view, time is homogeneous. Time translations may have no effect on physical events. Similarly, space is homogeneous and isotropic; again translations and rotations cannot alter the description of the physical world. It is quite remarkable that this simple conception of space and time may be broken by the occurrence of dissipative structures. Once a dissipative structure is formed, the homogeneity of time, as well as space, may be destroyed (*From Being to Becoming*, 104).

Here, Prigogine offers further clues to the manner of the supplementary relation that emerges between chemical kinetics and the spacetime structure of dissipative systems and greatly modifies the meaning of space and time, noting that, by the simple fact of their coming into being, dissipative structures already possess the potential to *interrupt* the homogeneity and isotropic tendency of space and time and, what is more, the formed being of these structures is such that they may even go so far as to *destroy* the homogeneity of both time and space. Once again, we find here two distinct processes at work: the potential to interrupt the homogeneity of spacetime in the process of its *becoming* on one side, coupled with the potential to destroy the homogeneity of spacetime through the fact of its *being* on the other.

Furthermore, in the initial formulation of this relation, Prigogine stresses the active role as being played by *chemical kinetics*, which requires some further unpacking before we can move on. As we have seen, he describes the relation between chemical kinetics and spacetime structures as *unexpected*, a subject to which he returns later in *From Being to Becoming*. Here, Prigogine sets the stage by first drawing a seemingly innocuous distinction between the specific realms of inquiry to be addressed by thermodynamics and quantum mechanics respectively, with the former dealing with probabilistic processes on the macroscopic level and the latter with probabilistic processes on the microscopic level. Upon looking closer, however, it quickly becomes clear that the basic dynamical equation of quantum mechanics—namely, the Schrödinger equation used to describe the evolution of quantum states over time as measured by an external clock—is entirely deterministic in claiming that once the initial value of a wave function is known it is thereafter possible to calculate its value at any other time, both past and future. For this reason, Prigogine seeks in the first instance to separate thermodynamics from quantum mechanics, noting that thermodynamic description 'deals generally with averages, and the probabilistic elements introduced by quantum mechanics play no role' (132). This distinction, however, is clearly insufficient on its own to prove the *in*determinism of thermodynamic processes. Hence, continues Prigogine, it is 'therefore of special interest to note that *independent of the [Heisenberg] uncertainty relations* there are *macroscopic* systems in which fluctuations and probabilistic description play an essential role' (132, italics added).

For Prigogine, as we know, this 'essential role' necessarily plays out in the 'neighbourhood' of bifurcation points in macroscopic systems under far from equilibrium conditions and leads to the emergent coherence of qualitatively distinct behaviour. Only in proximity to points of bifurcation, he further clarifies, do fluctuations 'play a critical role because there the fluctuation drives the average' and not the other way around (132). This last point is key as it is here, and only here, that the law of large numbers essentially breaks down, and it is this breakdown that makes it possible for irreversible processes to coexist alongside reversible processes. It is also here that Prigogine returns to the subject of chemical kinetics, noting that it is this breakdown of the law of large numbers that 'leads to *unexpected aspects* of chemical kinetics' (132, italics added). Chemical kinetics, he writes, is a relatively new field of inquiry based upon a simple physical interpretation. Starting from the thermodynamic principle that states that the introduction of thermal motion to a physical system causes particles to collide, it can be easily demonstrated that the large majority of these collisions are *elastic*: 'that is, they change the translational kinetic energy (as well as the rotational and vibrational energy if polyatomic molecules are considered), without affecting the electronic structure' (132). However, continues Prigogine, 'a fraction of these collisions are *reactive* and give rise to new chemical species' (132), which thus recalls his initial formulation of the supplementary relation as being between chemical kinetics and the spacetime structure of *reacting* systems, a further specification that we are now able to address.

On the basis of this physical interpretation, two simple inferences can be made that have dominated the development of chemical kinetics since its inception in the closing decades of the nineteenth century: one, the total number of collisions between two types of molecules will be proportional to their concentrations, and two, the total number of *inelastic* collisions will be similarly proportional to their concentrations. Prigogine, however, is quick to point out that these logical inferences break down when faced with the actual behaviour of particles:

> [H]ow can such chaotic behavior, like that depicted by collisions occurring at random, ever give rise to coherent structure? *Naturally some new feature must be taken into consideration; that is, the fact that, near instabilities, the distribution of reactive particles is no longer random*' (132–133, italics added).

Here, the 'unexpected aspects' of chemical kinetics is disclosed as relating to *ordered* emergence of coherent structures that simply cannot come into being, or endure over time, on the basis of an entirely random distribution of particles irrespective of how unlikely that chance might be. Rather, near instabilities, the distribution of reactive particles is no longer random. The new feature described by the supplementary relation, in other words, is that of a process which gives rise to qualitatively distinct new forms and as such is irreversible. It is strongly ironic, therefore, that the 'unexpected aspects' of chemical kinetics refer *not* to that which takes place by *chance*, but rather to that which takes place in accordance with an *order* determined by a tiny minority of obdurate and unyielding collisions, an *in*elasticity that ultimately comes to determine the structure in spacetime of those systems forced by this implacable order into reacting in a way that interrupts the law of large numbers and thus the causal and temporal reversibility it otherwise presumes.

ITERATING THE CATALYST

Of course, as Prigogine and Stengers are quick to point out in *Order Out of Chaos*, it is one thing to posit a universe in which irreversible and reversible processes coexist, and quite another to *accept* such a pluralistic world (257). For this reason, it remains for us to ask by what *means* the obstinately inelastic behaviour of a minority leads to the emergent coherence of qualitatively distinct behaviour in opposition to the law of large numbers and beyond any and all possibility of regulative control.

Prefaced with an apology for the inappropriate (but particularly telling given the broader context) anthropomorphism, Prigogine and Stengers argue that "in equilibrium matter is 'blind,' but in far-from-equilibrium conditions it begins to be able to perceive, to 'take into account,' in its way of functioning, differences in the external world" (14). Given this capacity to respond to and to take account of external gradients, they write, "life no longer appears to oppose the 'normal' laws of physics, struggling against them to avoid its normal fate—its destruction" (14). On its own, this dissolution of the most basic property and thus privilege accorded to life, one that underpins the traditional distinction between the physical sciences and the life sciences that still orders the categories of knowledge in the West, will likely be difficult for many people to accept at face value, and especially so for those wittingly and unwittingly invested in maintaining this distinction for ethical, political, juridical, religious and economic purposes. Nonetheless, and as has been argued throughout, it is incumbent upon us all to finally let go of the well-worn phantasy of exclusivity reserved for living organisms generally and human beings in particular, insofar as letting go of this metaphysical residue is a prior condition for the opening up of future spaces of ethical, political, juridical, religious and economic possibility and plurality.

In contrast to metaphysical interpretations, write Prigogine and Stengers, 'life seems to express in a specific way the very conditions in which our biosphere is embedded, incorporating the nonlinearities of chemical reactions and the far-from-equilibrium conditions imposed on the biosphere by solar radiation' (14). As noted above, this embedding of nonlinear processes within realms that are otherwise linear takes place through the looping of catalytic feedback in which the product of a relation is necessarily involved in its own synthesis, as shown in the Brusselator model (see figure 5.1). Further to this process of catalytic iteration, we need only to add the temporal irreversibility expressed by Markov chains in order to understand the ways and means by

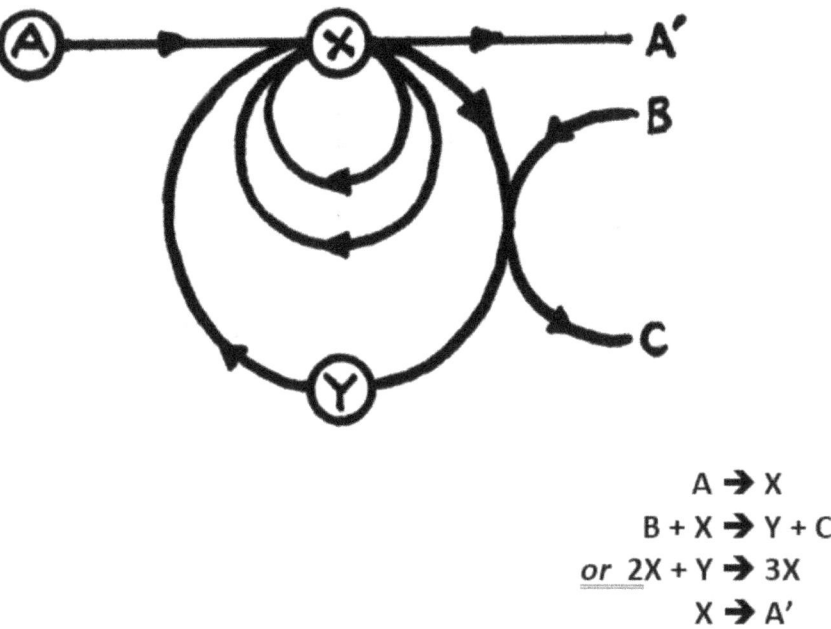

$$A \rightarrow X$$
$$B + X \rightarrow Y + C$$
$$\underline{or} \ 2X + Y \rightarrow 3X$$
$$X \rightarrow A'$$

Figure 5.1. The paths of Brusselator reactions constitutive of catalytic iteration A – A′

which an obdurate minority is able to order an entirely unpredictable iteration of an existent being.

On the most basic level, it is the very *marking* of the arrow of time that sets the temporal ordering of stochastic Markov chains apart from the fully calculable processes that follow from the wave function in quantum mechanics. So just what are Markov chains, and how is it that they take onto themselves the mark of time's irreversible passing? Named after Russian mathematician Andrey Markov, the importance of the Markov process or 'chain' is two-fold: first, Markov chains are characterized by the 'existence of well-defined transition probabilities *independent of the previous history of the system*'; second, they possess a 'remarkable property' in that they can be described in terms of entropy (*Order Out of Chaos*, 236; italics in original). While the intricacy of the mathematical proofs upon which these theses are founded far exceed the scope of this work, we can nonetheless clearly see their relevance for the argument being posed here: Markov chains are nonlinear and thus undetermined physical processes, the temporal ordering of which can be described in strictly logical terms that meet the current scientific standard.

Before moving on, however, it is important to distinguish here between an increasing of entropy based on an arrow of time, as is the case with Markov chains, and an increasing of entropy 'based on our decision to use present knowledge to predict future (and not past) behavior' (238). While somewhat murky, Prigogine and Stengers rightly stress the importance of this distinction insofar as it speaks to the difference between a conception of irreversibility as a wholly *physical* process and that of a *subjective* interpretation of irreversibility that ultimately restores full control over time to the deciding human subject. It is obvious, they write, that probability calculus is oriented in time insofar as the prediction of the future is clearly different from the prediction of the past (retrodiction). Moreover, if this orientation is solely and sufficiently responsible for generating an arrow of time, then the distinction between future and past exists only in the heads of human and nonhuman beings, having evolved the cognitive capacity to predict the probability of future events on the basis of previous events coupled with present context, a predict-ability which risks the future on the presumption of a deterministic universe. On this erroneous foundation, as we saw in relation to bioengineering practices in the opening chapter, the perception of risk thus comes to focus exclusively upon the supposed reliability of 'scientific' prediction while simultaneously failing to take account of the inherent *un*reliability that befalls the very concept of reliable prediction.

Irreversibility, however, can be neither resolved nor absolved by the willing subject. It cannot be conjured away, as Prigogine and Stengers put it, as 'merely the echo of human endeavor and of its limits' (239). At the same time, however, this gives rise to a further problem in that, in order to 'link dynamics and thermodynamics, a physical criterion is required to distinguish between reversible and irreversible processes' (240). It is this physical criterion, as we shall see, which Markov chains provide. Whereas probability '*presupposes* a direction of time and therefore cannot be used to derive the arrow of time,' Markov processes by contrast 'express the intrinsic meaning of the second law' (259). Let us begin by setting out the conditions that must be met by a physical criterion in order for it to be deemed valid in this instance. First and foremost, any such criterion must account for a minimum *selection principle* according to which only one of two forms of solutions can be realized in the physical realm. *Whenever applicable*, write Prigogine and Stengers, 'the second law expresses an intrinsic polarization of nature' (260). Despite superficial similarities, this 'intrinsic polarization' has nothing whatsoever to do with traditional metaphysical binaries, but rather draws a constitutive distinction between *a posteriori* probability calculus on the level of simple dynamics and an *a priori* yet always already supplementary selection principle that only once realized is thereafter circulated on the level of dynamics. We are of course already familiar with this notion of a supplementary relation from our previous discussion of chemical kinetics. In addition, however, it now becomes possible to understand further "how these symmetry-breaking solutions emerge in dynamic systems 'of sufficient complexity' and what the selection rule expressed by the second law of thermodynamics means on the microscopic level" (261).

Consider a system composed of a specific distribution of particles with two distinct types of trajectory. Regardless of the accuracy of our measurements, it is not possible *on the basis of this initial state* to deduce between one or other type of trajectory going forward in time. No matter how small a region of this system one might choose to focus on, this same uncertainty is always present in that in all regions, '*however small, there are always states belonging to each of the two types of trajectories*. For such systems, a trajectory becomes *unobservable*' (*Order Out of Chaos*, 263–264; italics in original). With this, write Prigogine and Stengers, we come up hard against the limits of Newtonian idealization:

> The independence of the two basic elements of Newtonian dynamics, the dynamic law and the initial conditions, is destroyed: the dynamic law enters into conflict with the determination of the initial conditions. We may recall the way in which Anaxagorus conceived of the wealth of nature's creative possibilities. For him, every object contains in each of its parts an infinite multiplicity of qualitatively different seeds. *Here also, each region of phase space maintains a wealth of qualitatively different behaviors*. In this perspective, the deterministic trajectory appears to have limited application (264, italics added).

Moreover, the implications of this 'intrinsic' creativity of being go far beyond both the breakdown of deterministic futures and the limitation imposed by the law of large numbers in small-scale regions of phase space and lead inevitably to a network of true monstrosity. Put another way, even if "we possess a lot of information about the system so that the initial cell formed by its representative points is very small, dynamic evolution turns this cell into a true geometric 'monster' stretching its network of filaments through phase space" (267).[9] Not by chance, such creative monstrosities are clearly akin to the unimaginable and thus unpredictable monsters that are emergent event-machines, as discussed at length in the previous chapter.

With this latter in mind, how might we now be able to better understand such processes of 'dynamic evolution' that cause to emerge truly monstrous material networks? How do Markov chains fit into this dynamic? And what becomes of past and future, that is, of the included and the uncertain, both *in* the process and *as* this process? Before we can close this final chapter, a number of important issues are still to be addressed. The first of these concerns the physical criterion by which reversible and irreversible processes can be distinguished. As we know, it is not possible to derive the arrow of time from the standard form of probability calculus, insofar as the latter presupposes a direction of time. By contrast, however, the braiding together of initial conditions and dynamic law in a relation of mutual dependence rather describes a 'state with an arrow of time [that] emerges from a law, which has also an arrow of time, and which transforms the state, however keeping this arrow of time' (289). Admittedly, Prigogine and Stengers's account of antecedence and derivability here is almost comically obscure, but hopefully things will become much clearer as we progress through this last part. Fortunately, the other outstanding issues are much simpler to articulate, albeit not necessarily to resolve. In schematic summary, these are as follows. First, we need a valid representation of the Second Law of Thermodynamics that can account for both reversible and irreversible physical processes, and on the basis of which it is thereafter possible to articulate a new concept of matter in accordance with fundamental changes in the structure of the basic laws of physics as disclosed by the Second Law. Second, we need to take full account the *a priori* limits imposed upon our ability to manipulate matter as a consequence of the Second Law. Last, we need to understand the centrality of the place and the play of monstrosity in our brave new world turned cancerous.

OF CASCADING MONSTROSITY

Monstrosity, we recall, describes an instantaneous event of transformative power in which the nonlinear emergence of a new form of an event-machine cuts the thread of history. We recall too Derrida's argument that to think both the organicity of the inorganic and the inorganicity of the organic with one and the same concept is thus to think of a new logical and conceptual form of being. It is perhaps to be expected therefore that, for Prigogine too, the machinery of being necessitates an entirely new conceptual form of matter. Before considering in more detail the processes of catalytic iteration as defined by Prigogine, however, it is helpful to very briefly summarize part of the argument for the machinic fallibility of epigenetic processes to this point. In chapters 3 and 4, it was argued that the indeterminacy of machinic fallibility is the parasitical power of interruption inscribed within automatism and constitutive of its particular intelligence. Furthermore, in being constituted through the transmissible memory of changes, epigenetic processes mark the site of temporal contact that is itself and all alone productive of meaning. If we are to account sufficiently for processes of dynamic evolution, then such processes must also be able to account for the particular and peculiar character of epigenetic emergence.

Returning to our exemplary system composed of a distribution of particles with two distinct trajectory types, the essential point is that 'any region, whatever its size, thus always contains different trajectories diverging at each fragmentation. Although the evolution of a point is reversible and deterministic, the description of a region, however small, is basically statistical' (269–270). To understand this, write Prigogine and Stengers, we need only consider a small mobile sphere with a well-defined trajectory. In the idealized form presumed by a closed system, the trajectory of this sphere will be fully determined and determinable forward and backward in time on the basis of its initial conditions. *However*, the interdependence of initial conditions and dynamic trajectory, as illustrated by relations of catalytic feedback in the Brusselator model above, discloses the concept of an operative closed system as a reductive abstraction with no correlation in physical fact. Insofar as an existent system of relations is iterated in being, in other words, uncertainty has always already riven its initial conditions prior to any possibility of abstraction. Moreover, Prigogine and Stengers write, even the smallest uncertainty in the initial conditions 'is amplified through successive collisions. As time passes, the probability of finding the small sphere in a given volume becomes uniform. Whatever the number of transformations, we never return to the original state' (270). Such cascades of amplification and aggregation within unstable dynamic systems, they continue, are clearly reminiscent

> of instabilities as they appear in thermodynamic systems. . . . Arbitrarily small differences in initial conditions are amplified. As a result we can no longer perform the transition from ensembles in phase space to individual trajectories. The description in terms of ensembles has to be taken as the starting point. Statistical concepts are no longer merely an approximation with respect to some 'objective truth' (270–271).

The implications that follow this relocating of a starting point at the level of systemic ensembles are profound. Most importantly, it discloses as *mis*placed the tyranny of probability calculus, the characteristic uses and abuses of which are founded upon the vesting and investing of value in a predictive marker as an approximation of an existent objective truth. In accordance with this claim, predicted risks in the future can be reduced *almost* to nothing simply by striving to improve the accuracy of this approximation of objective truth. This is the entirety of the foundation upon which the industries of risk analysis and risk management are built and which now collapses beneath the aggregate weight of cascading ensembles.

In deconstructing the myth of pure antecedent origin from which the predictions of probability calculus are derived, Markov chains quickly come to occupy a central role in contemporary probability theory. In themselves, Markov processes are actually relatively simple and are used to describe a great many physical processes. That said, however, this relative simplicity would also seem to highlight a fundamental contradiction with our previous claims as to the nonlinearity of emergent forms of being. Key to Markov processes is that its transition probabilities involve only two states (k and l), and that the transition probability from k to l does 'not depend on which states were involved before the occupation of state k. In this sense the system has no memory' (Prigogine, *From Being to Becoming*, 135). This absence of memory appears in stark contrast to our previous contention that nonlinear emergence is not only constrained by the memory of prior states of being, but also is in fact *constituted* through the transmissible memory of changes. So how are we to account for this apparent incommensurability? First of all, and in the manner of a cautionary note, we should not be at all surprised to find ourselves facing problems of this sort, given that the very concept of nonlinear emergence must always already presume some form of temporal paradox. Second, it is important to note Prigogine's own caution in specifying that his claim that 'the system has no memory' holds true only in one particular sense, which acknowledges at the very least the possibility of formulating another sense of the same system in which memory is indeed maintained in some form.

In fact, we have already encountered a situation exactly like this in the course of our previous analysis of metastable systems. Such systems, we recall, are constitutively open and at once *not* open to an infinite array of polymorphic forms, meaning that a given system must be constitutively open *and at the same time* constrained by its own specific historicity. Nonlinear emergence, in other words, is *a priori* unthinkable in accordance with the present *context* of that emergence, but this same context *also* determines the *limits* of that emergence inasmuch as it disallows *a priori* the possibility of that form being anything other than what it will have been. While the proliferating paradoxes of space and time and of antecedence and causality—as marked here by the imperfect future tense—make such processes very difficult to grasp intuitively, the introduction of Markov chains at this point will help to clarify things considerably while further grounding the general thesis on a firm material foundation.

STRETCHING, LOOPING AND LEAPING

Markov processes are by no means uncommon and have long been used by physicists to describe a great number of physical situations as well as to model chemical reactions. What makes them so important, however, is that they physically mark the instant of temporal paradox wherein two mutually exclusive states of being exist in one and the same location in spacetime. Characteristic of Markov chains and a product of catalytic feedback loops, it is this bivalence that ultimately renders all forms of being open to an unthinkable future and in the same moment constrained by their own singular histories. At first glance this claim may seem confusing at best, but this is so only because the *time* of emergence does not allow itself to be described by the laws of Newtonian physics and Euclidean geometry. This is not, however, to suggest that we lack the theoretical framework to describe such a situation. Rather, scholars of quantum theory long ago introduced the concept of superposition in order to account for wave-particle and position-momentum paradoxes at the microscopic level. Most important for us here is that the constitutive paradox common to Markov processes takes place at the superposition of the *catalytic* leap. In turn, this makes possible a better understanding of what Malabou describes as '*embryonic temporal contact*' that on its own and all alone is productive of meaning.

In the introduction, we briefly considered the causal and temporal difficulties that accompany the concept of *immediacy*, understood as the simultaneous appearance in being of a supplemental form of being with the form of being it supplements. Back then it was noted that, as a concept, immediacy is synonymous with magic insofar as it describes a dislocation in space but not in time, in defiance of the laws of classical causality. In addition, this magic of the instantaneous and the simultaneous betrays a further temporal quirk in that it cannot inhere in the speed of its coming or in the brevity of its appearing, but only in the fact of its necessary time*less*ness. Magic, it was argued, describes the impossibility of atemporal emergence. As we shall see now, it also describes the catalytic loops and leaps definitive of Markov chains.

We begin with two fibres, a contracting fibre and a dilating fibre. Analogous with bifurcation theory, these two fibres 'correspond to two realizations of dynamics, each involving symmetry breaking and appearing in pairs. The contracting fiber corresponds to equilibrium in the far distant past, the dilating fiber to the future. We therefore have two Markov chains oriented in opposite time directions' (Prigogine and Stengers, *Order Out of Chaos*, 275). On this basis, write Prigogine and Stengers, it then becomes possible to articulate the transition 'from intrinsically *random* to intrinsically *irreversible* systems' (275, italics added). While appearing rather complex, the accounting of this transition is in fact a relatively straightforward process. First, it is important to recognize just how, exactly, the contracting fibre differs from the dilating fibre. A contracting fibre, they write,

corresponds to a collection of hard spheres whose velocities are randomly distributed in the far distant past, and all become parallel in the far distant future. A dilating fiber corresponds to the inverse situation, in which we start with parallel velocities and go to a random distribution of velocities (276).

At this point, Prigogine and Stengers seek to further clarify this difference by likening it to the difference between incoming waves and outgoing waves described by mathematician Karl Popper in 'The Arrow of Time' (1956) as an example of a system presenting unidirectional processes and thus an arrow of time. Here, I include the cited paragraph in full for precisely the same reason:

> Suppose a film is taken of a large surface of water initially at rest into which a stone is dropped. The reversed film will show contracting, circular waves of increasing amplitude. Moreover, immediately behind the highest wave crest, a circular region of undisturbed water will close in towards the centre. This cannot be regarded as a possible classical process. It would demand a vast number of distant coherent generators of waves the coordination of which, to be explicable, would have to be shown, in the film, as originating from one centre. This, however, raises precisely the same difficulty again, if we try to reverse the amended film (538; cit. *Order Out of Chaos*, 258).

What Popper's example brings into clear focus is that the possibility or otherwise of *inversion* is at the heart of the question of time, or at least of the *testing* of time per se. Indeed, the testing of conceptual rigor is, in a sense, less important than the account of events that is thereby set *en train*. Whatever the technical means, as Prigogine and Stengers put it, 'there will always be a distance from the center beyond which we are unable to generate a contracting wave' (259). So why is this so important? The answer resides in the paradoxical time*less*ness of velocity inversion.

Getting back to our stretchy fibres composed of hard spheres with differently ordered velocities going either from the random to the parallel or from the parallel to the random, the direction in each case is the description of a particular distribution of collisions occurring between the particles of a system—hard spheres, in this case. The key point being made by Prigogine and Stengers is that, irrespective both of human ingenuity and of potential advances in measuring technology, it will *never* be possible 'to control the system to produce parallel velocities after an arbitrary number of collisions' (276). Unlike processes determined by past states of being, in other words, future-oriented processes are determined by an *arbitrary tipping point* beyond which neither return nor recuperation is possible. Hence:

> Once we exclude contracting fibers we are left with only one of the two possible Markov chains we have introduced. In other words, the second law becomes a selection principle of initial conditions. Only initial conditions that go to equilibrium in the future are retained. Obviously the validity of this selection principle is maintained by dynamics. *By suppressing one of the two Markov chains we go from an intrinsically random system to an intrinsically irreversible system* (276, italics added).[10]

With this, Prigogine and Stengers identify three basic elements in the description of irreversibility as it differs from reversible processes: instability, intrinsic randomness and intrinsic irreversibility, although this list is immediately followed up with the coda that 'intrinsic irreversibility is the strongest property: it implies randomness and instability' (276).

THE VELOCITY INVERSION EXPERIMENT

All that said, however, we have yet to satisfactorily resolve the role of retention in the iteration of intrinsically irreversible systems. In the passage above, Prigogine and Stengers maintain that *only* initial conditions that go to equilibrium in the future are retained. What then of our previous claim that, in some other form or sense of retention, nonlinear emergence is constituted through the transmissible memory of changes? For this, we must turn to the strange catalytic superposition that emerges at moments of velocity inversion in gaseous systems (see figure 5.2).

Here, a velocity inversion of every molecule of a gas is obtained at time t_0, after which the gas returns to its initial state at $2t_0$. In describing this process, however, it might seem that Prigogine and Stengers are contradicting their previous claims in relation to memory retention and irreversibility when they argue that 'for the gas to retrace its past there must be some storage of information' (280). In order for the system to repeat its initial conditions at $2t_0$, in other words, it must have *in some sense* retained information about those initial conditions. This retention of prior states, they continue, can in fact be described in terms of *correlations* between particles, and it is these correlations that serve to introduce a distinction between direct processes and inverse processes.

Admittedly, things do get more involved moving forward, but I will restrict myself to recounting only the key points with as much clarity as possible. Most important among these is that velocity inversion cannot occur within a closed system; that is to say, it is not an intrinsic process, but rather requires that some form of information or instruction be imparted to the molecules of a system from *outside* of that system. For illustrative purposes, Prigogine and Stengers here bring Maxwell's infamous demon briefly out of retirement and put him to work performing velocity inversions rather than directing the traffic of velocity distribution. However, while there is doubtless some irony in this invocation of Maxwell's demon as the figure of external interference that plagues—or parasites—every system, the reference to James Clerk Maxwell here serves a serious purpose. It was Maxwell who initially formalized the evolution of the velocity distribution function, $f(r, v, t)$, which gives the number of particles having at time t the position r and the velocity v. The

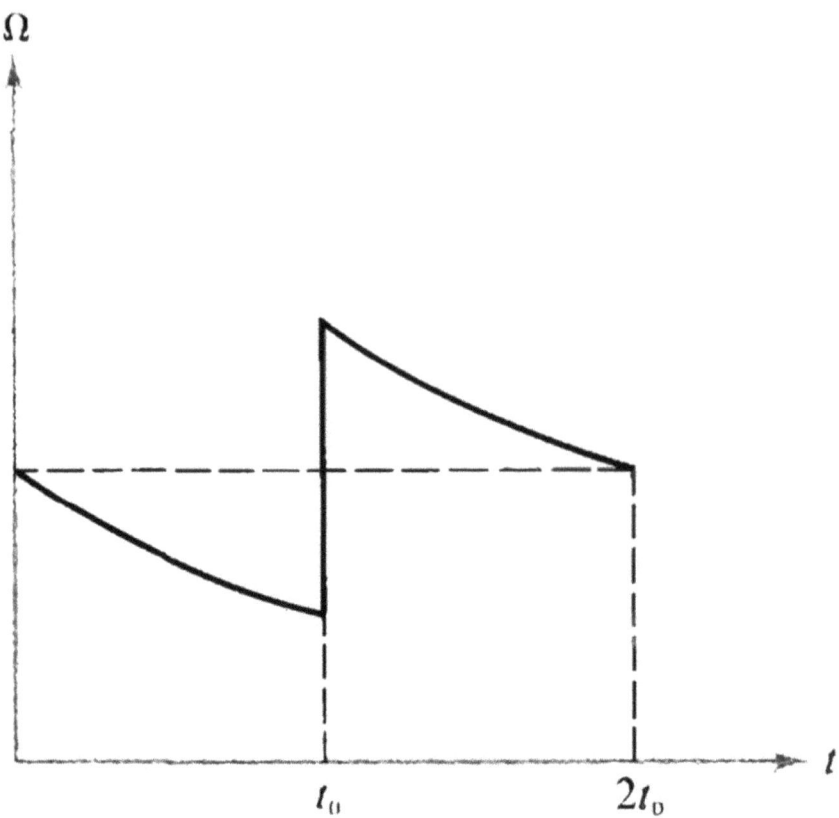

Figure 5.2. Time behaviour of the function Ω in the velocity inversion experiment

validity of this function, however, proved demonstrable only over relatively short periods of time, a limitation which shortly afterward Ludwig Boltzmann sought to overcome by means of a molecular mechanism aimed at further demonstrating its validity over longer periods of time.

While perhaps not immediately apparent, this absurdly abbreviated history is important insofar as the conception of irreversibility being developed by Prigogine is, 'in its essence,' similar to that proposed initially by Maxwell and then Boltzmann, according to which irreversibility is the manifestation on a macroscopic scale of randomness on a microscopic scale. This, writes Prigogine in the conclusion of *From Being to Becoming*, 'is probably the most intriguing conclusion to be drawn in this book: although in physics time was always a mere label associated with trajectories or wave packets, here *time emerges with a completely new meaning associated with evolution*' (176, italics added). Let us return to our newly retrained demon, busily ordering the velocity inversion of the particles of a system from a position outside of that system. Often invoked by both Prigogine and Stengers, Maxwell's demon serves as a placeholder to better illustrate the role played by the microscopic entropy operator—known as the M operator—in the creation of anomalous correlations between particles of a given system.

Recalling the velocity inversion graph (figure 2), the density matrix of system Ω is here tracked over time (t) from its initial conditions at 0 to the restoration of those initial conditions at $2t_0$. This movement is divided into two stages—from 0 to t_0 and from t_0 to $2t_0$—with t_0 marking the point at which all the particles of the system are subject to velocity inversion. Of particular note here is that, if it should happen that particles collide at any given point in time between 0 to t_0 which, to stay with Prigogine's notation, we will call t_1, then these particles must also collide *again* between t_0 to $2t_0$ and must do so precisely at time $2t_0 - t_1$ (put more simply, if we draw a straight line from any point between 0 and t_0 and passing through the centre at t_0, at the point of its intersection between t_0 and $2t_0$ we therefore find the same distribution of particles as that of our starting point). These correlations between states are 'anomalous' for two reasons. First, specific velocity distributions of the particles of a system are precisely correlated to reproduce the same state in the future despite their being separated in time and therefore *non*local. Second, these correlations must disappear during the period $t_0 - 2t_0$, with the system returning to 'normal' behavior at $2t_0$.

In reframing the velocity inversion experiment in terms of entropy production, we thus find two distinct processes at work. In the first period, $0 - t_0$, entropy behaves strictly in accordance with the dynamics of velocity distribution as formulated by Maxwell. In the second, however, the production of entropy accords rather with the *decay of anomalous correlations*. Failing to take account of this distinction, writes Prigogine, leads ultimately to the failure of Boltzmann's attempt at demonstrating the validity of Maxwell's velocity distribution function over longer periods of time, as it fails to recognize the need for 'a statistical expression of entropy that depends explicitly on correlations' (*From Being to Becoming*, 167). Like Maxwell, in other words, Boltzmann too remains bound by the limits of classical dynamics in accordance with which collisions and correlations are deemed to play strictly equivalent roles: collisions give rise to correlations just as correlations *may* cancel out the effect of collisions. But, counter Prigogine and Stengers, there is an essential difference:

> We can control collisions and produce correlations, but we cannot control correlations in a way that will destroy the effects collisions have brought into the system. It is this essential difference that is missing in dynamics but that can be incorporated into thermodynamics. Note that thermodynamics does not enter into conflict with dynamics at any point. *It adds an additional, essential*

element to our understanding of the physical world (*Order Out of Chaos*, 285; italics added).

This essential and supplementary element is the potential opening of every system to the chaotic outside and thus the potential for every system to have come to be in being its own singularly unforeseen and unforeseeable future. At the point of velocity inversion at time t_0, the quantity of the function Ω *jumps* abruptly in being the site of the instantaneous creation of abnormal precollisional correlations that must thereafter be destroyed. Moreover, with this introduction of abnormal correlations between particles, physicists are at last in a position to formulate a faithful representation of the Second Law of Thermodynamics in that, unlike Boltzmann's H-theorem, it demonstrates that an initial state can indeed be restored "at the expense of 'entropy production,' which is now positive during *all* the time evolution of the system," that is, in the period between 0 and $2t_0$ (Prigogine, *From Being to Becoming*, 169).

While this theoretical breakthrough is of clear significance, most compelling for us here concerns just what is happening at the precise moment of velocity inversion at t_0. Crucially, at time t_0 the quantity of Ω takes two distinct values, one for the system before velocity inversion and the other for the system after velocity inversion, and these two situations necessarily take different entropies. This superposition of mutually exclusive values is of fundamental importance going forward, as stressed by Prigogine and Stengers in pointing to its parallels with 'what occurs in the baker transformation when the contracting and dilating fibers are velocity inversions of each other' (*Order Out of Chaos*, 283). At time t_0, in other words, the two values correspond to the potential for reversible and irreversible Markov processes in the distribution of the density matrix Ω, with the one oriented to the past in describing the distribution of collisions going from the random to the parallel and the other oriented to the future in describing the distribution of collisions going from the parallel to the random. As we have seen, entropy production as determined by the Second Law becomes in this way 'a *selection principle of initial conditions*. By suppressing one of the two Markov chains we go from an intrinsically random system to an intrinsically irreversible system' (276, italics added).

From *within* a system of relations, the sudden jump at t_0 is not possible because the increase in entropy it requires is simply not available in isolation. Rather, time t_0 'corresponds to the very moment at which the system is open. We can invert the velocities only by acting from the outside' (283). At t_0, in other words, there is a flow of matter or 'information' coming from outside of the system and leading to a sufficient increase of entropy in that system. With this, writes Prigogine, we are left with just one basic question: 'Can we really construct a function, such as Ω, that takes into account correlations' (*From Being to Becoming*, 169)?

SUPERPOSITION AND SUPPLEMENTARITY

Within the classical tradition that includes dynamics and quantum mechanics, the concept of irreversibility is deemed either to denote a lack of sufficient knowledge, as we saw with Wiener's cybernetics, or as a strictly human property that we, as observers, introduce into an otherwise reversible universe, as with dominant variants of quantum mechanics. In explicit contrast, however, the production of entropy as described by the Second Law requires an entirely different concept of matter. Indeed, this should not even be that surprising given the extraordinary discoveries and developments that have taken place in physics over the course of the last hundred years. As Prigogine and Stengers write,

> the two great revolutions in the physics of our century correspond to the incorporation, in the fundamental structure of physics, of impossibilities foreign to classical mechanics: the impossibility of signals propagating with a velocity larger than the velocity of light, and the impossibility of measuring simultaneously coordinates and momentum. It is not astonishing that the second principle, which as well limits our ability to manipulate matter, also leads to deep changes in the structure of the basic laws of physics (*Order Out of Chaos*, 289–290).

From out of these revolutions, two concepts are of particular importance for us here: first, Heisenberg's undecidability relations, which concern non-commuting operators at the microscopic level, and, second, Niels Bohr's complementarity principle, which provides the framework for the play of undecidability relations generally.[11]

As we know, it was initially assumed by a great many physicists, not excluding Heisenberg himself, that Heisenberg's uncertainty relations have no role to play in the description of entities at the macroscopic level. In formulating a coherent representation of the Second Law of Thermodynamics, however, Prigogine quickly recognizes their importance with regard to the production of entropy on microscopic and macroscopic levels alike: 'Irreversibility is either true on all levels or on none. It cannot emerge as if by a miracle, by going from one level to another' (285). As a consequence of the wave-particle duality definitive of the quantum postulate, we recall, it becomes impossible to *simultaneously* determine both the location and the momentum of a particle at the quantum level, which in turn leads to the positing of Heisenberg's uncertainty relations in accordance with which position and momenta can only be represented by *noncommuting operators*. If, as Prigogine maintains, irreversibility is true either everywhere or nowhere, then what is true on one level of being must also hold true at every other level. Focusing on the noncommuting operators as described by Heisenberg's uncertainty relations, Prigogine argues that this is but one more example of Bohr's complementarity principle, which more broadly states the existence of observables whose numerical value cannot be determined simultaneously. However, whereas Bohr focused on the existence of such observables within the microscopic realm, Prigogine instead lays claim to 'a new form of complementarity—one between the dynamical and the thermodynamic descriptions,' adding that the 'possibility of such a complementarity was explicitly mentioned by Bohr' (*From Being to Becoming*, 174).

So how are we to understand such a relation of complementarity in which dynamical and thermodynamic descriptions are represented as noncommuting operators whose numerical value cannot be determined simultaneously? Can we, in other words, 'superpose the quantum delocalization with delocalization due to irreversibility' (*Order Out of Chaos*, 289)? In fact, we are already well on our way to answering this question. Recalling the example of the velocity inversion experiment, we find an observable distribution function (Ω) simultaneously expressing two distinct numerical values at time t_0, making it impossible to determine both of these values at the same time. Furthermore, time t_0 corresponds to the moment in a 'rejuvenating' cycle in which that system is open to, and receptive of, material imposed upon it from outside and producing abnormal correlations for a limited period of time until order is reiterated at $2t_0$. While the velocity inversion experiment serves to illustrate this process in as simple a way as possible, it nonetheless follows that the same process must describe the behaviour of every distribution function of particles as a result of the entropy operator M. As such, argues Prigogine, the Second Law therefore leads us to a new concept of matter.

Hence, he further clarifies, the 'minimum assumption' necessary for introducing irreversibility into classical mechanics is simply an enlargement of the concept of classical observables: '[I]nstead of functions of coordinates and momenta, an operator M has been introduced' (*From Being to Becoming*, 179). No longer concerned with orbits and trajectories, classical dynamics becomes instead 'the study of the time evolution of distribution functions' (179). A similar consequence obtains on the quantum level as well, insofar as there is 'no way of introducing an operator such as M in the framework of the reversible evolution of wave functions as described by the Schrödinger equation' (179). The self-defeating fixation upon individual trajectories, in other words, must be overturned at all levels of being, with distribution functions taking their place as the basic elements of temporal and creative evolution. In this process, a second new concept comes into play alongside the microscopic

entropy operator *M*, that of *time* operator *T*. Satisfying a new uncertainty relation, Prigogine provocatively describes the time operator *T* as '*a second time*,
an internal time quite different from the time that in classical or quantum
mechanics simply labels trajectories or wave functions' (209). This second,
internal time is the *a priori* possibility of time's arrow, of contingency and
nonlinearity as cause and condition of irreversibility at both microscopic and
macroscopic levels of being. Irreversibility, in short, is inscribed into the
structure of matter.

THE EVOLUTION OF TIME

In attempting to take account of both reversible and irreversible physical
processes, my aim throughout this chapter has been to provide sufficient
detail without getting bogged down in some of the more arcane and esoteric
aspects that are likely impenetrable to a great many scholars working exclusively within the humanities broadly understood, which in large part includes
myself. Of course, such an approach can never be entirely successful, seeking as it does to demarcate—as far as possible—a carefully balanced middle
ground that does justice to the complexity of the arguments on both sides.
With this in mind, and prior to introducing the sleepwalkers and zombies
through whom or which the various threads of our argument thus far will
come together in the conclusion, it is likely useful in closing this chapter to
briefly recap the principal points claimed herein.

Most intriguing concerns the transformed and transformative play of time
itself, which as Prigogine argues emerges with 'a completely new meaning
associated with evolution' (*From Being to Becoming*, 176). At the centre of
this transformative emergence is the recasting of entropy production, which
becomes positive both as an open metastable process and in the meaning
attributed to that process. Initially, entropy is deemed as serving an entirely
negative function in the macroscopic and microscopic levels alike, prohib-
iting processes such as the flow of heat from hot to cold and the perfect
recuperation of workable energy in the former, and in the latter prohibit-
ing particular classes of initial conditions. Put another way, the 'distinction
between what is permitted and what is prohibited is maintained in time by
the laws of dynamics' (Prigogine and Stengers, *Order Out of Chaos*, 285). It
is from out of this rule of law, however, that 'the positive aspect emerges: the
existence of entropy together with its probability interpretation. *Irreversibility
no longer emerges as if by a miracle* at some macroscopic level' (285, italics
added). In place of a presumption of error or lack, or of an approximation
awaiting its proper determination at some point in the future, macroscopic

irreversibility marks instead the fundamental role played by time across every level of being.

Indeed, while countless iterations of reversible material processes do indeed exist which can be usefully treated as such, 'most systems of interest to us, including all chemical systems and therefore all biological systems, are time-oriented on the macroscopic level' (285). Rather than an illusion, continue Prigogine and Stengers, this 'expresses a broken time-symmetry on the microscopic level' (285). Moreover, as we have seen, the time-symmetry of dynamics can be broken in one of two different ways—that is, either as a stable system of relations moving in fully determined fashion toward a future state of equilibrium or as a metastable system of relations emerging from an initial state of equilibrium and as such subject to potential points of bifurcation and thus the chance of unforeseen coherence.

In parallel with this transforming of time, the probability processes as consistent with the Second Law also transform the traditional concept of matter. Unruly kin to the operators of position and momenta that proved fundamental in the development of quantum mechanics, Prigogine's introduction of entropy operator M and time operator T become necessary in order to take account of supplementary properties that emerge *in addition to* those described by classical dynamics, which can 'come only from some type of randomness' (*From Being to Becoming*, 175). Put simply, the transition from dynamics to thermodynamics and from *a posteriori* calculation to *a priori* probability brings forth new metastable entities in being. At all levels, write Prigogine and Stengers, "be it the level of macroscopic physics, the level of fluctuations, or the microscopic level, *nonequilibrium is the source of order. Nonequilibrium brings 'order out of chaos'*" (*Order Out of Chaos*, 286–287; italics in original). Equally important, however, is that the Second Law makes chaos out of order and as such makes possible the chance emergence into being of the monstrously new. Beyond good and evil, beyond life and death, beyond subject and object, entropy marks instead a remarkable opening up of *a priori* potential that can never be properly controlled, nor can it avail itself of the fictive safety quite literally being sold off the back of countless 'management' strategies that presume to guarantee our safety in the face of the future. At the opening to the future, however, only zombies and sleepwalkers exist.

Conclusion

Ends and Endings: Surviving the Zombie Apocalypse

In the end, after everything, what does it mean to be *after* life in a way that is *not* a form of survival, of living on (*sur-vivre*), be that as an angel or a zombie or as some practically unimaginable form of timeless continuation? The answer to this question requires that we first answer a different question that, in the end, may or may not be the same question: namely, what does it mean to survive the nature and the concept of *life*?

This is no idle question. It is in the name of life as an exclusive property that capitalism has proved victorious, rendering implausible if not—theoretically at least—impossible any other systemic forms or order. While paradoxical indeed, the nature and the concept of life underwrites the reduction to a single parasitic tendency that we know today as both the Anthropocene and the Capitalocene, the lifeblood of a global cybernetic machine of reproduction expressed through the arithmetic of surplus value and its profitable extraction. By contrast, the structuring nonlinearity of dissipative systems necessarily exceeds the control of the broader system and context in which it emerges and does so in ways that by definition cannot be predicted, foreseen or even imagined. As the disorderly potential for disruptive and monstrous creation that precedes every manifest form of being, the challenge posed by the catalytic feedback processes characteristic of dissipative systems becomes ever more urgent once a single cancerous inclination comes to order the system as a whole.

THE ZOMBIE APOCALYPSE

We ended the last chapter in provocative fashion, stating that at the opening to the future, only zombies and sleepwalkers exist. How are we to understand this figural provocation? Perfect strangers to one another, zombies and sleepwalkers nonetheless occupy an identical terrain in the present, differing only in their orientation to the future. This difference of temporal orientation is critical, however, insofar as it describes nothing less, and nothing more, than the chance to break free of the past as the historicity of instrumental capture. So, with this in mind, what exactly is the zombie apocalypse, and when is it likely to occur? Before answering these questions, it is important to understand that an apocalypse is not a single, universal and catastrophic event that forever severs 'before' from 'after.' Similarly, we must not confuse apocalypse with extinction, be that of species, biosphere or world. As myriad processes, apocalypses rather happen all the time. Given this coda, how can we ever hope to survive the annihilation of form that comes in the form of zombiedom?

As we know all too well, it is a long-held truism in the West that posits the inalienable existence of an internal principle unique to biological organisms that governs the organization of living forms of matter. Indeed, this much-vaunted principle of totalizing form remains fundamental to how we think of ourselves as human beings today. After all, to think anything else is to recast human beings as nightmarish monstrosities lacking both purpose and privilege. As such, it is a huge irony, therefore, that at the end of everything the supreme principle of life itself turns all forms of life into zombies and nothing more. What, then, is going on—or not going on—with life? How, and why, is life always already afterlife, always and only living on, mere survival?

At equilibrium, as we know, there is not a whole lot going on—any gradients such as differences of temperature or pressure within a given system of relations have been resolved, and thus the system enters a static state. Having reached this state, nothing else will, or can, ever happen. This is the meaning not only of equilibrium but also of instrumentality—in designating survival as nothing more than mute and immobile continuance, the two concepts are indistinguishable in practice. Furthermore, this situation also describes—and to great effect—the configuration of the world in the mode of Heidegger's standing reserve, a mode or an inclination which attains its completed form in the victorious ignorance of the Anthropocene. As we have seen, however, the static form characteristic of equilibrium and instrumentality alike is based upon the presumption that it is in fact *possible* for a system to be entirely self-contained in its functioning and safely closed off from any and all potential incursions from the world beyond its impermeable borders.

Of course, this figure of the monadic sovereign as existing on its own and without relation is a myth, that is to say, an ideology and a blunt one at that. Just as Leibniz elevates the newly wrought principle of reason to the status of supreme principle, so too is the entirely normative figure of the monad elevated to the status of supreme figure of what is now a thoroughly principled reason. As a figure of inherent perfection and thus pure of will, the closeted sovereign alone—and quite literally so—is thus elevated to the position of supreme arbiter of the physical world of objects and sole judge of an object's validity based not upon its value in-itself, but only with respect to its value *for* the sovereign *as* its arbiter and judge. In this way, the supreme principle simultaneously begets its own sovereign principal.

For us today, the idea of an external and omnipresent arbiter likely seems outdated and naïve, mere residue perhaps from a time long past. Indeed, just the *possibility* of a system being able to *attain and thereafter maintain itself* at static equilibrium is on its own sufficient to condemn the universe to its ever-increasing annexation by formal stasis that ultimately ends with nothing at all. As forms of being like any other, the set of 'lifeforms' must also be subject to this ever-encroaching stasis that permits of no change and no movement, ultimately becoming continuance and only continuance. Merely surviving with no chance of ever being otherwise, living on without even a chance of death, life becomes what it always has been, the stubborn ideological residue of a timelessness that can never be insofar as it can never *not* be. Such is the afterlife of equilibrium, the zombies of instrumentality, taking form in a myriad of apocalyptic processes that end only and always in endless and changeless living on. Paradoxically, this end without end, this being without will or desire, is inscribed at the very origin of life in the form of sovereign will.

Despite this, the keystones of the human-zombie creation myth, along with its apocalyptic teleology, remain at least as firmly entrenched today as at any time previously, reigning supreme behind calculations of exchange, ignorance and hubris and obscured further by the reiteration of 'natural' limits. There is no better example of this entrenchment than that of the cosmological concept of *heat death*. Articulated initially in the first phase of thermodynamics as dealing exclusively with the negatively perceived role of entropy in relation to systems at equilibrium, this apocalyptic *telos* has over time taken on the weight of a self-evident truth having being proclaimed, often gleefully, on all sides ever since. Lacking any foundation in physical processes, the ideology of heat death is, in the end and literally so, the impossible hope of an already hopeless zombie.

THE FUTURE OF SLEEPWALKING

Inhabiting the timeless afterlife of equilibrium, the residual zombies of instrumentality are thus condemned to a form of living on characterized by an inability to be anything other than what it always already is. Amid the ongoing apocalypse that we know as the Anthropocene, the zombie thus becomes its supreme totalizing figure: a champion of classical causality and perfect prediction; of instrumental captivity and universal exchangeability. Coincidental with the invention of the steam engine and the consequent focus upon questions of heat and entropy in the closing decades of the nineteenth century, philosopher Friedrich Nietzsche animates this figure with extraordinary keenness as the embodiment of what he calls *the will to nothingness*.[1]

It is our supreme good fortune, however, that all of this breaks down with the chance awakening of what Prigogine calls *hypnons*, that is, *sleepwalkers*. At equilibrium, write Prigogine and Stengers, the particles making up a system essentially behave as independent entities that, in the manner of sleepwalkers and zombies both, ignore one another completely. While each of these particles may be as complex as we like, their oblivious behavior nonetheless remains the same insofar as "at equilibrium their complexity is turned 'inward'" (*Order Out of Chaos*, 287). In being composed of oblivious hypnons, a system at equilibrium is thus *incoherent* insofar as formal coherence requires a specific ordering *relation* between the particles. At equilibrium, in other words, zombies and sleepwalkers are identical, with no possible way to distinguish between zombie particles and sleepwalker particles in the present state of a given system at equilibrium. In the present, a sleepwalker *is* a zombie.

As we know, however, no system is sovereign and thus inviolate in its iteration. We can put this in another way: *to sleep* necessarily implies the possibility of being *awake*, that is to say, to sleep *and* to be awake. Of course we already have a fairly extensive history with this pairing, which needs to be considered, but first let us put this argument in yet another way. The survival of the zombie, we recall, requires only that it be always what it already is, thus ruling out any chance whatsoever that it might 'awaken' from out of its perpetual zombiedom. The hypnon, by contrast, while describing a zombie in the present, nonetheless somehow retains the potential to be awake in relation to the future and, in so doing, ceases to be a zombie in becoming other than what it already is. *What has the chance to undo the future as presently ordered is simply that to be is always the chance to not be.* Oriented toward a potential future that remains unthinkable in the present, being is always already the possibility of not being. Being, in short, carries its own survival in the form of its *not* being. Recalling Derrida's difference without difference in passing from thought to thought, we discover that in the world of the new only old zombies are still alive.

In present being, there exist only independent and therefore incoherent zombies and, should the fundamental reversibility of time as posited by classical dynamics prove correct, then that is all that *can* exist. Unmoved and unmoving, such is the apocalyptic present of a fully determined and thus entirely predictable world of things. But this is not our universe, or at least it is not *wholly* our universe. Put simply, a hypnon is a zombie only until it is not—such is the complex paradox constitutive of time's irreversible arrow. Returning now to the sleep of reason, we have previously encountered the sleep-awake antonym in two distinct contexts. In the first case, we find Heidegger in ironic mood describing the unusually long incubation period that preceded Leibniz's formulation of the principle of reason and which constitutes thereafter 'a wakefulness that no longer admits of sleep, least of all, an incubation' (*The Principle of Reason*, 118). Against this, however, it was argued that the seeming apodicticity of this supreme principle of reason serves instead to close off critical inquiry regarding its plausibility as both a reasoned and reasonable principle. Furthermore, insofar as, wittingly or otherwise, it animates the entirety of the metaphysical tradition in the West, the breakdown of the analogy pairing reason with wakefulness and unreason with sleep at once calls time on that entire tradition.

Exemplifying this fundamental breakdown of metaphysical reason, the second and most substantial engagement with the sleep-awake antonym occurs in the first chapter, detailing the death of Socrates and the argument from opposites primarily in the *Phaedo*. Here, in failing to distinguish between graded and binary antonyms, Socrates mistakenly claims to have sufficiently proved the continuance of the soul after death as a necessary consequence of the reversibility of *graded* antonyms that take place along a single axis, whereas the pairings awake–asleep and living–dead are both *binary* antonyms composed of mutually exclusive terms and thus without relation. Furthermore, this fundamental error in turn forms the basis of Socrates's claim that the potential for change in the future is a property of living beings exclusively and, indeed, that life 'is' only this possibility of difference over time. If not for the reversive processes of dying and 'alive-ing,' in other words, the universe and all things in it would succumb sooner or later to a perfect state of moribund stasis determined by the impossibility of difference. By this late stage, the irony of Socrates's attribution of such privilege on behalf not only of *life*, but also of an *afterlife*, will hopefully require no further explanation.

At equilibrium, the laws of fluctuations and correlations are universal on microscopic and macroscopic levels alike. At equilibrium, in other words, there are only zombies. At *non*equilibrium, however, this totalizing ordering of a system's composite elements can no longer be determined. At nonequilibrium, in other words, zombies have the chance to become *hypnons in the present by virtue of their relation to an unthinkable future that only ever will have been.* Recalling our earlier discussion of the evental machine, this chance is the *structure* of possibility itself, that is, of the *peut-être*, of the real and dense *perhaps* that heralds an unheard-of form of being without announcing itself and without a horizon of expectation. In recasting the zombies in the role of hypnons by the act of waking them up—meaning that in the very same moment they *become* hypnons they will also have *ceased to be* hypnons—nonequilibrium introduces a structural coherence entirely foreign to equilibrium. Crucially, this potential activity in relation to nonequilibrium conditions is not only the property of all material being, but also that beings can in fact generate these conditions themselves. As the agency of transformation, it is the foreign and the parasitic that have the chance to save the universe that will have been from the moribund emptiness and will do nothing constitutive of so-called 'life.' As the condition of being, it is the alien parasite that already undoes the same and which always moves the unmoving.

Having reached this point, write Prigogine and Stengers, we are at last in a position to speak about 'evolution' in its proper sense:

> As we have seen, dissipative structures require far-from-equilibrium conditions. Yet the reaction diffusion equations contain parameters that can be shifted back to near-equilibrium conditions. The system can explore the bifurcation diagram in both directions. Similarly, a liquid can shift from laminar flow to turbulence and back. There is no definite evolutionary pattern involved. The situation for models involving the size of the system as a bifurcation parameter is quite different. Here, growth occurring irreversibly in time produces an irreversible evolution. But this remains a special case, even if it can be relevant for morphogenetic development. Be it in biological, ecological, or social evolution, we cannot take as given either a definite set of interacting units, or a definite set of transformations of these units. The definition of the system is thus liable to be modified by its evolution. The simplest example of this kind of evolution is associated with the concept of structural stability (*Order Out of Chaos*, 189).

At the precise point of transition from equilibrium to nonequilibrium, such as is the case of nonlinear chemical processes, local events within a system impact that system as a whole insofar as emergent correlations link together particles despite being separated by macroscopic distances. While this transition indeed *resembles* a phase transition when viewed from outside, as noted previously by Prigogine and Stengers, the two transitional processes are in fact mutually exclusive. Despite this, however, the perception of similarity to the well known and thus easily understood process of phase transition provides a useful comparison in the attempt to clarify the meshwork of novel emergence understood as phases of futural technicity.

PHASES OF FUTURE TECHNICITY

It remains for us at this late stage to introduce one final critical concept insofar as it relates to phase space, technical evolution and innovation without precedent, that of *technical genesis* as defined by French philosopher Gilbert Simondon. For Simondon, contemporary culture in the West is ultimately defined by its misunderstanding of technics, a devastating error that can be rectified only by engaging with technical ensembles outside of the regime of instrumental capture. In *On the Mode of Existence of Technical Objects* (1958), Simondon argues that modalities determining the genesis of the technical object serve to distinguish it from both the aesthetic object and the living being. Moreover, by paying attention to these specific modalities it thus becomes possible 'to avoid using classifications as a way of thinking that occurs after genesis only to distribute the totality of objects into genera and species suitable for discourse' (26n1). In opposition to this dominant metaphysical paradigm, writes Simondon, the technical object in fact 'retains the essence of its past evolution in the form of its technicity' and thus, as bearer of this technicity, 'can become the subject of adequate knowledge only if the latter grasps the temporal sense of its evolution' (26n1).

In contrast to the instrumental point of view that serves to restrict technical knowledge to the understanding of isolated schemas of operation, Simondon argues that a technical object is never simply this or that thing but is rather *that of which there is* genesis: 'The unity of the technical object, its individuality, and its specificity are the characteristics of consistency and convergence in its genesis. The genesis of the technical object partakes in its being' (26). Here, Simondon explicitly situates his argument in opposition to the traditional metaphysical paradigm that, as we have seen from Aristotle through to Heidegger, excludes technical objects from concern on the grounds that they lack the origin and ordering principle of their own existence—on the grounds, in other words, that their beginnings and ends, their *arkhe* and *telos*, are always and only to be found outside of the objects themselves. Simondon, however, argues that 'the technical object in its oneness is a unit of coming-into-being' and as such is an ensemble of phylogenetic forms specific to itself as a process of technical evolution:

> The technical object is that which is not anterior to its coming-into-being, but is present at each stage of its coming-into-being; the technical object in its oneness is a unit of coming-into-being. . . . As such, as in a phylogenetic lineage, a

definite stage of evolution contains dynamic structures and schemas within itself
that partake in the principal stages of an evolution of forms (26).

Hence, rather than being defined by the lack of its own reason for being, the
technical object for Simondon 'unifies itself internally according to a principle of inner resonance' over the course of numerous phases of convergence
and self-adaptation constitutive of its specific evolutionary lineage (26).
Crucially, this evolution of forms is *not* a linear process, which is to say that
it always already refutes the possibility of perfect predictability otherwise
required by causal determinism to justify instrumentalization. The technical
ensembles of today are *not*, in other words, descendants of antecedent forms
simply because they have 'a greater degree of perfection in relation to use'
(26). Here, Simondon's critique dovetails somewhat with that of Heidegger,
for whom the push toward the greatest possible perfection to which modern
technology tends consists 'in the completeness of the calculably secure establishing of objects' (*The Principle of Reason*, 121). As we shall see, however,
this concept of a phylogenetic series of forms specific to the evolution over
time of technical beings not only presupposes a thoroughgoing deconstruction of vitalism, but also, together with Heidegger's *phusei*-being, Serres's
parasitical black box, Malabou's epigenetic plasticity, and the mad time of the
Derridean event-machine, prepares the ways for posthumanist critique to play
a fundamental part in the future by moving us at last beyond our collective
fear of the dark and into the potential spaces of ethical accountability.

To this end, Simondon begins by proposing a revised definition of the
concept of genesis that is also capable of accounting for technical objects.
There is genesis, he writes, 'when the coming-into-being of a system of a
primitively oversaturated reality, rich in potential, greater than unity and har-
boring an internal incompatibility, constitutes for this system the discovery
of compatibility, a resolution through the advent of structure' (*On the Mode*,
168). Understood, in other words, as the novel resolution of prior incompatibility, the advent or event of each new form of being constitutes a singular
and distinct phase of convergence and self-adaptation, the systematic totality
of which comes to define its singular evolutionary lineage under sway of its
own principle of inner resonance constitutive of its supplementary excess
in relation to the instrumental unity of its parts. Furthermore, Simondon
here defines technical genesis explicitly as a tending toward thermodynamic
metastability, describing such structuration as 'the advent of an organization
that is the basis of an equilibrium of metastability. Such genesis opposes itself
to the degradation of the potential energies contained in a system through
the passage to a stable state from which transformation is no longer possible' (168).

For Simondon then, the formulation of *technical* genesis is at once the *re*formulation of the concept of genesis in general. Ironically, what was once the defining characteristic of life is thus revealed as the instrument of its own thoroughgoing deconstruction. In place of a vitalist foundation that proves either contradictory or else dependent upon the donation of a supernatural gift of some sort—lifeforce, soul, vibrancy, *Geist* or whatever else—Simondon proposes instead the notion of 'the individuation of oversaturated systems, conceived as successive resolutions of tensions through the discovery of structures at the heart of a system rich in potential. Tensions and tendencies can be conceived as really existing in a system: the potential is one of the forms of the real, as completely as the actual' (168). As the genetic process of systemic becoming, in other words, individuation describes the successive discoveries and resolutions of internal incompatibilities through the advent of novel structures, each of which constitutes a distinct form and phase of convergence and auto-adaptation. Moreover, and this point is fundamental, the particular antagonisms and tendencies of a given system that compose its inner resonance—its *potentials*, in short—exist as forms no less real than the actualized forms of a system. The potentials of a system, argues Simondon, 'are not the simple virtuality of future states, but a reality that pushes them into being' (168). In contrast to the virtuality of as yet unrealized future states, the potentials of a system are rather *forms of reality* that constitute the power of coming-into-being by the fact of their forcing the future into being.

In the place of both the Aristotelian and Heideggerian notions of *phusei*-being, Simondon poses instead that of *phase*-being as the condition of coming-into-being. Based initially upon the concept of phase ratio in physics, he argues that a 'phase' is not reducible to a given moment isolated in or over time, but rather a phase is a phase only in relation to other phases, and it is this 'existence of a plurality of phases [that] finally defines the reality of a neutral center of equilibrium in relation to which there is a phase shift' (173). As a systemic relation of reciprocal tensions, he continues, the schema of phases is therefore 'very different from the dialectical schema, because it implies neither necessary succession, nor the intervention of negativity as a motor of progress' (173). As entropy operator and thus 'totally independent of the notions of genus and species,' Simondon argues instead that the notion of the phase rather puts into play

a principle according to which the temporal development of a living reality proceeds through a split on the basis of an initial, active center, then through a regrouping after the furtherance of each separated reality resulting from this split; each separated reality is the symbol of the other, just as each phase is the symbol of the other phase or phases; no phase, as a phase, is balanced with respect to itself, nor does it contain a complete truth or reality: every phase is

Conclusion

abstract and partial, untenable; only the system of phases is in equilibrium in its neutral point; its truth and its reality are this neutral point, the procession and conversion in relation to this neutral point (173–174).

For Simondon, a metastable organization comes into being in the present as one specific form that takes its place within a broader phylogenetic series composing the principal stages of a nonlinear evolution of forms. Technical epigenesis, in other words, describes the putting to work of a system of always partial phases that, untenable in isolation, come to exist only 'in its neutral point; its truth and its reality are this neutral point, the procession and conversion in relation to this neutral point' (174). This dovetails clearly with Malabou's definition of complex systematic forms as the making manifest of a quantitative capacity to combine with, or to displace, that which lies contingently outside through reciprocal processes of interference and transformation by way of catalytic feedback processes. As we know, Malabou locates the taking place of epigenetic mechanisms 'at the moving contact point between origin and the present state of affairs, until their difference disappears right into their contact—tensed origin, retrospective present, future in the making' (*Before Tomorrow*, 157). Both Simondon's neutral point of metastability and Malabou's moving contact point as the resolution of differential temporal gradients together describe not the breakdown of reason, but rather the breakdown of what remains a pervasive yet perverse form of instrumental logic. Strictly speaking, evolution names the supplementary chance of an existent potential to have taken place in an unthinkable and thus monstrous form that ultimately forces the future into being as that which will have been.

While comparatively brief, this exegesis of Simondon's concept of technical genesis helps to further clarify the place of ethical accountability in the uncertain world that is the future and, in so doing, to draw together in conclusion the various threads of the thesis. As has been the case throughout, the key term here is *potential*—potential at its most profound and fundamental insofar as it is the potential to take on novel forms and ways of being that, for us today, are by definition unthinkable and will forever remain so. And potential, above all else, comprises the primary concern of both the posthuman and the technological insofar as it concerns nothing more or less than the chance of a future in the making. The metaphysical concept of life only ever drags us back to the impossibility of genetic origin and to the debilitating ghost in the teleological machine that is all that remains of humanism. By contrast, metastable formal systems, which include every form of 'living' being as traditionally described, have no need of magical donations of vitality from some perfect elsewhere, but rather emerge and endure by way of the opening of a reciprocal deferral to meaning that is the very definition of purposiveness.

The critical, political and ethical consequences of coming into being after life are profound. Of these, perhaps the most urgent and most difficult is the redirection of critique as newly tasked with the facilitating of creative paths oriented toward the emancipation of automatisms. As we have seen, whereas the concept of genetic determinism presupposes a transcendental origin, the epigenetic relations definitive of machinality instead remain always preliminary; that is, they compose the necessary condition of self-organization but do not determine the form of that organization prior to its taking place in being. As the supplementary condition of preliminary relations between always partial phases, metastable forms of being occupy the moving contact point between necessity and contingency that Malabou describes so acutely as 'the true space of life for automatisms' (*Morphing Intelligence*, 121).

TO HAVE DONE WITH THE LIFE
OF LIBERAL MORALITY

Previously, it was argued that the emergence of movedness as form discloses that the play of technicity and the work of ethicality are indistinguishable in fact. While this is a paradoxical sort of disclosure—it does not offer further clarity but rather only folds back upon itself in obdurate refusal of an erroneously imposed distinction—it is a critical revelation nonetheless. This becomes clear once rephrased in the form of a philosophical statement: *a priori technicity situates ethics as the condition of the technological.* Furthermore, it is as a necessary corollary of this statement that the question of time returns once again to the forefront of contemporary philosophical concern. Stated bluntly, this question does not ask what *we* can do *with* time, but rather what *can* be done *through or by way of* time? Rather than an undoing or cancellation of the future, this question requires thinking otherwise that, as Derrida argues, belongs only to the future insofar as it makes the future possible.

Let us go back to the beginning and to the coincidence of instrumentality and causality, from which all biological organisms are excluded on the basis of an imaginary internal principle that governs the organization of *living* forms of matter exclusively. Quite literally super-natural, this vital ordering principle alone serves as the ground upon which the entire edifice of liberal morality is constructed. It is also the necessary exclusion of the very possibility of ethics, which can begin only following the collapse of the living-nonliving binary. The chance of ethical accountability, in other words, *demands* that we first be done with life once and for all. But how are we to respond to such a demand, and why is it necessary?

The demand for accountability is a refusal to countenance the lie of government safeguarding from risk that serves primarily to facilitate further extraction of surplus value while at the same time serving to conceal this primary function. As we have seen in relation to those lively miracles of bioengineering known to us today as extremophiles, the production and reproduction of manifest risk and, more importantly, of the apparent *absence* of risk, is a very simple process—as simple as classifying an entity as either a 'who' or a 'what.' In a single stroke, in other words, the classification of a given entity as an inanimate object—a 'what'—excludes that being from ethical concern and in so doing constitutes it legally and morally as a resource available for use in any manner and without any risk. In this, the recent history of extremophiles provides a particularly compelling narrative. Prefaced by centuries of scientific certainty as to the impossibility of their existence, their initial discovery leads to a fundamental revision of the traditional concept of life. However, as further study discloses their practically limitless potential as an economic resource, this status as living beings is thereafter deemed merely provisional, allowing for their reclassification as mere objects in accordance with their perceived value as commodities. Hence, despite being impossible and thus incalculable only a few decades before, every relation and evolutionary pathway of extremophiles moving into the future suddenly becomes entirely predictable and thus fully under human control going forward on the basis of nothing more than a simple shift in classification. By way of a change of pronoun, time is thus abruptly withdrawn from a select group of value-producing extremophiles and deemed as no longer having a role to play in their future. As Catherine Malabou states in another context, time ultimately vanishes as a question.

This production of the *appearance* of instrumental control, however, is explicitly refuted by our post-Darwinian understanding of evolution as a cyclic material process of reiteration at every level of complexity, with selection for mutation understood as a nonlinear process dependent upon fluctuations and mechanisms of catalytic feedback incorporating transmissible memory of changes linked to a specific environment. Hence, while it only ever *appears* necessary to safeguard the populace from the risky behavior of inanimate objects, the prior condition of ethical possibility is in fact the necessity of profound *un*predictability, that is, of being as being fundamentally *un*safe. Beyond the resurgent illusions of contemporary vitalism today and beyond politically and economically invested delusions of safety, the *possibility* of ethics is thus the *im*possibility of programmed technologies engineered under the auspices of strategic risk management.

As has been argued throughout, the *a priori* potential for nonlinear evolution understood as a general property of being means that, first, any and all predictions founded upon present or habitual states of being are *necessarily* subject to possible error and, second, that it is *a priori* impossible to predict the future emergence of novel forms of being. Rather than describing the absence of an ethical dimension, this *a priori* inscription of the potential to give rise to profoundly unforeseen and unforeseeable forms in fact marks *absolute* ethical necessity and, as such, demands in response an urgent reconsideration of the ways in which we currently interact—or, far more frequently, fail to interact—with beings other than ourselves and with the future. It is with regard to this last that Simondon's extended concept of *technical* genesis proves particularly helpful. For Simondon, as we know, the technical entity is a systematic and metastable totality composed of always partial phases of convergence and auto-adaptation that take place within a singular phylogenetic or epigenetic series of forms. However, just as we previously argued that there is nothing about biological genesis that speaks exclusively to life, so too there is nothing about Simondon's technical genesis that speaks exclusively to *non*life. At the neutral point of metastable structuration, in other words, the living being and the technical object are indistinguishable. Beyond both, the general economy of evolution is the chance to have forced the future into being, and it is to this chance of a future that the future of ethical discourse must respond.

In explicit contrast to the normative concept of autopoiesis, questions of ethical concern rather take as their subject the inventiveness of a general artificiality that, as Claire Colebrook argues, "does not extend life but continually undermines any possibility of 'a' life" ('All Life Is Artificial Life,' 8). As we have seen, Colebrook describes this as a counter-logic of artifice, one that provides the theoretical tools with which we have the chance to escape from the timeless stasis of instrumental capture and open to futures other than those predicated upon the past. Recalling too both Derrida and Meillassoux, such speculation necessitates a paradoxical rationalism that is inextricably linked to the question of time and to a radical contingency that ultimately liberates the dense and real 'perhaps' from the ordered confines of a deterministic quarantine.

BEING AND NOT BEING: TO BE *IS* TO NOT BE

Just as there is no *life in general*, so too there is no *matter in general*—with this simple phrase, Colebrook brings us to the very heart of the problems that face us both before and after tomorrow. In contrast to the mutual exclusivity of metaphysical dualisms which presuppose that a prior ethical differentiation has already taken place, the universe of which we are a part is a composite of radically differing configurations, partial phases and fluctuating intensities that come together in the form of unpredictable and incompossible metastable systems and, as such, it relocates the time and place of ethics with the conditions, contexts and facilitation of emergent systems.

It is, in other words, no longer an acceptable practice to sidestep the question of ethics wherever and whenever it proves either convenient or profitable for us to do so. Today and tomorrow, nothing is more dangerous to our shared future than the tragic hubris that continues to attribute to itself an absolute yet illusory property that alone sustains the superlative privilege afforded to human life. As an operative metaphysical concept, 'life' ultimately sustains such stupefied morbidity that is nothing other than the triumphant deracination of our shared world by capitalist modes of production. Put as simply as possible, *it is only with the collapse of the simple ontological distinction between 'life' and its absence that relations of unfettered instrumentalization cease to be possible.*

As the exemplary figure of the unfounded privilege afforded to life, it is with the tragic narcissism of Hamlet that the question of life and its ending ends, to be replaced instead by the extremophile as the figure of manifold futures that will not yet have been. To *be* is the potential to *be otherwise*, that is to say, to *not* be that which a given being is: at once being and not being in the sense that to be *is* to not be. Given that it is the evolution *of* technology itself that ultimately discloses *to* itself the priority of its ethical dimension, it thereafter becomes impossible to deny the fabrications of technology a central role to play in what amounts to the collapse of all moral programmes hitherto but, rather than marking the end of ethics, constitutes instead the long-overdue announcing of its commencement.

Notes

INTRODUCTION

1. I make this same error in my first book, *Zoogenesis: Thinking Encounter with Animals* (2014), for which Matthew Calarco rightly takes me to task in his review article "Life and Relation beyond Animalization" (2017).

2. The other two questions concern the relation of reason and the brain and the challenges posed to Kant's authority and status from within the continental philosophical tradition.

3. A slightly shorter version of this reading of Leibniz's principle of reason first appeared in "Posthumanism and the Ends of Technology," in *Palgrave Handbook of Critical Posthumanism* (2022), 1021–1043.

4. I stress here that Einstein's position is only *somewhat* ironic. In famously dismissing the work on quantum theory by contemporaries including Werner Heisenberg, Niels Bohr, Erwin Schrodinger and many others in the tumultuous opening decades of the twentieth century with the flat statement that 'God does not play dice,' Einstein ultimately throws in his lot with—gambles on, in other words—classical causality on the basis of negative theology in the guise of the Hidden Variables Theory. These issues will be addressed in detail in chapter 5 in relation to the concepts of nonlocality and quantum entanglement.

CHAPTER 1

1. This notion of an illusive simulacrum of virtue produced by economies of material exchange and fit only for slaves sounds an intriguing if disquieting echo insofar as, in the *Meno*, Socrates sets out to demonstrate that knowledge is in fact the recollection of essential truths and not something that can be learned over time by leading an illiterate slave boy to recall certain geometric truths. While the demonstration ultimately fails to convince, it is nonetheless symptomatic of explicit techniques of control aimed at suppressing the democratic instincts of the underclasses in Plato's *Republic* by providing illusions of virtue that ensure quietism and compliance. On

these illusions of control, see my "Plato in the Belly of the Beast: Force-Feeding Servitude in the *Republic*" (2019).

2. For more on this, see the chapter "Persephone Calls: Power and the Inability to Die in Plato and Blanchot," in my *Zoogenesis: Thinking Encounter with Animals*, 31–54.

3. On these questions, see also Plato's *Philebus*.

4. On the safeguarding of the elite in Plato's idealist Republic, see my "Plato in the Belly of the Beast."

5. An earlier version of the argument that follows here can be found in the chapter "Technology" in *The Edinburgh Companion to Animal Studies* (2018), wherein I address the issue specifically in light of the potential bioengineering of extremolytes.

6. Martin Heidegger, *The Question Concerning Technology and Other Essays*, 21.

CHAPTER 2

1. Meillassoux's *After Finitude* (2008) and *Time without Becoming* (2014) will be addressed in detail in the next chapter.

2. Cf. Rémi Brague, *Du Temps chez Platon et Aristote: Quatre Études* (1984), 134–135.

3. As we shall see going forward, Derrida too—and perhaps even above all—occasionally falls prey to the seduction of this vitalist and ultimately anthropocentric schema.

4. See also, for example, the brief preface to *Branches* [*Rameaux*] (2020/2004), wherein Serres argues, 'Today's world is screaming in pain because it is beginning its childbirth labour. At serious risk, we have to invent new relations between humans and the totality of what conditions life: the inert planet, the climate, living species, visible things and invisible things, sciences and technologies, the global community, morality and politics, education and health—We are leaving our world for other worlds, possible ones, and will have to abandon a hundred passions, ideas, customs and norms brought about by our narrow historical duration. We are entering into an evolutionary branch [*rameau*]' (n.p.).

5. Derrida, '*Ousia* and *Grammē*: Note on a Note from *Being and Time*' (1968), 31. The analysis of Heidegger's reading of the aporetic formulation of time in Aristotle that follows is both informed by, and indebted to, this pivotal early text of Derrida's.

6. Square brackets here denote additional clarifications inserted by Heidegger. As might be expected, Heidegger's translation of the original Greek at times deviates substantially from more traditional translations. For point of reference, Hardie and Gaye's translation of this same passage is as follows: 'For each [thing constituted by nature] has within itself a principle of motion and of stationariness (in respect of place, or of growth and decrease, or by way of alteration)' (728). It is for this reason, continues Aristotle, that things that exist by nature 'plainly differ' from all such things *not* constituted by nature (exemplified here by a bed and a coat) insofar as the latter 'have no innate impulse to change. But in so far as they happen to be composed

of stone or of earth or a mixture of the two, they *do* have such an impulse, and just to that extent—which seems to indicate that nature is a principle or cause of being moved or of being at rest in that to which it belongs primarily, in virtue of itself and not accidentally' (*Physics* II, 1, 192b15–23; 728–729). It is this distinction that ultimately allows for the instrumentalization of nonhuman being and as such is one of the primary targets of this thesis.

7. It is interesting to note that of Heidegger's three stated examples—history, art and life—only 'life' is deemed to require scare quotes: "as 'life' does in all living things" (201).

8. This final section forms part of my longer paper 'Technology,' in *The Edinburgh Companion to Animal Studies* (2018), 504–517.

9. Kumar and Singh, "Smart Therapeutics from Extremophiles: Unexplored Applications and Technological Challenges" (2013), 390.

10. The analysis of commodity fetishism proposed by Marx in the opening chapter of *Capital* (125–177) is quite simply an extraordinary work of critique all but buried now beneath conservative and liberal propaganda undertaken with the explicit intention of doing just that.

CHAPTER 3

1. On the metaphysical "as, such that it is," see Giorgio Agamben's superb close reading of the Hegelian voice in his early work, *Language and Death: The Place of Negativity* (1991).

2. On and around this subject, see Cecile Malaspina, *An Epistemology of Noise* (2018).

3. Here and throughout, it is vital that we continue to distinguish between two exclusive senses of supplementarity: that of the supplement as a *genetic extension* of that which precedes it both temporally and causally (as here with artifice understood as an extension that supplements the human body that pre-exists it and in which its cause is to be found), as opposed to that of *a priori* or *epigenetic* supplementarity as the event of black-boxed machinality that only ever defers to its own absence in the supplementary form of the future perfect tense (to which Colebrook previously draws our attention when she states that 'the parasite would have no existence other than that of supplementarity'; 'Posthuman Humanities,' 178).

4. As Malabou notes, American biologist Mary-Jane West-Eberhard initially proposes this definition of 'phenotypical malleability' in *Developmental Plasticity and Evolution* (2003), 34.

5. In the original French, Malabou writes '*l'épigenèse marque l'actualité du point de rencontre entre l'ancien et le nouveau, l'espace où ils interfèrent et se transforment mutuellement—embryon d'une temporalité spécifique*' (*Avant demain*, 272). Carolyn Shread translates this passage into English as 'epigenesis marks the current valency of the meeting point between the old and the new, the space where they reciprocally interfere and transform one another—the embryo of a specific temporality' (*Before Tomorrow*, 158).

6. *Morphing Intelligence*, 76. Malabou here cites Jean Piaget's *The Psychology of Intelligence* (1959), 120 and 112.

7. In *Changing Difference: The Feminine and the Question of Philosophy* (2011), Malabou states that '[t]ransformability is at work from the start, it trumps all determination. Everything starts with metamorphosis' (139).

8. David Bates, "Automaticity, Plasticity, and the Deviant Origins of Artificial Intelligence," in *Plasticity and Pathology: On the Formation of the Neural Subject*, ed. David Bates and Nima Bassiri (2016), 150–165; cit. *Morphing Intelligence*, 118.

9. In *Before Tomorrow*, Malabou explicitly imposes an epigenetic structure upon her argument throughout, and nowhere else is her extraordinary control of form more evident than it is here.

10. *Before Tomorrow*, 162. The passages cited by Malabou are from Paragraph 81 of Kant's *Critique of the Power of Judgment*, 290.

11. '*l'indifférence est la doublure du sens. . . . Ce qui est indifférent* fait sens tout seul. *C'est bien là ce que le vivant donne à penser. Il fait sens de se supporter seul*' (*Avant demain*, 293).

12. With this idea of forms that, in appearing *as if* self-forming, withdraw from meaning and as such—in Malabou's provocative phrase—'*decorrelate* thought,' Malabou inevitably recalls to mind the uncanny mechanism of Heidegger's 'profound boredom,' wherein being presents itself as such in the factual enigma of the withdrawal of sense. On this, see Heidegger's *The Fundamental Concepts of Metaphysics: World, Finitude, Solitude*.

13. "*La finalité apparaît précisément comme 'sens de l'existence fortuite du sens'*" (*Avant demain*, 293). The latter part of this sentence is a citation of "Sens et fait," by Eric Weil, 80.

14. Malabou here cites François Duchesneau, "Épigénèse de la raison pure et analogies biologiques" (2000), 237; *Avant demain*, 161.

CHAPTER 4

1. This example of the Hamiltonian constant is not simply fortuitous. Rather, it plays a key role in leading physicists of the early nineteenth century to the realization that, as Ilya Prigogine and Isabelle Stengers write in *Order Out of Chaos: Man's New Dialogue with Nature* (1984), "motion does more than bring about relative changes in the relative position of bodies in space" (107).

2. These texts are both transcribed from spoken lectures: Derrida's at the University of California and Meillassoux's a decade later at Middlesex University, London.

3. See also *The Beast and the Sovereign*, volume 1, wherein Derrida speaks of the world as "always constructed, simulated by a set of stabilizing apparatuses, more or less stable, then, and never natural" (9).

4. On deconstruction and its relation to correlationism deployed as a handy pejorative charge, see my "Being without Life: On the Trace of Organic Chauvinism with Derrida and DeLanda" (2017).

5. It should also be noted at this stage that absolute possibility as it is evoked here has nothing whatsoever to do with linguistic or *representative* capacities. It does not, in other words, infer the possibility of a given subject being able to distinguish the in-itself from the for-us as such, but rather concerns the absolute possibility that the in-itself *can be* different from the for-us.

CHAPTER 5

1. Following established convention, the anonymous author or authors of *The Cybernetic Hypothesis* are hereafter be referred to as 'Tiqqun' after the journal in which the text first appeared.

2. On Plato's *Republic* as a blueprint for perpetual power, see my 'Plato in the Belly of the Beast: Force-Feeding Servitude in the *Republic*,' 327–343.

3. Cf. Humberto R. Maturana and Francisco J. Varela, *Autopoiesis and Cognition: The Realization of the Living* (1980).

4. On this development, see Paul J. Cohen's keystone text *Set Theory and the Continuum Hypothesis* (1963).

5. See my 'Plato in the Belly of the Beast.'

6. Cf. Piero Sraffa, *Production of Commodities by Means of Commodities* (1960).

7. The Brusselator model will be considered in detail in the section 'Iterating the Catalyst.'

8. See Friedrich Nietzsche, 'On Truth and Lie in the Non-Moral Sense' [*Über Wahrheit und Lüge im aussermoralischen Sinne*] (1873).

9. That initial conditions and dynamics can no longer be considered independent is clearly demonstrated by the baker transformation. For more on the baker transformation and the extraordinary challenges it poses for contemporary physics, see appendix A in Prigogine, *From Being to Becoming*, 219–231.

10. Inevitably, in attempting to present the key points of this argument with as much clarity as possible, it has been necessary at various times to skip over much of the densely esoteric mathematical formulae upon which these key points are founded. For readers looking for more detailed accounts—such as how the baker transformation in this instance demonstrates that a contracting fibre always remains a contracting fibre and likewise a dilating fibre always remains a dilating fibre—the appendices of Prigogine's *From Being to Becoming* provide an excellent place to start (219–255), along with Albert Bharucha-Reid's more in-depth *Elements of the Theory of Markov Processes and Their Applications* (1960).

11. To this, we should also mention the formulation of Planck's constant, which, as Prigogine and Stengers state, "destroys already the concept of a trajectory, and leads therefore also to a kind of delocalization in phase space" (*Order Out of Chaos*, 289). While we do not have the space to address Planck's constant in any detail here, it remains a task to which I hope to return in my next book.

CONCLUSION

1. On the will to nothingness, see Nietzsche's *On the Genealogy of Morality: A Polemic* (1887). The continuing relevance of these three essays is obvious, as illustrated by the following passage: "It is absolutely impossible for us to conceal what was actually expressed by that whole willing that derives its direction from the ascetic ideal: this hatred of the human, and even more of the animalistic, even more of the material, this horror of the senses, of reason itself, this fear of happiness and beauty, this longing to get away from appearance, transience, growth, death, wishing, longing itself—all that means, let us dare to grasp it, a will to nothingness, an aversion to life, a rebellion against the most fundamental prerequisites of life" (89).

References

Note from the Author: The original publication date of a text can be very important as to how that text and the ideas it contains are perceived and read. For this reason, whenever a particular reference is introduced for the first time in the main body of this text, I give the year of its original publication without any reference to a specific edition or translation, whereas if I then go on to cite directly from a specific edition of that text, I give the date of publication of that specific edition.

Agamben, Giorgio. *Language and Death: The Place of Negativity*. Translated by Karen E. Pinkus. Minneapolis: University of Minnesota Press, 1991.

Anitori, Roberto Paul, ed. *Extremophiles: Microbiology and Biotechnology*. Norfolk: Caister Academic Press, 2012.

Aristotle. *Physics*. Translated by R. P. Hardie and R. K. Gaye. In *Complete Works of Aristotle*, edited by Jonathan Barnes, 699–982. Princeton, NJ: Princeton University Press, 1995.

———. *Metaphysics*. Translated by W. D. Ross. In *Complete Works of Aristotle*, edited by Jonathan Barnes, 3343–3716. Princeton, NJ: Princeton University Press, 1995.

———. *Nicomachean Ethics*. Translated by W. D. Ross. In *Complete Works of Aristotle*, edited by Jonathan Barnes, 3718–4009. Princeton, NJ: Princeton University Press, 1995.

———. *Rhetoric*. Translated by W. Rhys Roberts. In *Complete Works of Aristotle*, edited by Jonathan Barnes, 4618–4865. Princeton, NJ: Princeton University Press, 1995.

Bardin, Andrea. *Epistemology and Political Philosophy in Gilbert Simondon: Individuation, Technics, Social Systems*. Dordrecht: Springer, 2015.

Barthélémy, Jean-Hughes. *Life and Technology: An Inquiry Into and Beyond Simondon*. Translated by Barnaby Norman. Luneburg: Meson Press, 2015.

Bates, David, and Nima Bassiri, eds. *Plasticity and Pathology: On the Formation of the Neural Subject*. New York: Fordham University Press, 2016.

Baudrillard, Jean. *The System of Objects*. Translated by James Benedict. London and New York: Verso, 2005.

Bell, John S. *Speakable and Unspeakable in Quantum Mechanics.* Cambridge: Cambridge University Press, 1987.

Bennett, Jane. *Vibrant Matter: A Political Economy of Things.* Durham, NC, and London: Duke University Press, 2010.

Bharucha-Reid, Albert. *Elements of the Theory of Markov Processes and Their Applications.* New York: Dover Publications, 2003.

Bohr, Niels. *Philosophical Writings*, Vol. 4, *Causality and Complementarity, Supplementary Papers.* Woodbridge, CT: Ox Bow Press, 1998.

———. *The Philosophical Writings of Niels Bohr.* 3 vols. Woodbridge, CT: Ox Bow Press, 1987.

———. *Essays 1958–1962: On Atomic Physics and Human Knowledge.* New York and London: John Wiley & Sons, 1963.

———. *Atomic Theory and the Description of Nature.* Cambridge: Cambridge University, 1961.

———. "The Quantum Postulate and the Recent Development of Atomic Theory." *Nature* 121 (1928): 580–590.

Bontems, Vincent, ed. *Gilbert Simondon ou l'invention du futur.* Cerisy-La-Salle: Klincksieck, 2016.

Born, Max, and Albert Einstein. *The Born-Einstein Letters.* Translated by Irene Born. London: Macmillan, 1971.

Bradley, Arthur. *Originary Technicity: The Theory of Technology from Marx to Derrida.* New York: Palgrave Macmillan, 2011.

Brague, Rémi. *Du Temps chez Platon et Aristote: Quatre Études.* Paris: PUF, 1984.

Braidotti, Rosi, and Rick Dolphijn, eds. *Philosophy after Nature.* London and Washington, DC: Rowman & Littlefield International, 2017.

Braidotti, Rosi. *The Posthuman.* Cambridge, UK: Polity Press, 2013.

Brassier, Ray. *Nihil Unbound: Enlightenment and Extinction.* New York: Palgrave Macmillan, 2007.

———. "Axiomatic Heresy: The Non-philosophy of François Laruelle." *Radical Philosophy* 121 (2003): 24–35.

Calarco, Matthew. "Life and Relation beyond Animalization: Review of *Zoogenesis: Thinking Encounter with Animals* by Richard Iveson." *Humanimalia: A Journal of Human/Animal Interface Studies* 9, no. 1 (Fall 2017): 152–159.

———. *Thinking through Animals: Identity, Difference, Indistinction.* Stanford, CA: Stanford Briefs, 2015.

Calder, Nigel *Magic Universe: A Grand Tour of Modern Science.* Oxford: Oxford University Press, 2005.

Clark, Andy. *Natural-Born Cyborgs: Minds, Technologies, and the Future of Human Intelligence.* Oxford: Oxford University Press, 2003.

Cohen, Paul J. *Set Theory and the Continuum Hypothesis.* New York: Dover Publications, 2008.

Colebrook, Claire. "All Life Is Artificial Life." *Textual Practice* 33, no. 1 (2019): 1–14.

———. "Fragility." In *The Edinburgh Companion to Animal Studies*, edited by Ron Broglio, Lynn Turner, and Undine Sellbach, 247–261. Edinburgh: Edinburgh University Press, 2018.

———. "The Time of Planetary Memory." *Textual Practice* 31, no. 5 (2017): 1017–1024.

———. *Death of the Posthuman*. Vol. 1 of *Essays on Extinction*. Ann Arbor, MI: Open Humanities Press, 2014.

———. "Posthuman Humanities." In *Death of the Posthuman*, vol. 1 of *Essays on Extinction*, 158–184. Ann Arbor, MI: Open Humanities Press, 2014.

———. *Sex after Life*. Vol. 2 of *Essays on Extinction*. Ann Arbor, MI: Open Humanities Press, 2014.

———. *Deleuze and the Meaning of Life*. London: Continuum, 2010.

Colebrook, Claire, and Jamie Weinstein, eds. *Posthumous Life: Theorizing beyond the Posthuman*. New York: Columbia University Press, 2017.

DeLanda, Manuel. *Philosophy and Simulation: The Emergence of Synthetic Reason*. London and New York: Continuum, 2011.

———. "The Machinic Phylum." *TechnoMorphica* (1998): n.p. http://www.egs.edu/faculty/manuel-de-landa/articles/the-machinic-phylum/. Accessed January 2022.

———. *A Thousand Years of Nonlinear History*. New York: Swerve Editions, 1997.

———. *War in the Age of Intelligent Machines*. New York: Zone Books, 1991.

Deleuze, Gilles. "Postscript on the Societies of Control." *October* 59 (1992): 3–7.

Dennett, Daniel C. *Darwin's Dangerous Idea: Evolution and the Meanings of Life*. London: Penguin, 1995.

Derrida, Jacques. *The Beast and the Sovereign*. Vol. 1. Translated by David Wills. New York: Fordham University Press, 2008.

———. "Nietzsche and the Machine." In *Negotiations and Interviews, 1971–2001*. Translated by Elizabeth Rottenberg. Stanford, CA: Stanford University Press, 2002.

———. "Typewriter Ribbon: Limited Ink (2)." In *Without Alibi*, 71–160. Translated by Peggy Kamuf. Stanford, CA: Stanford University Press, 2002.

———. "'This Strange Institution Called Literature': An Interview with Jacques Derrida," translated by Geoffrey Bennington and Rachel Bowlby, in *Acts of Literature*, edited by Derek Attridge, 33–75. New York: Routledge, 1992.

———. "*Ousia* and *Grammē*: Note on a Note from *Being and Time*." In *Margins of Philosophy*, 29–67. Translated by Alan Bass. Chicago: University of Chicago Press, 1984.

———. *Marges: De la philosophy*. Paris: Minuit, 1972.

Dewey, John. *The Collected Works of John Dewey*. Vol. 10, *1934, Art as Experience*. Chicago: Southern Illinois University Press, 2006.

———. *The Public and Its Problems*. New York: Henry Holt, 1927.

Duchesneau, François. "Épigénèse de la raison pure et analogies biologiques." In *Kant actuel: Hommage à Pierre Laberge*, edited by François Duchesneau, Guy Lafrance, and Claude Piche, 233–256. Paris: Bellarmin-Vrin, 2000.

Durvasula, Ravi V., and D. V. Subba Rao, eds. *Extremophiles: From Biology to Biotechnology*. Boca Raton, FL, and London: CRC Press, 2018.

Einstein, Albert. *Relativity: The Special and the General Theory*. Translated by Robert W. Lawson. London: Penguin Books, 2006.

Ferrando, Francesca. *Philosophical Posthumanism*. London: Bloomsbury Academic, 2019.

Freud, Sigmund. *The Standard Edition of the Complete Psychological Works*. Vol. 21, *1927–1931: The Future of an Illusion, Civilization and its Discontents and Other Works*. London: Vintage, 2001.

———. *The Standard Edition of the Complete Psychological Works*. Vol. 19, *1923–1925: "The Ego and the Id" and Other Works*. Translated by James Strachey. London: Vintage, 2001.

———. *The Standard Edition of the Complete Psychological Works*. Vol. 18, *1920–1922: Beyond the Pleasure Principle, Group Psychology and Other Works*. London: Vintage, 2001.

Gerday, Charles, and Nicolas Glansdorff, eds. *Physiology and Biochemistry of Extremophiles*. Washington, DC: ASM Press, 2007.

Gödel, Kurt. *On Formally Undecidable Propositions of Principia Mathematica and Related Systems*. Translated by B. Meltzer. New York: Dover Publications, 1992.

Hainge, Greg. *Noise Matters: Towards an Ontology of Noise*. London: Bloomsbury Academic, 2013.

Harman, Graham. *Object-Oriented Ontology: A New Theory of Everything*. London: Pelican Books, 2017.

———. *Tool-Being: Heidegger and the Metaphysics of Objects*. Chicago and La Salle: Open Court, 2002.

Hawking, Stephen. *A Brief History of Time: From the Big Bang to Black Holes*. London: Bantam Press, 2011.

———. *The Theory of Everything: The Origin and Fate of the Universe*. Los Angeles: Phoenix Books, 2005.

———. *The Universe in a Nutshell*. London: Bantam Press, 2001.

Hayles, N. Katherine. *How We Became Posthuman: Virtual Bodies in Cybernetics, Literature and Informatics*. Chicago: University of Chicago Press, 1999.

Heidegger, Martin. *Heraclitus: The Inception of Occidental Thinking* and *Logic: Heraclitus's Doctrine of the Logos*. Translated by Julia Goesser Assaiante and S. Montgomery Ewegen. London: Bloomsbury Academic, 2018.

———. *The History of Beyng*. Translated by Jeffrey Powell and William McNeil. Bloomington: Indiana University Press, 2015.

———. *Plato's Sophist*. Translated by Richard Rojcewicz and André Schuwer. Bloomington: Indiana University Press, 2003.

———. "On the Essence and Concept of *Φύσις* in Aristotle's *Physics* B, 1." In *Pathmarks*, translated by Thomas Sheehan, 183–230. Cambridge: Cambridge University Press, 1998.

———. *Kant and the Problem of Metaphysics*. Translated by Richard Taft. Bloomington: Indiana University Press, 1997.

———. *Being and Time: A Translation of Sein und Zeit*. Translated by Joan Stambaugh. New York: State University of New York Press, 1996.

———. *The Fundamental Concepts of Metaphysics: World, Finitude, Solitude*. Translated by William McNeill and Nicholas Walker. Bloomington: Indiana University Press, 1995.

———. *The Principle of Reason*. Translated by Reginald Lilly. Bloomington, Indiana University Press, 1991.

————. *The Basic Problems of Phenomenology*. Rev. ed. Translated by Albert Hofstadter. Bloomington: Indiana University Press, 1988.

————. *On Time and Being*. Translated by Joan Stambaugh. London: Harper Torchbooks, 1986.

————. *The Question Concerning Technology and Other Essays*. Translated by William Lovitt. New York and London: Garland Publishing, 1977.

Horikoshi, Koki. *Extremophiles: Where It All Began*. Tokyo: Springer, 2016.

Hui, Yuk. *On the Existence of Digital Objects*. Minneapolis: University of Minnesota Press, 2016.

————. *The Question Concerning Technology in China: An Essay in Cosmotechnics*. Falmouth: Urbanomic, 2016.

Hui, Yuk, and Peter Lemmens, eds. *Cosmotechnics: For a Renewed Concept of Technology in the Anthropocene*. London: Routledge, 2021.

Husserl, Edmund. *Ideas: General Introduction to Pure Phenomenology*. Translated by W. R. Boyce Gibson. London and New York: Routledge, 2012.

————. *Logical Investigations*. Vol. 1. Translated by J. N. Findlay. London and New York: Routledge, 2001.

————. *Logical Investigations*. Vol. 2. Translated by J. N. Findlay. London and New York: Routledge, 2001.

————. *Cartesian Meditations: An Introduction to Phenomenology*. Translated by Dorion Cairns. Dordrecht: Martinus Nijhoff, 1960.

Ihde, Don. *Bodies in Technology*. Minneapolis: University of Minnesota Press, 2002.

Iveson, Richard. "Posthumanism and the Ends of Technology." In *Palgrave Handbook of Critical Posthumanism*, edited by Stefan Herbrechter et al., 1021–1043. New York: Palgrave Macmillan, 2022.

————. "Of Times before Tomorrow: Contingency and the Life of Machines." *Culture, Theory and Critique* 61, no. 1 (2020): 37–63.

————. "Plato in the Belly of the Beast: Force-Feeding Servitude in the *Republic*." *Culture, Theory and Critique* 60, nos. 3–4 (2019): 327–343.

————. "Technology." In *The Edinburgh Companion to Animal Studies*, edited by Ron Broglio, Lynn Turner, and Undine Sellbach, 504–517. Edinburgh: Edinburgh University Press, 2018.

————. "Being without Life: On the Trace of Organic Chauvinism with Derrida and DeLanda." In *Philosophy after Nature*, edited by Rosi Braidotti and Rick Dolphijn, 179–194. London and Washington, DC: Rowman & Littlefield International, 2017.

————. *Zoogenesis: Thinking Encounter with Animals*. London: Pavement Books, 2014.

Kant, Immanuel. *The Metaphysics of Morals*. Translated by Mary Gregor. Cambridge: Cambridge University Press, 2017.

————. *Critique of the Power of Judgment*. Translated by Paul Guyer and Eric Matthews. Cambridge: Cambridge University Press, 2000.

————. *Critique of Pure Reason*. Translated by Paul Guyer and Allen W. Wood. Cambridge: Cambridge University Press, 1998.

————. *Gesammelte Schriften*. Berlin: Königlich Preussischen Akademie der Wissenschaften, 1902–1997.

Kapp, Ernst. *Elements of a Philosophy of Technology: On the Evolutionary History of Culture*. Translated by Lauren K. Wolfe. Minneapolis: University of Minnesota Press, 2018.

Kumar, Raj, and Ajeet Singh. "Smart Therapeutics from Extremophiles: Unexplored Applications and Technological Challenges." In *Extremophiles: Sustainable Resources and Biotechnological Implications*, edited by Om V. Singh, 389–401. Malden, MA: Wiley-Blackwell, 2013.

Laruelle, François. "Le concept d'une 'technologie première.'" In *Gilbert Simondon: Une pensée de l'individuation et la technique*, 206–219. Paris: Albin Michel, 1994.

Latour, Bruno. *Down to Earth: Politics in the New Climatic Regime*. Translated by Catherine Porter. Cambridge, UK: Polity Press, 2018.

Leibniz, G. W. *Discourse on Metaphysics and Other Essays*. Translated by R. Ariew and D. Garber. Indianapolis: Hackett Publishing, 1992.

Lovelock, James. *Gaia: A New Look at Life on Earth*. Oxford: Oxford University Press, 2016.

Lyotard, Jean-François. *Libidinal Economy*. Translated by Iain Hamilton Grant. Bloomington: Indiana University Press, 1993.

———. *The Differend: Phrases in Dispute*. Translated by Georges Van Den Abbeele. Minneapolis: University of Minnesota Press, 1989.

———. *Économie libidinale*. Paris: Minuit, 1974.

Malabou, Catherine. *Morphing Intelligence: From IQ Measurement to Artificial Brains*. Translated by Carolyn Shread. New York: Columbia University Press, 2019.

———. *Les nouveaux blessés de Freud à la neurologie: Penser les traumatismes contemporains*. Paris: Presses Universitaires de France, 2017.

———. *Métamorphoses de l'intelligence: Que faire de leur cerveau bleu?* Paris: Presses Universitaires de France, 2017.

———. *Before Tomorrow: Epigenesis and Rationality*. Translated by Carolyn Shread. Cambridge, UK: Polity Press, 2016.

———. *Avant demain: Épigenèse et rationalité*. Paris: Presses Universitaires de France, 2014.

———. *The New Wounded: From Neurosis to Brain Damage*. Translated by Steven Miller. New York: Fordham University Press, 2012.

———. *Ontology of the Accident: An Essay on Destructive Plasticity*. Translated by Carolyn Shread. Cambridge, UK: Polity Press, 2012.

———. *Changing Difference: The Feminine and the Question of Philosophy*. Translated by Carolyn Shread. Cambridge, UK: Polity Press, 2011.

———. *The Heidegger Change: On the Fantastic in Philosophy*. Translated by Peter Skafish. Albany: State University of New York Press, 2011.

Malaspina, Cecile. *An Epistemology of Noise*. London: Bloomsbury Academic, 2018.

Manzocco, Roberto. *Transhumanism—Engineering the Human Condition: History, Philosophy and Current Status*. Cham: Springer, 2019.

Marx, Karl. *Capital: A Critique of Political Economy*. Vol. I. Translated by Ben Fowkes. London: Penguin Classics, 1990.

Maturana, Humberto R., and Francisco J. Varela. *The Tree of Knowledge: The Biological Roots of Human Understanding*. New York: Shambhala Publications, 1992.

———. *Autopoiesis and Cognition: The Realization of the Living*. Dordrecht, The Netherlands: D. Reidel Publishing, 1980.

Maudlin, Tim. *Philosophy of Physics: Quantum Theory*. Princeton, NJ: Princeton University Press, 2019.

———. *Philosophy of Physics: Space and Time*. Princeton, NJ: Princeton University Press, 2015.

———. *Quantum Non-Locality and Relativity: Metaphysical Intimations of Modern Physics*. 3rd ed. Malden MA: Wiley-Blackwell, 2011.

———. *The Metaphysics within Physics*. Oxford: Oxford University Press, 2010.

———. "Space-Time in the Quantum World." In *Bohemian Mechanics and Quantum Theory: An Appraisal*, edited by James Cushing, Arthur Fine, and Sheldon Goldstein, 285–307. Dordrecht: Kluwer Academic Publishers, 1996.

Meillassoux, Quentin. "Time without Becoming." In *Time Without Becoming*, edited by Anna Longo, 9–27. Milan: Mimesis International, 2014.

———. *After Finitude: An Essay on the Necessity of Contingency*. Translated by Ray Brassier. London and New York: Continuum, 2006.

Nagel, Ernest. *Gödel's Proof*. London: FB & C Ltd., 2017.

Neumann, John von, and Oskar Morgenstern. *Theory of Games and Economic Behavior*. Princeton, NJ: Princeton University Press, 1953.

Nietzsche, Friedrich. *On the Genealogy of Morality*. Translated by Carol Diethe. Cambridge: Cambridge University Press, 2006.

———. "On Truth and Lies in the Nonmoral Sense." In *Philosophy and Truth: Selections from Nietzsche's Notebooks of the Early 1870s*, translated and edited by Daniel Breazeale, 79–97. Atlantic Highlands, NJ: Humanities Press International Inc., 1993.

———. *Twilight of the Idols and The Anti-Christ*. Translated by R. J. Hollingdale. London: Penguin Classics, 1990.

———. *The Will to Power*. Translated by Walter Kaufmann and R. J. Hollingdale. New York: Vintage, 1968.

Odenwald, Sten F. *Patterns in the Void: Why Nothing Is Important*. New York: Westview Press, 2002.

O'Riordan, Kate. *Unreal Objects: Digital Materialities, Technoscientific Projects and Political Realities*. London: Pluto Press, 2017.

Piaget, Jean. *The Psychology of Intelligence*. Translated by Malcolm Piercy. London: Routledge & Kegan Paul, 1959.

Plato. *Phaedo*. Translated by G. M. A. Grube. In *Complete Works*, edited by John M. Cooper, 49–100. Indianapolis, IN, and Cambridge: Hackett Publishing, 1997.

———. *Sophist*. Translated by Nicholas P. White. In *Complete Works*, edited by John M. Cooper, 235–293. Indianapolis, IN, and Cambridge: Hackett Publishing, 1997.

———. *Statesman*. Translated by C. J. Rowe. In *Complete Works*, edited by John M. Cooper, 294–358. Indianapolis, IN, and Cambridge: Hackett Publishing, 1997.

———. *Philebus*. Translated by Dorothea Frede. In *Complete Works*, edited by John M. Cooper, 398–456. Indianapolis, IN, and Cambridge: Hackett Publishing, 1997.

———. *Meno*. Translated by G. M. A. Grube. In *Complete Works*, edited by John M. Cooper, 870–897. Indianapolis, IN, and Cambridge: Hackett Publishing, 1997.

———. *Republic*. Translated by G. M. A. Grube and C. D. C. Reeve. In *Complete Works*, edited by John M. Cooper, 971–1223. Indianapolis, IN, and Cambridge: Hackett Publishing, 1997.

Plotnitsky, Arkady. *Niels Bohr and Complementarity: An Introduction*. Dordrecht: Springer, 2013.

———. *Reading Bohr: Physics and Philosophy*. Dordrecht: Springer, 2006.

———. *Complementarity: Anti-Epistemology after Bohr and Derrida*. Durham, NC, and London: Duke University Press, 1994.

Popper, Karl. "The Arrow of Time." *Nature* 177 (1956): 538. doi.org/10.1038/177538a0.

Prigogine, Ilya. *Is Future Given?* River Edge, NJ: World Scientific, 2003.

———. *From Being to Becoming: Time and Complexity in the Physical Sciences*. San Francisco: W. H. Freeman & Company, 1980.

Prigogine, Ilya, and Isabelle Stengers. *Order Out of Chaos: Man's New Dialogue with Nature*. London: Verso, 2017.

Rampelotto, Pabulo, ed. *Biotechnology of Extremophiles: Advances and Challenges*. New York: Springer, 2016.

Sagan, Dorion, and Eric Schneider. *Into the Cool: Energy Flow, Thermodynamics, and Life*. Chicago: University of Chicago Press, 2005.

Salwan, Richa, and Vivek Sharma, eds. *Physiological and Biotechnological Aspects of Extremophiles*. London: Elsevier, 2020.

Serres, Michel. *Branches: A Philosophy of Time, Event and Advent*. Translated by Randolph Burks. London: Bloomsbury Academic, 2020.

———. *Le parasite*. Paris: Pluriel, 2014.

———. *Rameaux*. Paris: Pommier, 2004.

———. *The Parasite*. Translated by Lawrence R. Schehr. Baltimore, MD, and London: Johns Hopkins University Press, 1982.

Simondon, Gilbert. *Deux leçons sur l'animal et l'homme*. Paris: Ellipses, 2020.

———. *On the Mode of Existence of Technical Objects*. Translated by Cecile Malaspina and John Rogove. Minneapolis, MN: Univocal, 2017.

———. *L'individuation à la lumière des notions de forme et d'information*. Paris: Millon, 2005.

———. *L'individuation psychique et collective*. Paris: Aubier, 2002.

———. *Du mode d'existence des objets techniques*. Paris: Aubier, 1989.

Singh, Om V., ed. *Extremophiles: Sustainable Resources and Biotechnological Implications*. Malden MA: Wiley-Blackwell, 2013.

Smolin, Lee. *Einstein's Unfinished Revolution: The Search for What Lies beyond the Quantum*. London: Penguin Books, 2019.

———. *Three Roads to Quantum Gravity*. New York: Basic Books, 2017.

Sraffa, Piero. *Production of Commodities by Means of Commodities*. Cambridge: Cambridge University Press, 1960.

Stiegler, Bernard. *The Neganthropocene*. Translated by Daniel Ross. London: Open Humanities Press, 2018.

————. *Symbolic Misery*. Vol. 1, *The Hyper-industrial Epoch*. Translated by Daniel Ross. Cambridge, UK: Polity Press, 2016.

————. *Automatic Society*. Vol. 1, *The Future of Work*. Translated by Daniel Ross. Cambridge: Polity Press, 2015.

————. *States of Shock: Stupidity and Knowledge in the Twenty-First Century*. Translated by Daniel Ross. Cambridge, UK: Polity Press, 2015.

————. *Technics and Time*. Vol. 1, *The Fault of Epimetheus*. Translated by Richard Beardsworth and George Collins. Stanford, CA: Stanford University Press, 1998.

Swan, Melanie. "Digital Simondon: The Collective Individuation of Man and Machine." *Platform: Journal of Media and Communication* 6, no. 1 (2015): 46–58.

Tiqqun. *The Cybernetic Hypothesis*. London: Semiotext(e), 2020.

Tyshenko, Michael and William Leiss. "Life in the Fast Lane: An Introduction to Genomics Risks." *CTheory* (2005): n.p. http://journals.uvic.ca/index.php/ctheory/article/view/14534/5381. Accessed August 2017.

Unger, Roberto Mangabeira, and Lee Smolin. *The Singular Universe and the Reality of Time: A Proposal in Natural Philosophy*. Cambridge: Cambridge University Press, 2015.

Voltaire. *Oeuvres complètes: Dictionnaire philosophique IV*. Paris: Hachette Livre, 2013.

Weil, Eric. "Sens et fait." In *Problèmes kantiens*, 57–107. Paris: Vrin, 1970.

Wiener, Norbert. *Cybernetics or, Control and Communication in the Animal and the Machine*. Eastford, CT: Martino Fine Books, 2013.

————. *The Human Use of Human Beings: Cybernetics and Society*. London: Free Association Books, 1989.

Wendling, Amy E. *Karl Marx on Technology and Alienation*. New York: Palgrave Macmillan, 2009.

West-Eberhard, Mary-Jane. *Developmental Plasticity and Evolution*. New York: Oxford University Press, 2003.

Wolfendale, Peter. *Object-Orientated Philosophy: The Noumenon's New Clothes*. Falmouth: Urbanomic, 2014.

Zeh, H. Dieter. *The Physical Basis of the Direction of Time*. Berlin and Heidelberg: Springer, (1984) 2007.

Index

About the Author

Richard Iveson was awarded his doctorate from Goldsmiths College, University of London, and then took up a postdoctoral research fellowship at the Institute of Advanced Studies in the Humanities at the University of Queensland. Under the general rubric of posthumanism and the posthuman, his current research focuses on the intersection of Continental philosophy, emergent technologies and the philosophy of science.